IMAGES
of America

SHARON HILL

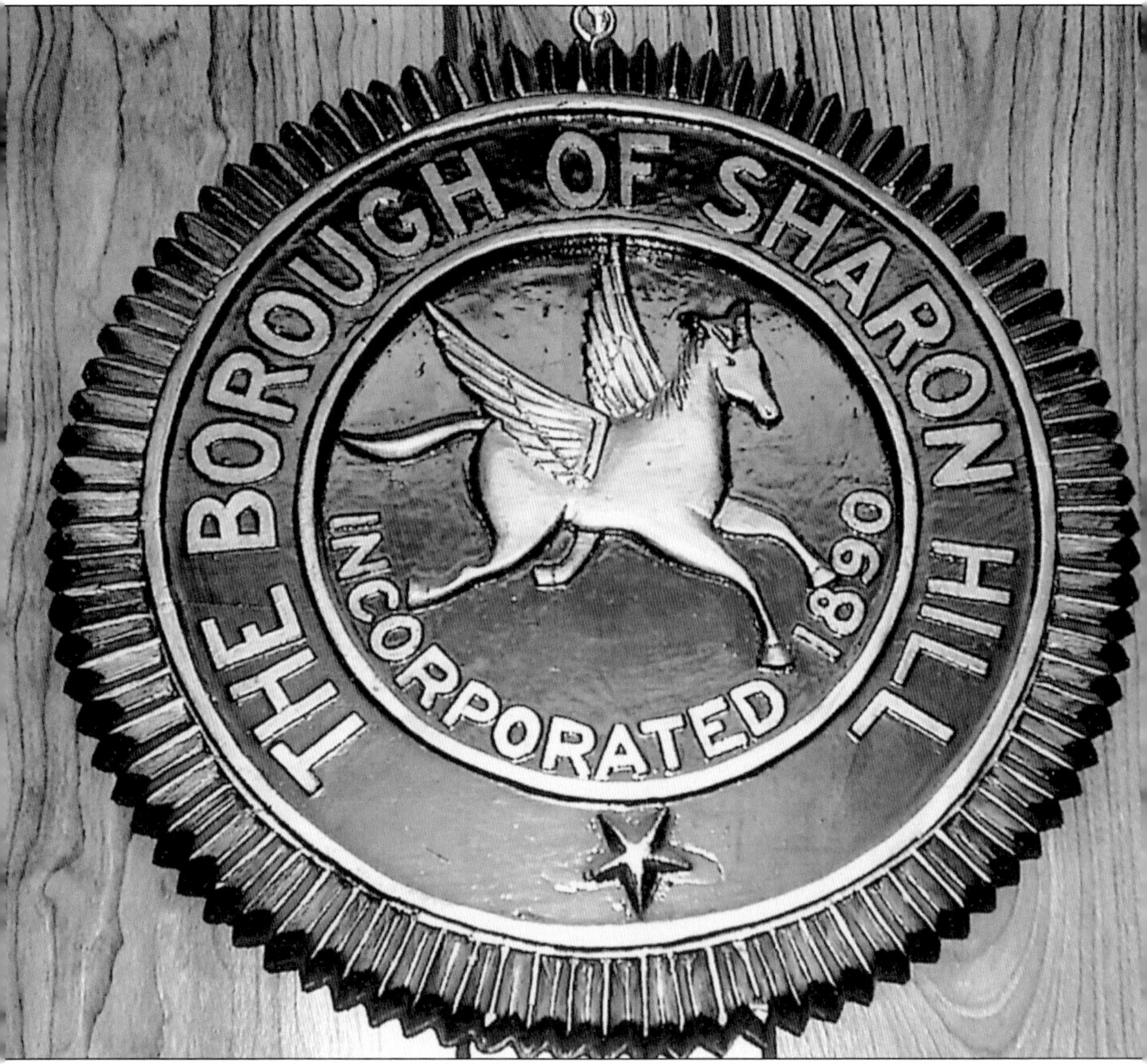

THE SHARON HILL SEAL. On May 25, 1891, Sharon Hill Borough Council adopted as its seal a circle inscribed with the borough's name and date of incorporation, 1890, with a device of a winged horse in the center. The chief burgess was William Douglass. Council members were John Muldoon, Robert Barry Jr., William J. Canning, J. Franklin Winner, William Cook, and Craig R. Arnold. The treasurer was Thomas Garvin and the solicitor Edward W. Bliss. The secretary was George W. Chapman. (Courtesy of the Sharon Hill Historical Society.)

On the cover: **THE SHARON HILL TROLLEY STATION.** The Sharon Hill trolley station was completed by August 1, 1917. The lines of the Philadelphia and West Chester Traction Company leased from the Philadelphia and Garrettford Street Railway Company provided service from Sixty-ninth Street in Upper Darby to Sharon Hill. The fare was 5¢. In 1937, the trademark "Red Arrow" was adopted. In 1970, the rail lines that had been the last independent interurban transportation system were sold to SEPTA, the Southeastern Pennsylvania Transportation Authority. (Courtesy of the Hagley Museum and Library.)

IMAGES
of America

SHARON HILL

Kathleen Clarke and Jean Shiber for the
Sharon Hill Historical Society

ARCADIA
PUBLISHING

ISBN 978-0-7385-5686-4

Published by Arcadia Publishing
Charleston, South Carolina

Printed in the United States of America

Library of Congress Control Number: 2008921751

For all general information contact Arcadia Publishing at:
Telephone 843-853-2070
Fax 843-853-0044
E-mail sales@arcadiapublishing.com
For customer service and orders:
Toll-Free 1-888-313-2665

Visit us on the Internet at www.arcadiapublishing.com

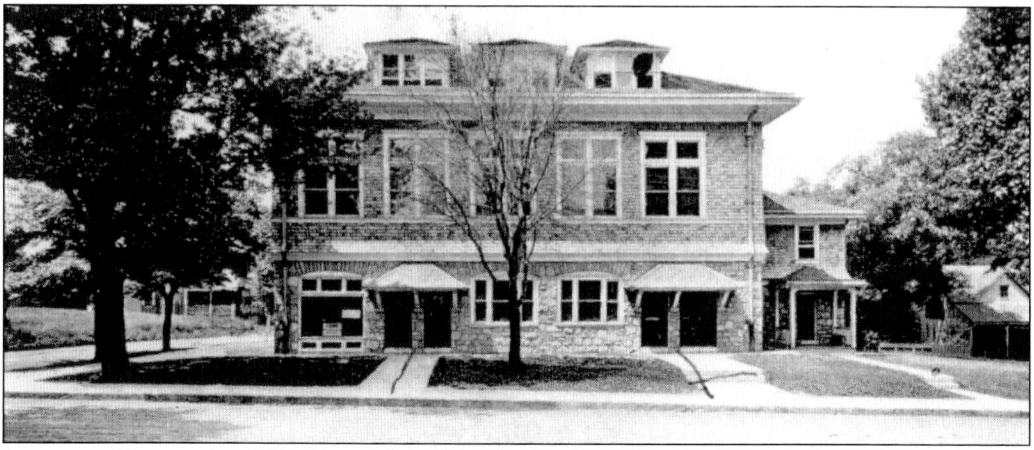

BOROUGH HALL, 1906. The borough hall was built by the Sharon Hill Improvement Association for public and private purposes. The borough council met there for the first time in 1906 for an annual rent of $250. It became the permanent meeting place for local government when the borough purchased the building in 1928 for $10,500 at a sheriff's sale. In 1912, the firehouse became headquartered here and eventually the police station. The historic building is located at Sharon Avenue and Spring Street. (Courtesy of the Sharon Hill Historical Society and the Sharon Hill Historical Commission.)

Contents

ACKNOWLEDGMENTS

The Sharon Hill Historical Society would like to give special thanks to Robert Clarke, who personally scanned all the images in this book and assisted with the editing. We would also like to thank John Wessels and Don Weldon for their technical advice. A special thanks to Kate Kelly, historian, for her assistance in editing and the use of her informational resources. We would like to express our sincere appreciation to Kathleen Fitzgerald Sharkey, Kimberly Carson McGowan, Victoria Donohue Welch, and Maida Barton Follini for their contributions of photographs of their families, Sharon Hill sites, and background information. We would also like to express our gratitude to the members of the historical society and all others who contributed their photographs and advice. We appreciate the kind assistance we received from the Sharon Hill Historical Commission, Holy Spirit Church, Delaware Historical Society, Delaware County Planning Department, Free Library of Philadelphia, and Hagley Museum and Library. Unless otherwise noted, all images are courtesy of the Sharon Hill Historical Society and the Sharon Hill Historical Commission.

Introduction

The impact that the coming of railroads had on communities all over the country was readily evident in the little town of Sharon Hill. Not yet incorporated in the 1870s, the town obtained its name from the famed institute established by Rachael and John Jackson known as Sharon Female Seminary. The town at that time was a sparsely populated, undeveloped stretch of land that was part of an original land grant by William Penn. It established the town of Darby and included the area of Sharon Hill.

The Philadelphia, Wilmington and Baltimore Railroad, which had been operating its lines along the Delaware River, decided to move its railroad farther inland along the lines that exist as Amtrak today. Soon enterprising businessmen seized the opportunity to develop the land along the railway lines and formed a corporation called the Sharon Land Association. A town plan was formulated, and 390 lots in varying sizes were mapped out that offered a scintillating endorsement "for the business men of town or city, the desirable requisites of a country home are health, accessibility, proximity to the city, beauty of scenery, cultivated surroundings and if possible cheapness."

Affluent city folk found this to be true and built their summer homes along the Queen's Highway and were able to enjoy "the fine plateau on which Sharon Hill is laid out; one of the most beautiful stretches of the farm highlands of Delaware County . . . an elevated rich table land, naturally drained, rolling with gentle undulations to the river's edge and swept by pure country air by a rapid little stream of fresh water." It was touted as resembling the "finest and healthiest portions of Lancaster and Chester Counties, the garden of Pennsylvania."

Little by little, the town expanded. Roads were laid out, new homes were built, churches and schools were established, and of course a suitable railroad passenger station and freight siding were built. The convenience to both Chester and Philadelphia gave the residents quick access to the city. While the borough was still forming, the station became the hub of the town. Not merely housing the ticket agency, it became the first post office, the place to pick up the daily mail, and a place to meet and socialize with neighbors.

Railroad communities such as Sharon Hill sprang up all over the nation and allowed people an opportunity to take advantage of the suburban living in areas that developed along the rail lines while maintaining employment at working facilities within their reach in the cities.

From just such situations and events evolved the .77-square-mile borough of Sharon Hill. When the town seceded from Darby in 1890, it was established officially as its own entity, the borough of Sharon Hill.

The culture of this small town was shaped by its churches, schools, and community events.

One

INFLUENCE OF TRANSPORTATION

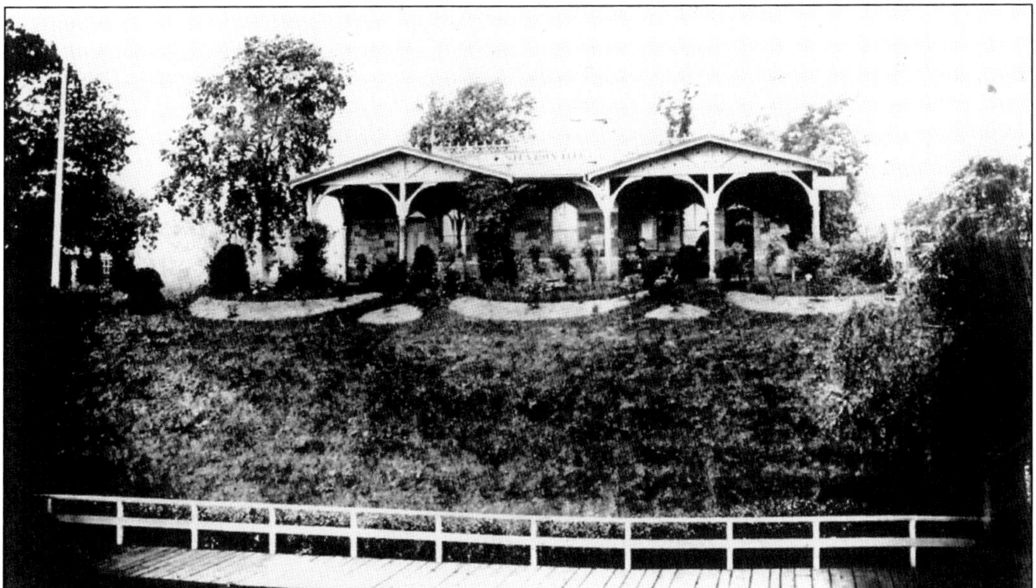

SHARON HILL TRAIN STATION, 1878. The Sharon Hill train station, built in 1872 by the Philadelphia, Wilmington and Baltimore Railroad, was located on the corner of the railroad and Sharon Avenue. The building's interior was finished with highly polished hardwood. The waiting rooms were models of comfort and elegance. A. C. Nolan was the station agent in 1876.

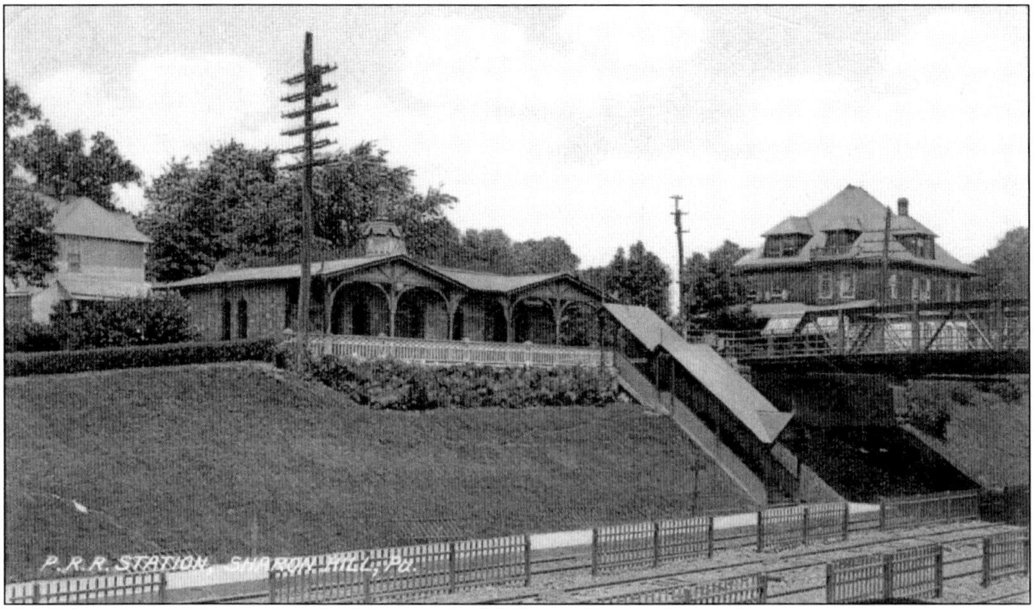

SHARON HILL TRAIN STATION, 1910. An authentic railroad community emerged in 1871 when the Philadelphia, Wilmington and Baltimore Railroad announced that its path would run through Sharon Hill. The railroad station shown in this 1910 postcard was constructed of serpentine stone obtained from local quarries. The station became a focal point of the town and a meeting place for its residents as well as providing transportation to and from Philadelphia, Wilmington, and Baltimore.

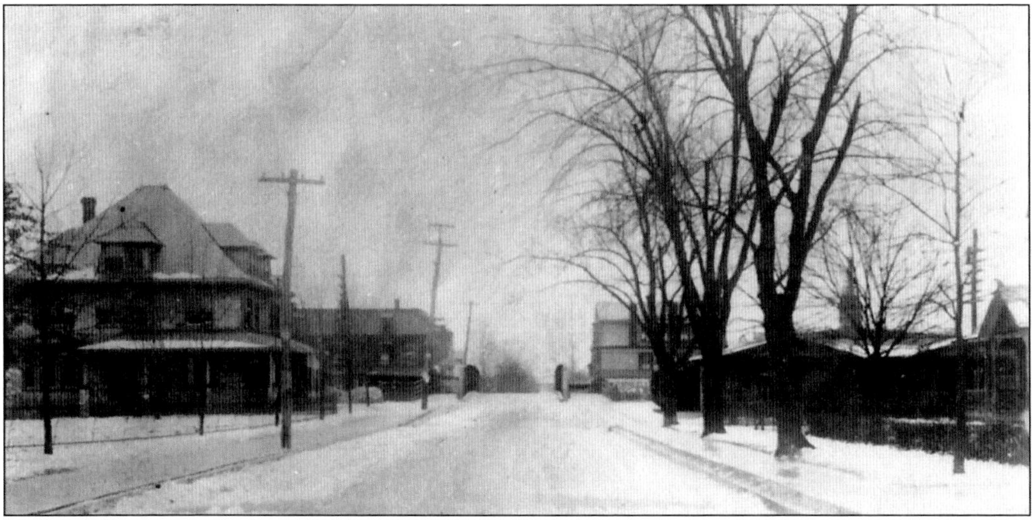

SHARON AVENUE, LOOKING SOUTH, 1910. In 1894, Sharon Hill had 14 streets. Only Sharon Avenue and Calcon Hook Road were paved; the others were dirt roads or paths. Road grading was just beginning. Oyster shells were used for fill on Clifton Avenue. Small bridges were constructed to get across some streets. Residents were required to build foot walks of lumber, which looked like small boardwalks. There were no street signs or numbered houses. Railroad transportation was preferred because the roads were blocked by snow and mud for months. This 1910 scene of Sharon Avenue shows the railroad depot on the right and Dr. David Dalton's Drug Store on the left.

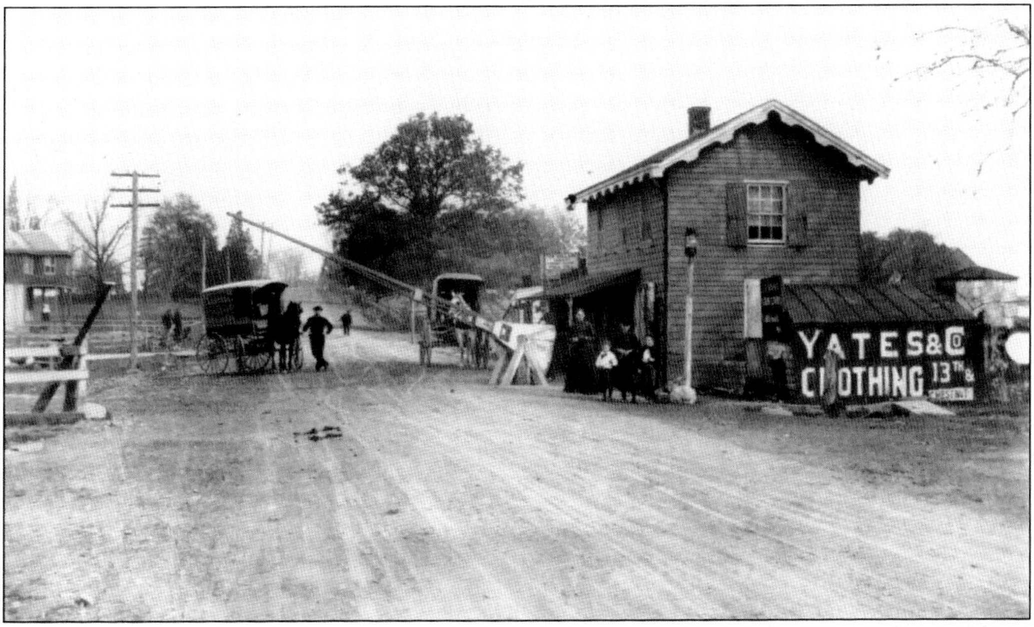

TOLL GATE NO. 6, 1892. Tollgates were established in Pennsylvania by an act of assembly in 1799. The act authorized the commissioners to erect the gates along what is known today as Chester Pike for a period of five years in an effort to raise money to maintain bridges. Toll gate No. 6 was located at Calcon Hook Road. Tolls were collected for single (10¢) and double (17¢) teams of horses, single horses (1¢), and bicycles (1¢).

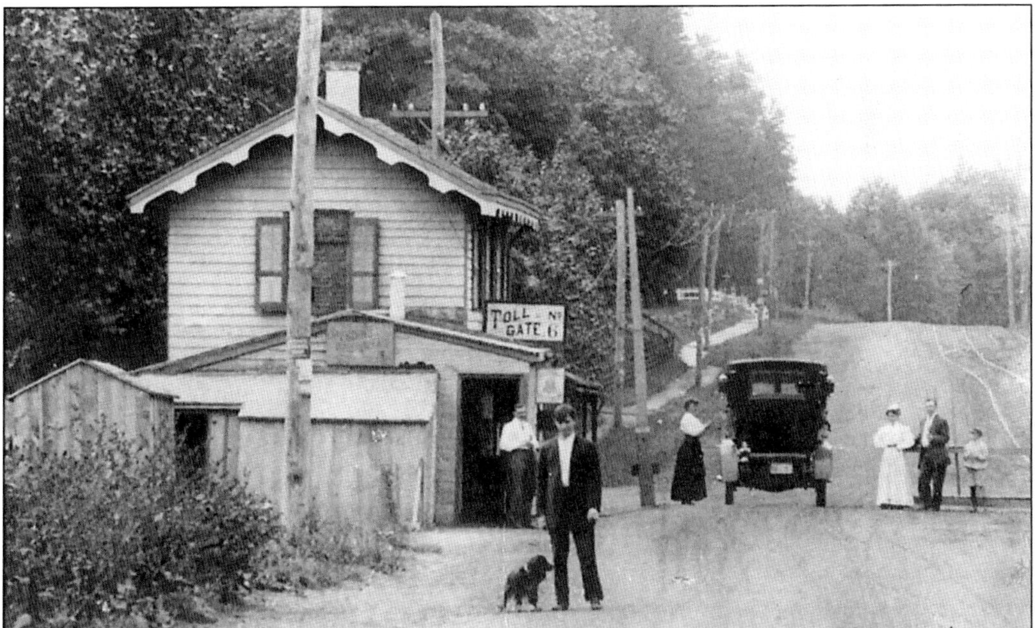

TOLL BOOTH NO. 6, 1900S. The building was a five-room wooden dwelling that served as a home for the toll taker. Harry Garton was the toll keeper in 1920. The tollhouse that was located on the Reese property was privately owned and financed by money collected from the users. It was opened as a fee road on August 12, 1926.

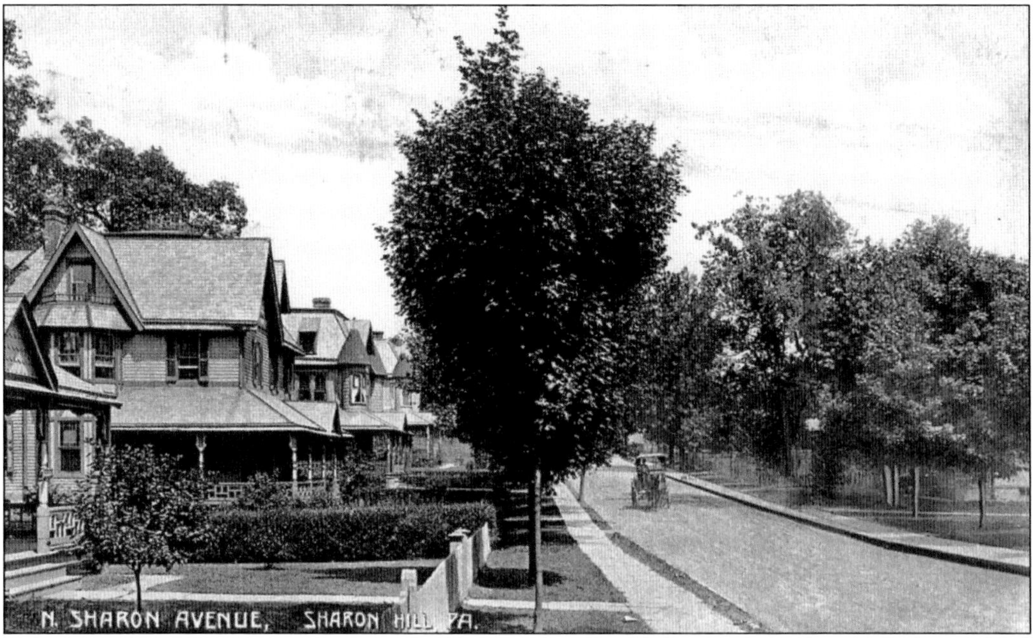

SHARON AVENUE, 1910. This postcard view of the west side of Sharon Avenue is looking north toward Chester Pike. It shows lovely Victorian homes with wraparound porches and a tree-lined street. Sharon Avenue and Calcon Hook Road were the only paved roads in the town. (Courtesy of Marcy Hinchcliff.)

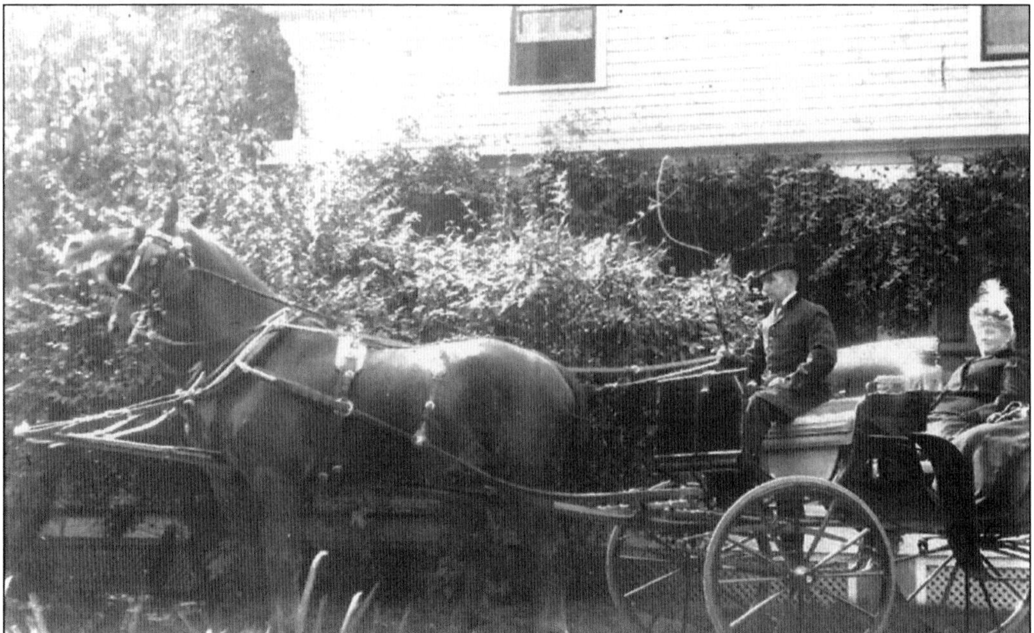

FOLWELL HORSE AND CARRIAGE, 1905. The Folwell home (Twin Oaks) is the setting for the coachman, who is about to take the lady of the house and the family for a traditional Sunday ride, a trip to the train station, or to the Delaware River area for fishing or dining. (Courtesy of Maida Barton Follini.)

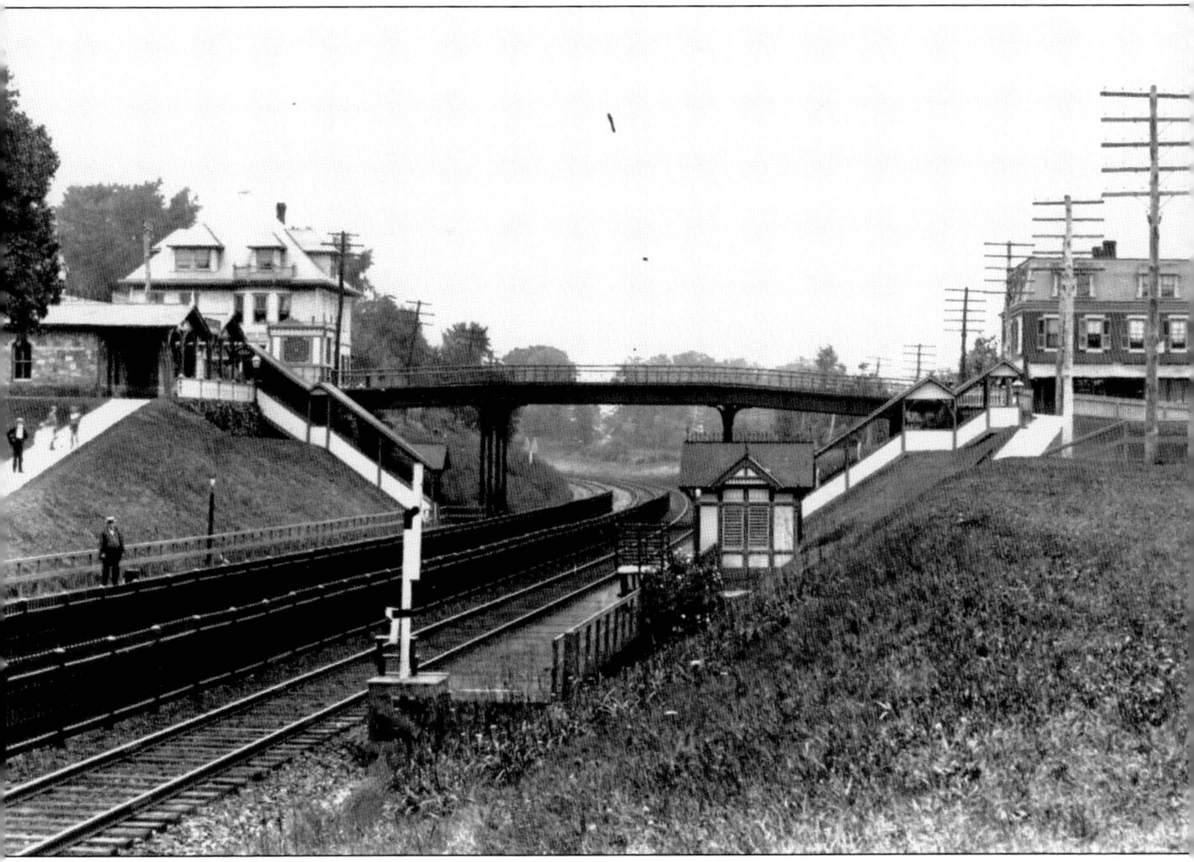

SHARON HILL STATION, 1907. Amenities included a covered stairway leading to the boarding platform. The double rails in the center were there to discourage passengers from crossing the tracks. The bridge in the background was widened to accommodate foot traffic.

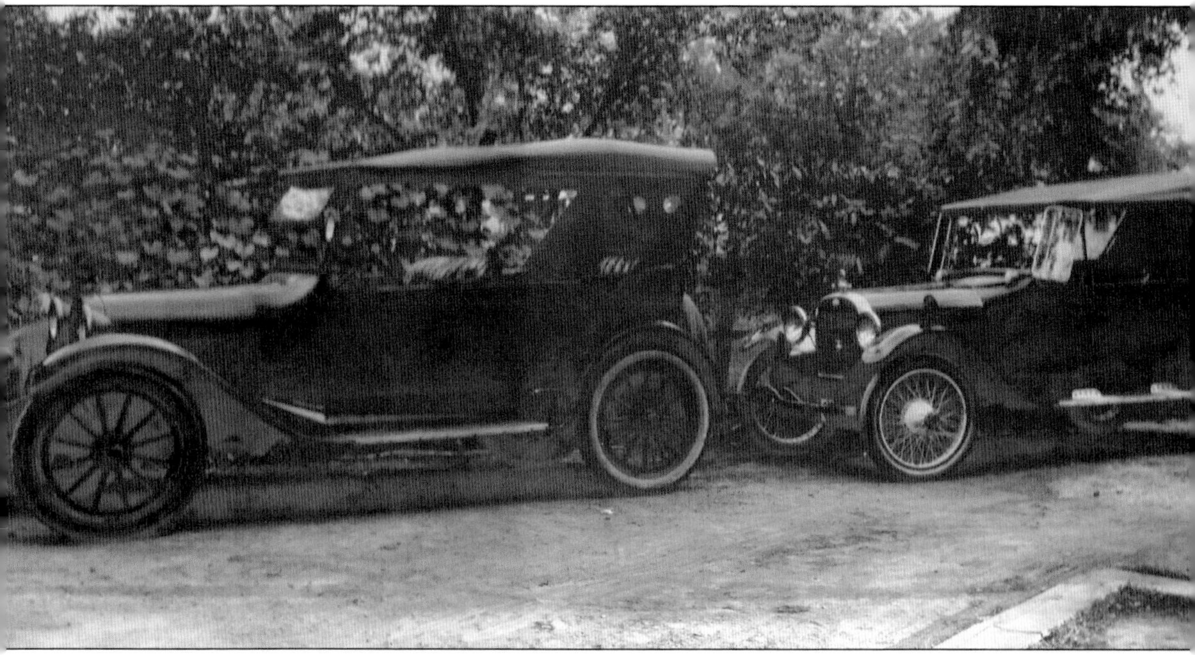

EARLY AUTOMOBILES, 1920S. These convertibles are parked outside the home of the Wellemeyers at Chester Pike and Cherry Street. Automobiles, horses and carriages, delivery trucks, and bicycles traveled along the pike and stopped to pay tolls at Calcon Hook Road. (Courtesy of Gerri Jackson.)

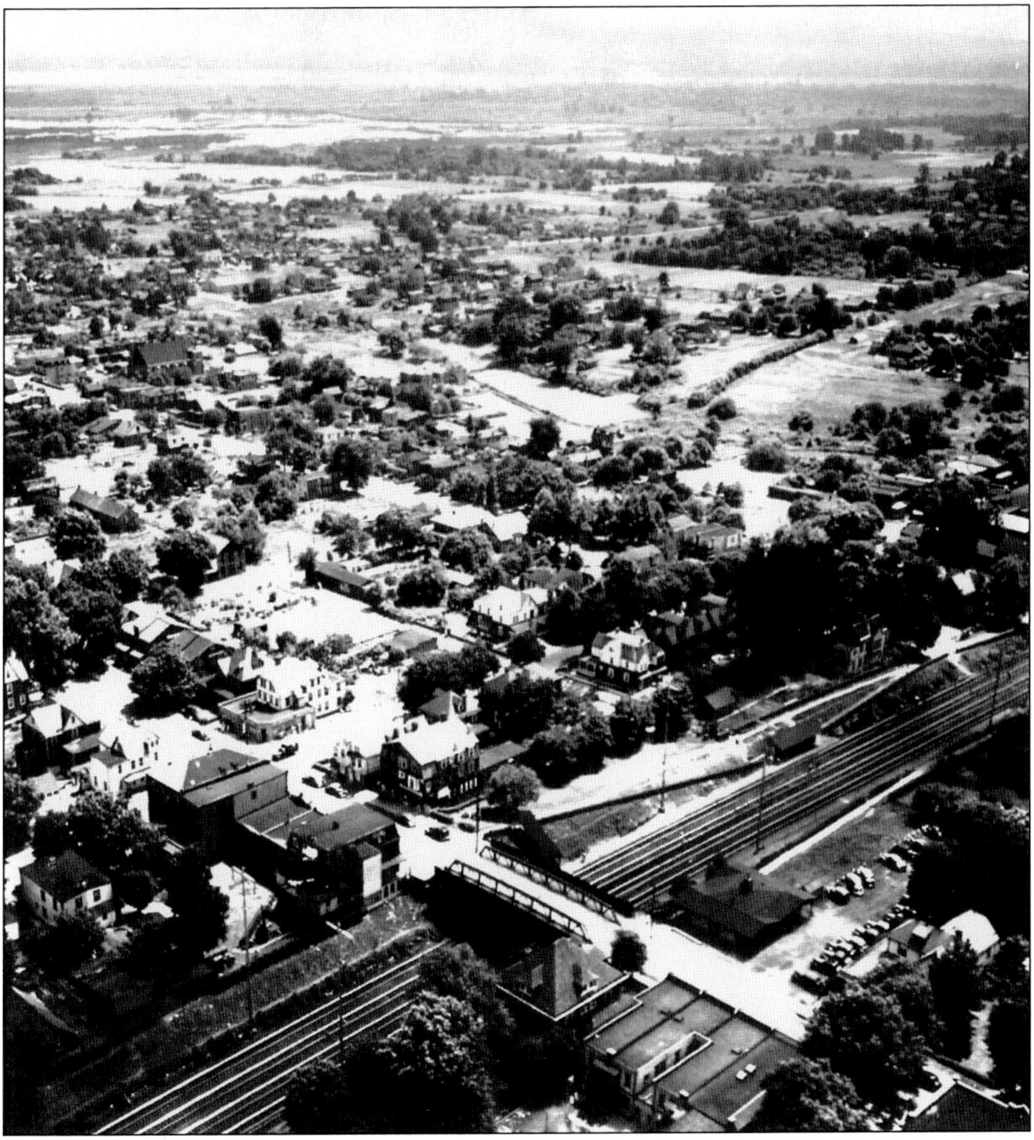

Aerial View of Sharon Avenue and Bridge, 1944. This view of Sharon Avenue shows the 1872 train station on the west side before the bridge. Across from the station is Dr. David Dalton's Drug Store. Across the bridge on the east side of the road toward Elmwood Avenue is a row of 1890s buildings that once housed Adam Rose Plumbing, Tuppenney's Bakery, Rankin's Grocery Store, Dr. Dalton's first drugstore, George Justice's Tobacco Store, Miss Hartnett's Millinery Store, and Winner's Hall where the borough council held its meetings. On October 27, 1897, a fire caused $30,000 worth of damage to the property. Sharon Hill had no fire company or fireplugs. Nearby fire companies did not hear the alarm.

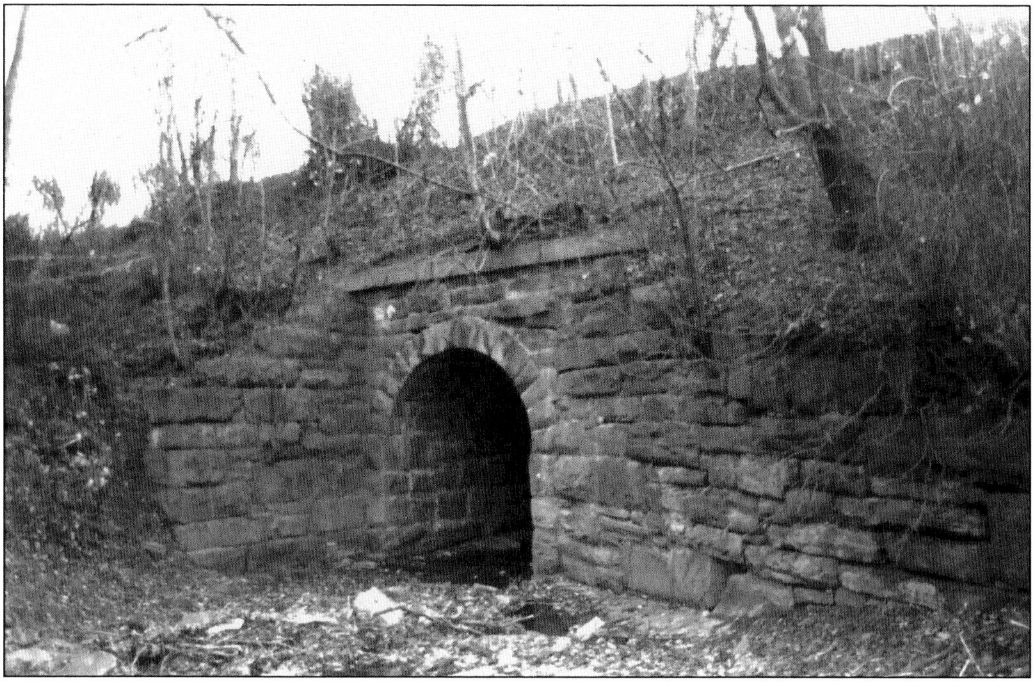

COW TUNNELS, 1870S. When the Philadelphia, Wilmington and Baltimore line cut through the fields of farmers, it was necessary for the railroad to build cow tunnels so that the cattle could have access to their grazing pastures. A small stream of water ran underneath as well and provided water for the grazing cattle. Two tunnels exist. One is on grounds behind the Spring Village apartment complex at Poplar Street, and a second one is along the Hermasprota Creek below High Street and Woodland Avenue.

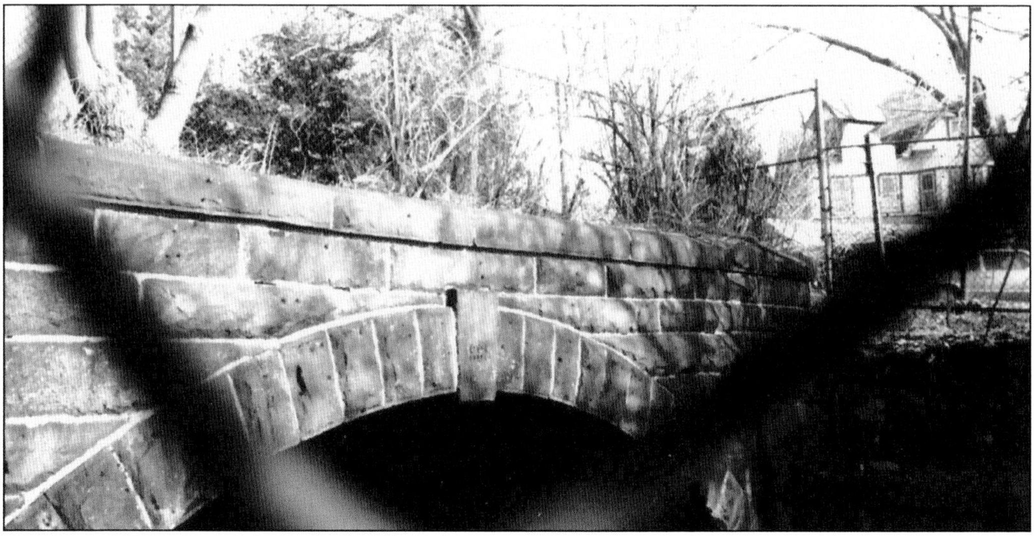

BALTIMORE AND OHIO TUNNEL, C. 1883. When the Baltimore and Ohio Railroad came through Sharon Hill, it was necessary for it to build a tunnel under Chester Pike. The tunnel had to be covered with earth, and the people of Sharon Hill had a new man-made hill. The tunnel is known as the Boone Tunnel. The hill is at Cherry Street and Laurel Road. The railroad divided most of the large estates along Chester Pike.

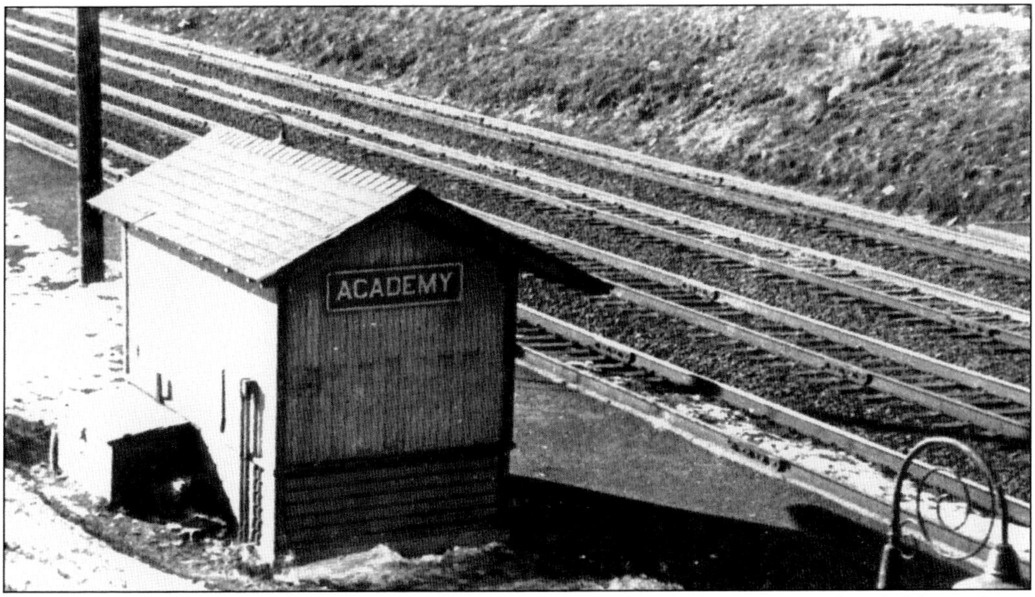

ACADEMY STATION, 1949. The academy station provided easy access to Holy Child Academy and was built to accommodate the students and teachers of the school. Passengers boarded trains using the Pennsylvania Railroad lines. While named on many early maps of the town, the exact date of construction is unknown.

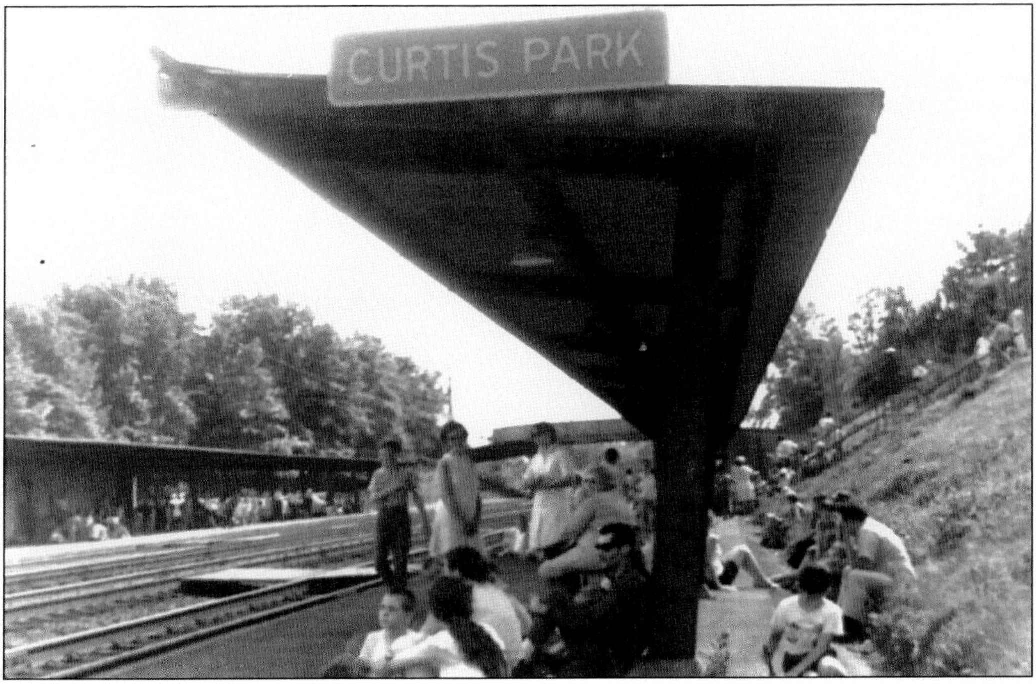

CURTIS PARK STATION, 1968. Citizens all along the Penn Central line from New York to Washington, D.C., gathered to view the train bearing the body of Sen. Robert Kennedy after his June 6 assassination in Los Angeles. Shown are local residents at the Curtis Park station awaiting the train that took Robert Kennedy to his final resting place in Arlington National Cemetery. (Courtesy of Joseph McCalla.)

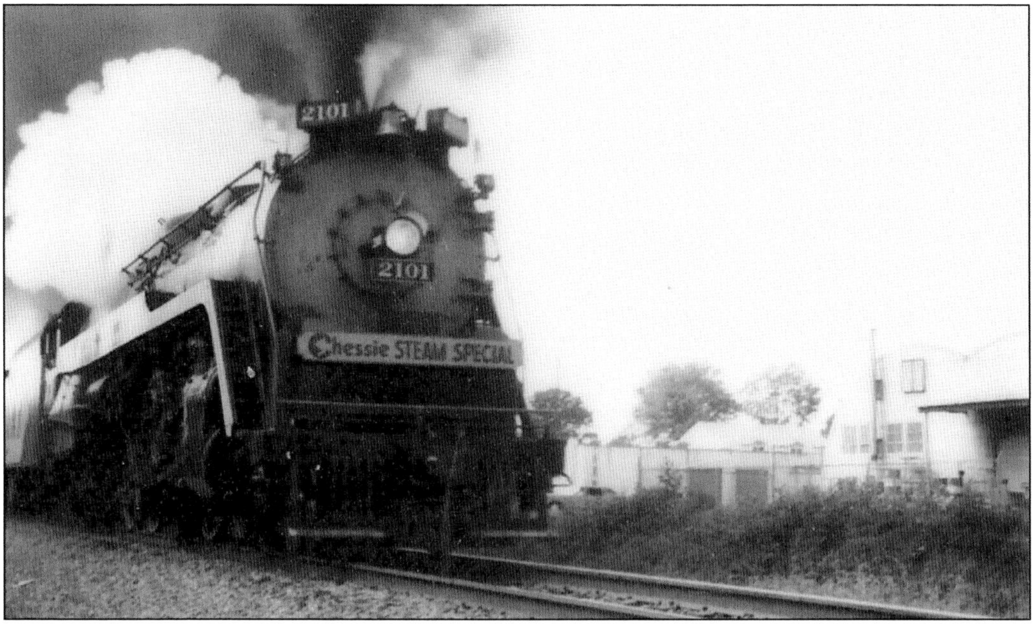

BALTIMORE AND OHIO LOCOMOTIVE, 1980S. Traveling on the Baltimore and Ohio Railroad is the *Chessie Steam Special.* It was part of a promotional tour operated by the Chessie System, predecessor to CSX, in the early 1980s. The train, which only ran once, visited all major Chessie terminals, including Philadelphia. The photograph shows the train passing through Sharon Hill behind Marshall Road facing the neighboring community of Collingdale. (Courtesy of Kathleen Fitzgerald Sharkey.)

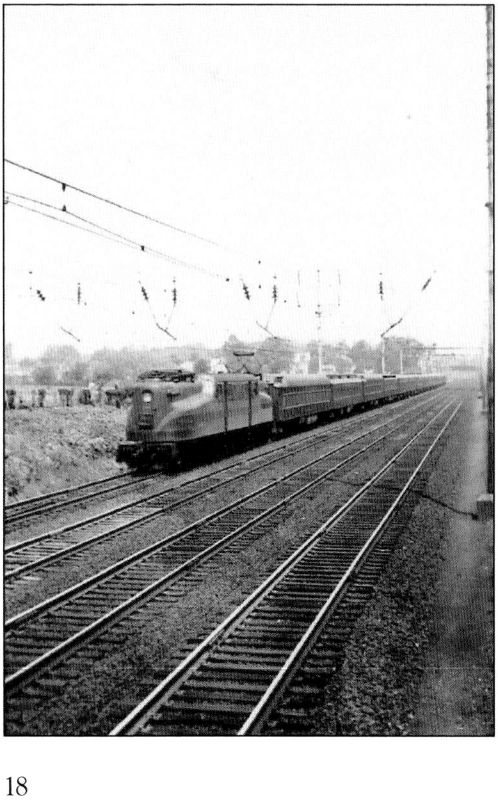

PENNSYLVANIA RAILROAD PASSENGER TRAIN, 1940S. The passenger train going through Sharon Hill depicted in this photograph is a GG-1 electric locomotive produced for the Pennsylvania Railroad between 1934 and 1942. This train was designed by famed industrial designer Raymond Lowery, who also designed the Coke bottle.

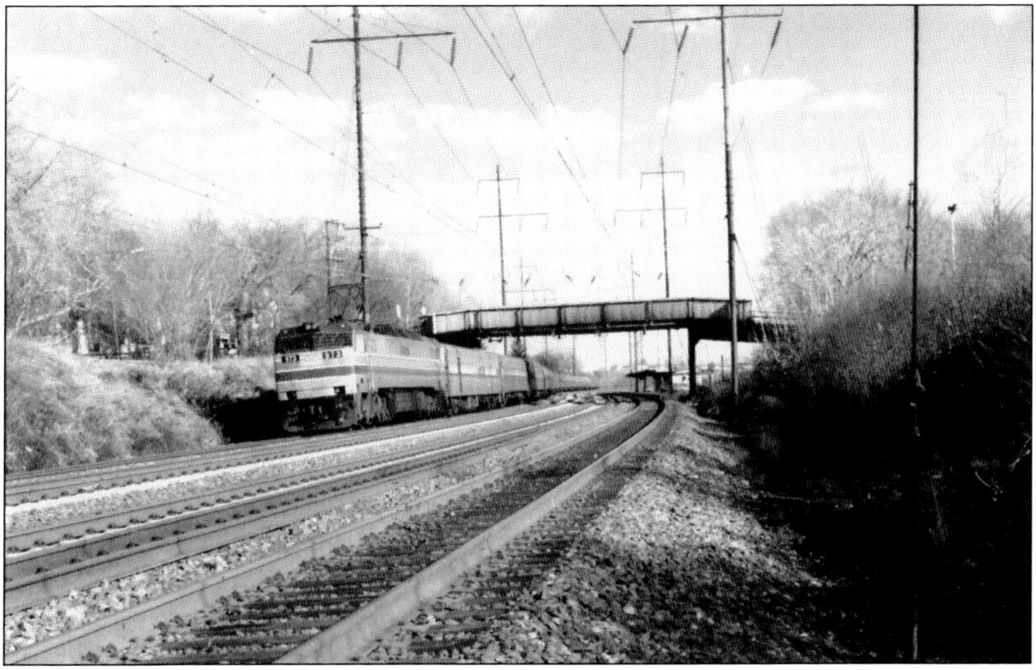

E60CP, 1980s. This photograph shows an Amtrak E60CP locomotive on one of the long-distance trains. The train is traveling under the Calcon Hook Bridge, sometimes referred to as the Academy Bridge, which crosses the tracks at Hook Road.

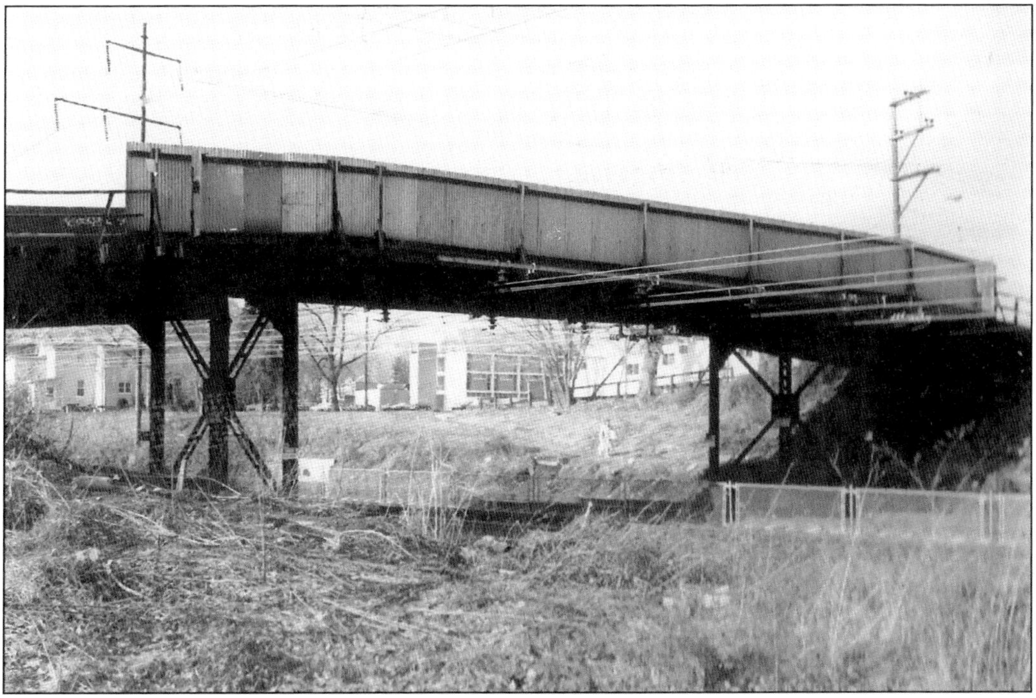

Calcon Hook Bridge. Built in 1896 with a 15½-foot-wide roadway and a seven-ton weight limit, it was replaced in 1985 with a 28-foot-wide structure and no weight restrictions. The bridge crosses the Conrail lines from Woodland Avenue to Elmwood Avenue.

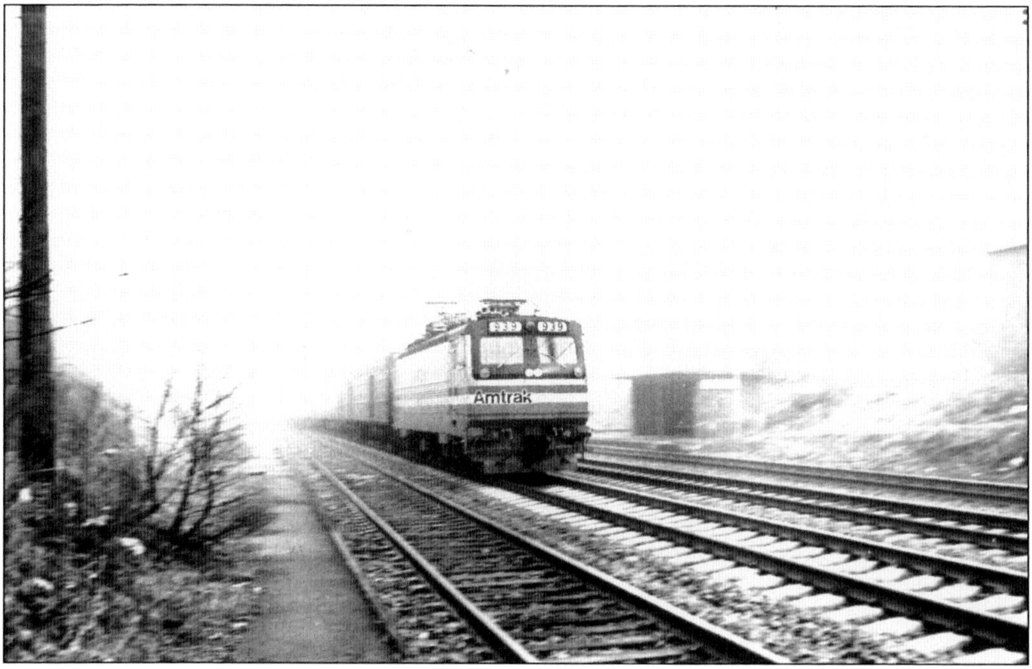

AMTRAK LOCOMOTIVE, 1980S. Pictured is an AEM-7 locomotive No. 939 passing through Sharon Hill. Produced in Sweden for Amtrak in the mid-1980s, they were affectionately referred to by the crews as "Swedish meatballs."

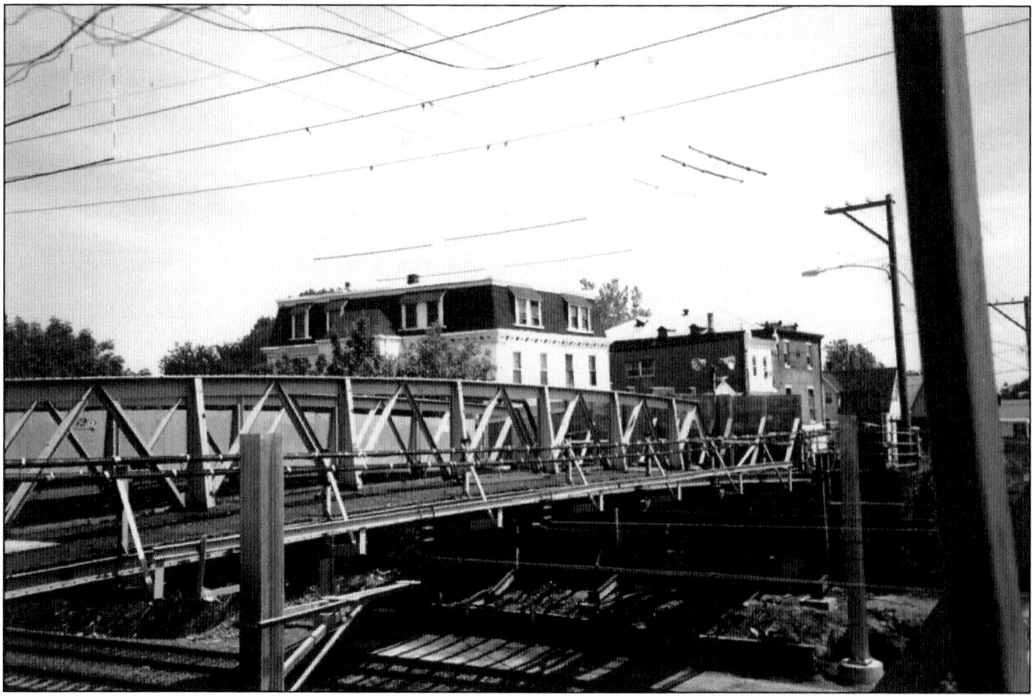

SHARON AVENUE BRIDGE, 1984. Shown is the Sharon Avenue Bridge being dismantled to be replaced with a wider bridge to allow for foot traffic and automobile traffic near the Sharon Hill train station.

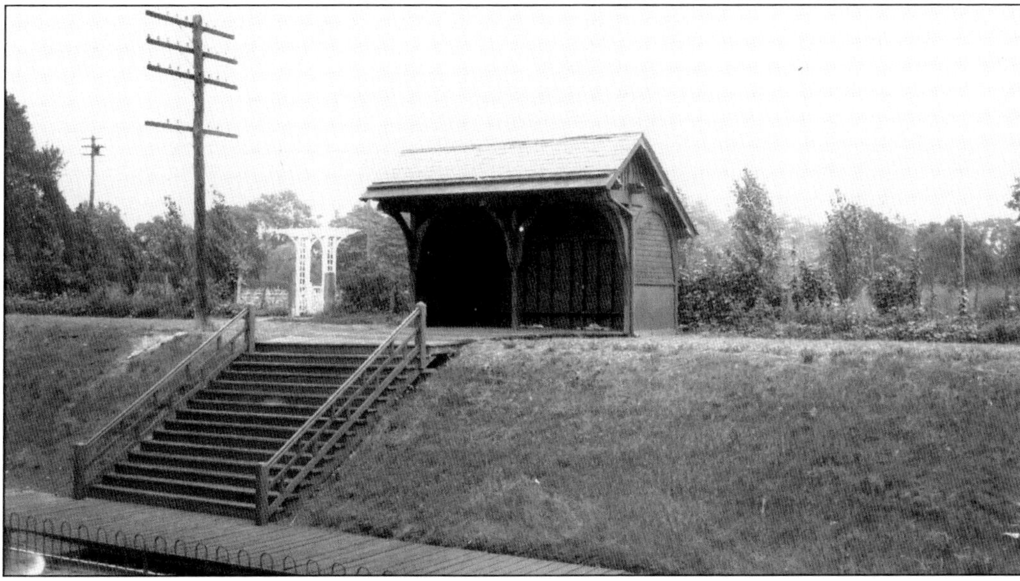

BALTIMORE AND OHIO STATION, 1880S. Construction of the Baltimore and Ohio Railroad station began in 1883 and was opened for freight service on July 11, 1896. This station was located off Clifton Avenue and was just behind the Folwell estate. The railroad divided most of the large estates along Chester Pike.

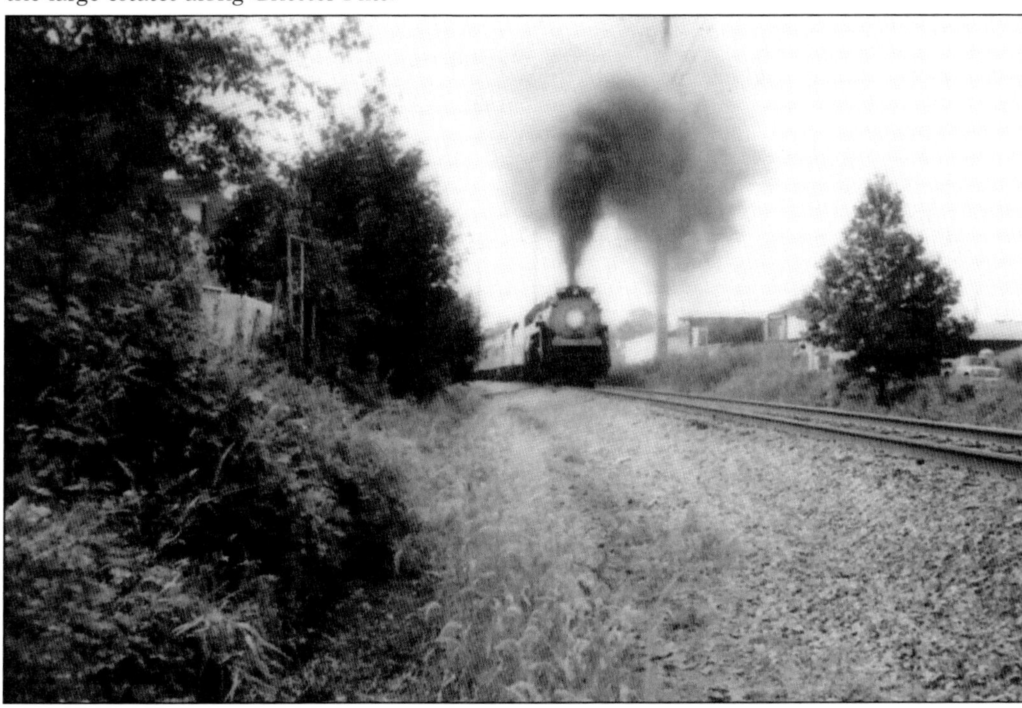

LOCOMOTIVE ON THE BALTIMORE AND OHIO RAILROAD, 1980S. This steam locomotive with its thick, black smoke traveled on the former Baltimore and Ohio Railroad line through Sharon Hill from Philadelphia. The smoke from these engines passing through was enough to send local children scrambling to their cellars until the smoke cleared. (Courtesy of Kathleen Fitzgerald Sharkey.)

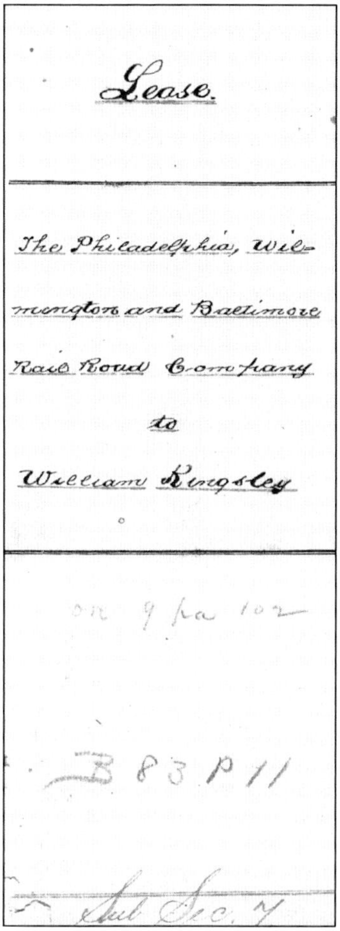

Lease.

The Philadelphia, Wilmington and Baltimore Rail Road Company

to

William Kingsley

B 83 P 11

RENTAL LEASE, 1875. This lease is between the Philadelphia, Wilmington and Baltimore Railroad and William Kingsley, dated September 25, 1875. The rent was $1 at the termination of the lease. It was signed by Isaac Hinkley, president of the railroad and the Sharon Land Association. (Courtesy of John and Barbara Kahler.)

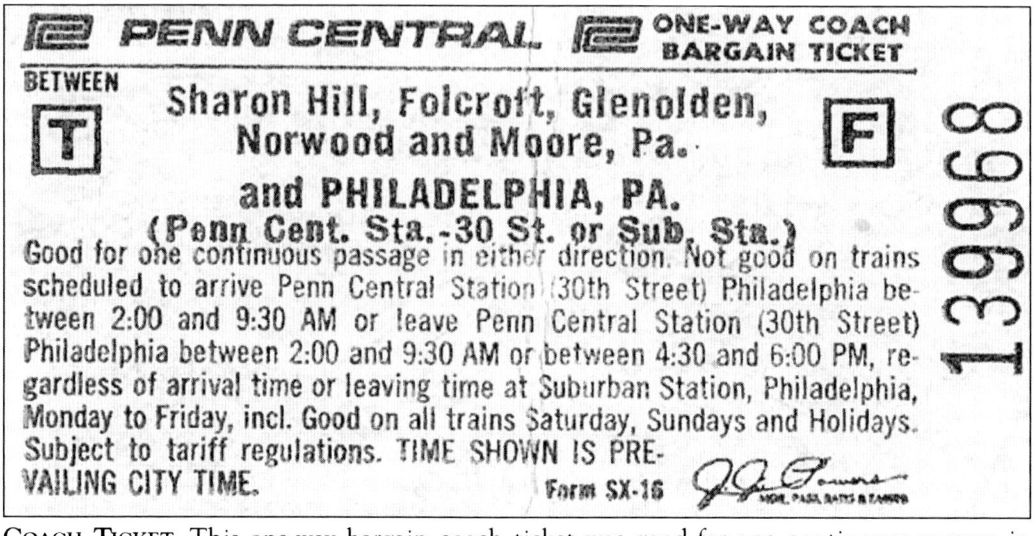

PENN CENTRAL ONE-WAY COACH BARGAIN TICKET

BETWEEN

T

Sharon Hill, Folcroft, Glenolden, Norwood and Moore, Pa.

F

13968

and PHILADELPHIA, PA. (Penn Cent. Sta.-30 St. or Sub. Sta.)

Good for one continuous passage in either direction. Not good on trains scheduled to arrive Penn Central Station (30th Street) Philadelphia between 2:00 and 9:30 AM or leave Penn Central Station (30th Street) Philadelphia between 2:00 and 9:30 AM or between 4:30 and 6:00 PM, regardless of arrival time or leaving time at Suburban Station, Philadelphia, Monday to Friday, incl. Good on all trains Saturday, Sundays and Holidays. Subject to tariff regulations. TIME SHOWN IS PREVAILING CITY TIME.

Form SX-16

COACH TICKET. This one-way bargain coach ticket was good for one continuous passage in either direction between Philadelphia and Sharon Hill except for rush hours, Monday through Friday. It was good on all trains on Saturdays, Sundays, and holidays and cost 15¢.

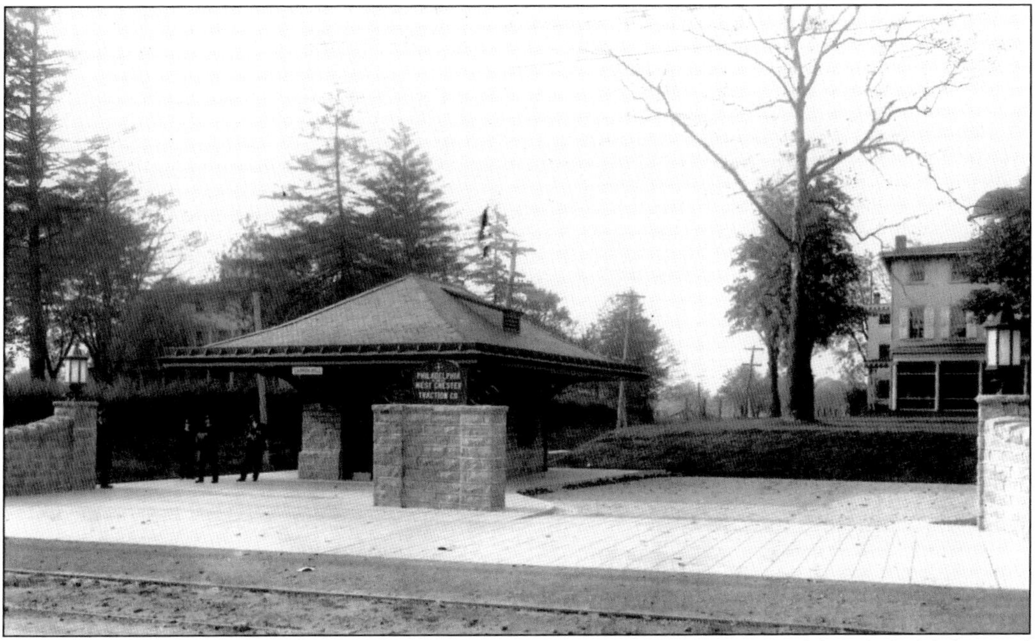

SHARON HILL TROLLEY STATION, 1917. The station at this time was part of the Philadelphia and West Chester Traction Company. The line carried passengers from Sharon Hill to Sixty-ninth Street in Upper Darby. The mansion on the left was the Carson home, and on the right was the property of Edward P. Timmons, who sold his land for construction of the station. (Courtesy of the Hagley Museum and Library.)

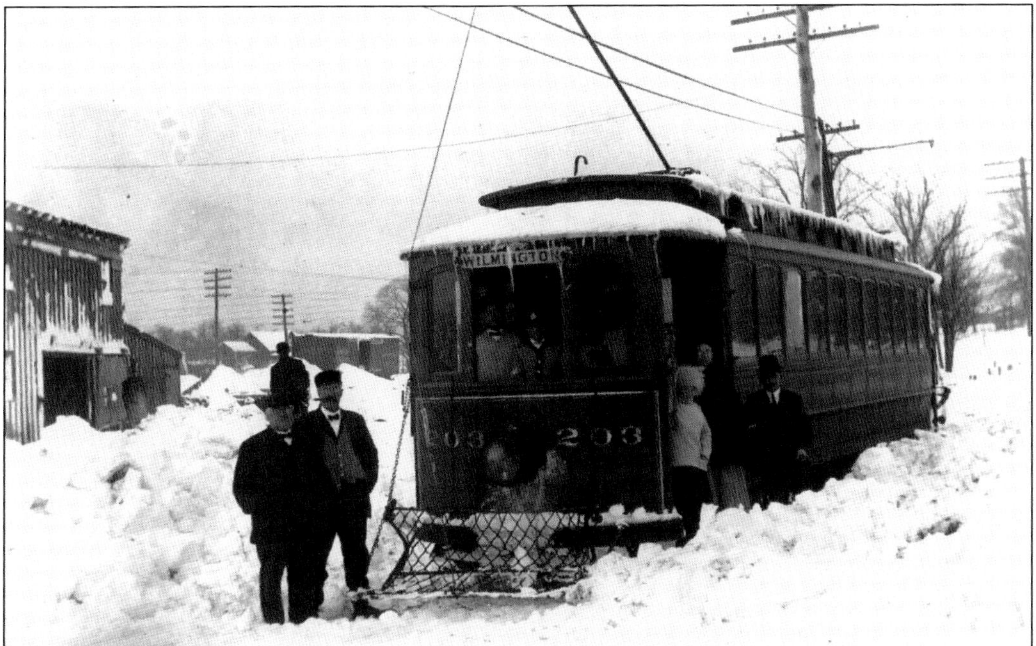

TROLLEY, 1900S. This trolley on its way to Wilmington from Darby is stuck in the snow at Calcon Hook Road and Chester Pike. The cowcatcher on the front was supposed to clear snow off the tracks. Motormen in 1910 worked 12½ hours a day and earned $17 per week.

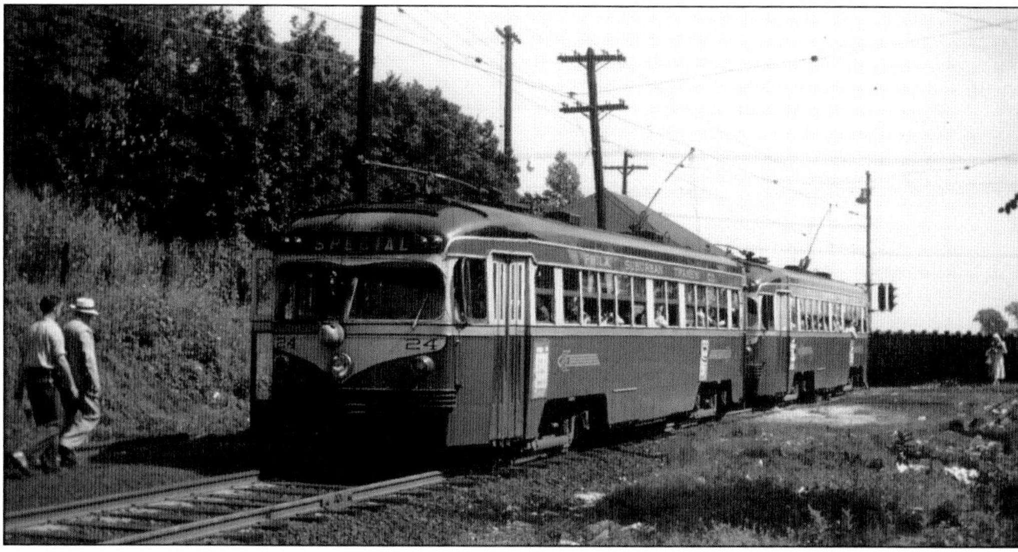

TROLLEY DEPARTURE, 1950S. Trolleys are waiting to depart the Sharon Hill trolley station. This photograph shows the typical trolley made by the Brill Company and was used almost exclusively by the Red Arrow Division of what is now known as SEPTA (Southeastern Pennsylvania Transportation Authority).

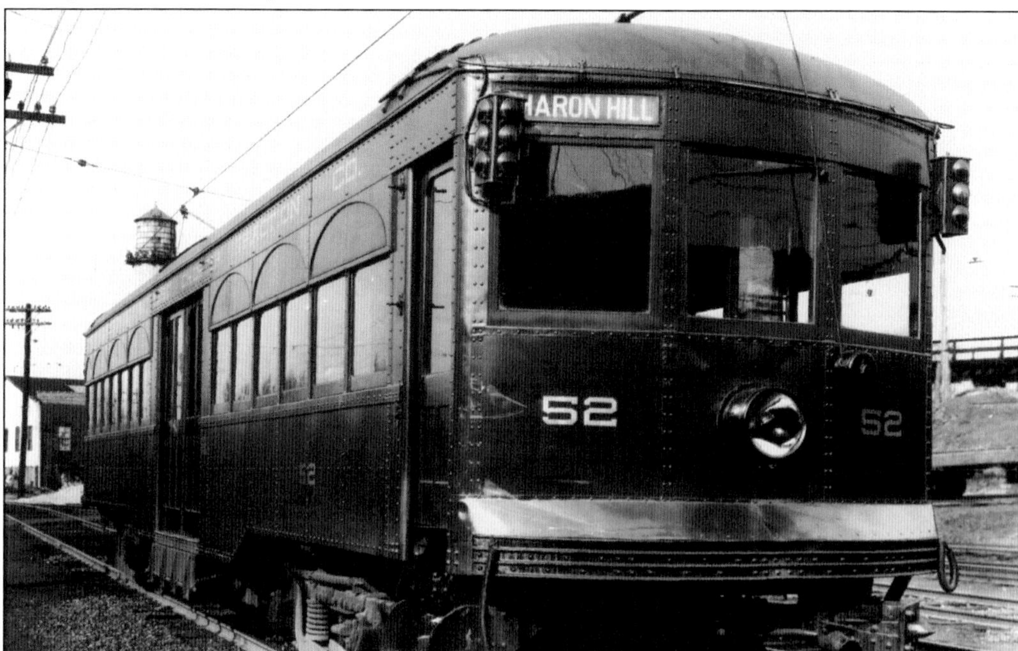

BRILL COMPANY TROLLEY, C. 1931. Electric railways ran down the middle of Chester Pike. Residents used the trolleys to go to Philadelphia to shop. In 1892, the Chester, Darby and Philadelphia Railway Company constructed lines on the pike, which was then known as the Chester, Darby and Telford Road. In 1899, the Chester Traction Company laid a double track, which was completed by 1919 and used by the trolley shown here. The trolleys on the pike could not survive the onslaught of motor vehicles and were removed in 1934. (Courtesy of the Hagley Museum and Library.)

Two

RESIDENTIAL VISTAS

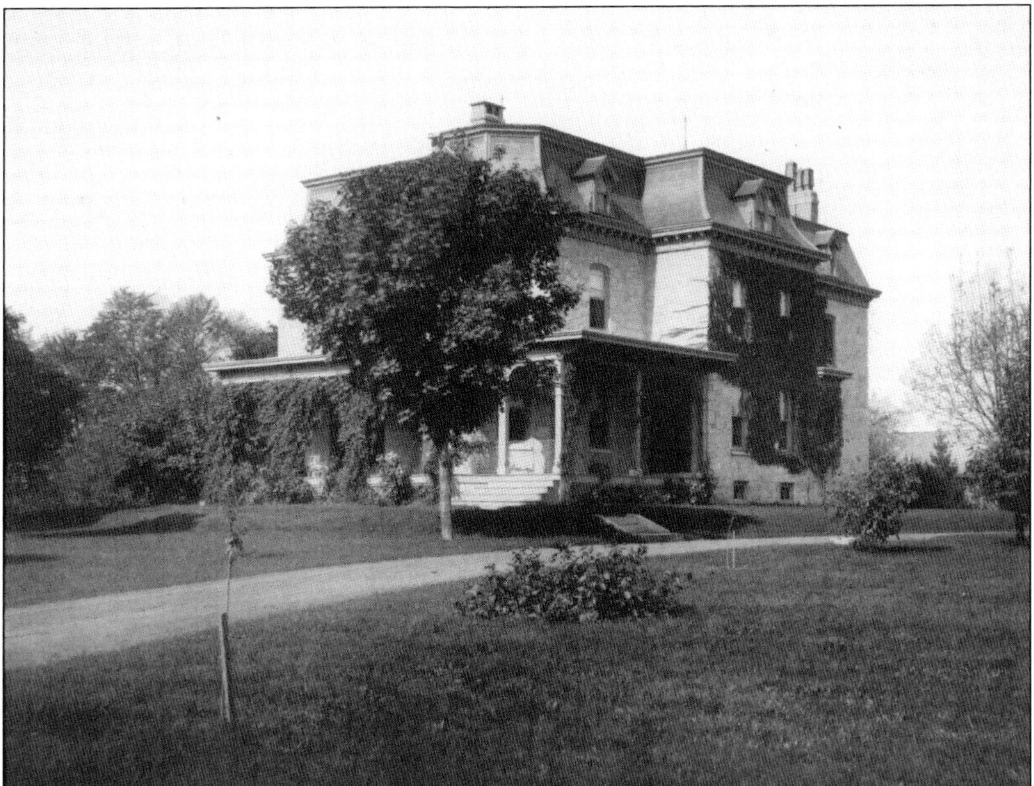

ISAAC CLOTHIER MANSION, C. 1875. Isaac Clothier of Strawbridge and Clothier, a department store in Philadelphia, built his mansion on Chester Pike and High Street. Each year Isaac Clothier sent hay wagons to the end of the trolley car line in Darby to transport his employees to his home for a Fourth of July party. The store's delivery horses grazed at the farm each summer. Thomas Lee purchased the home in 1892. (Courtesy of the Print and Picture Collection, Free Library of Philadelphia.)

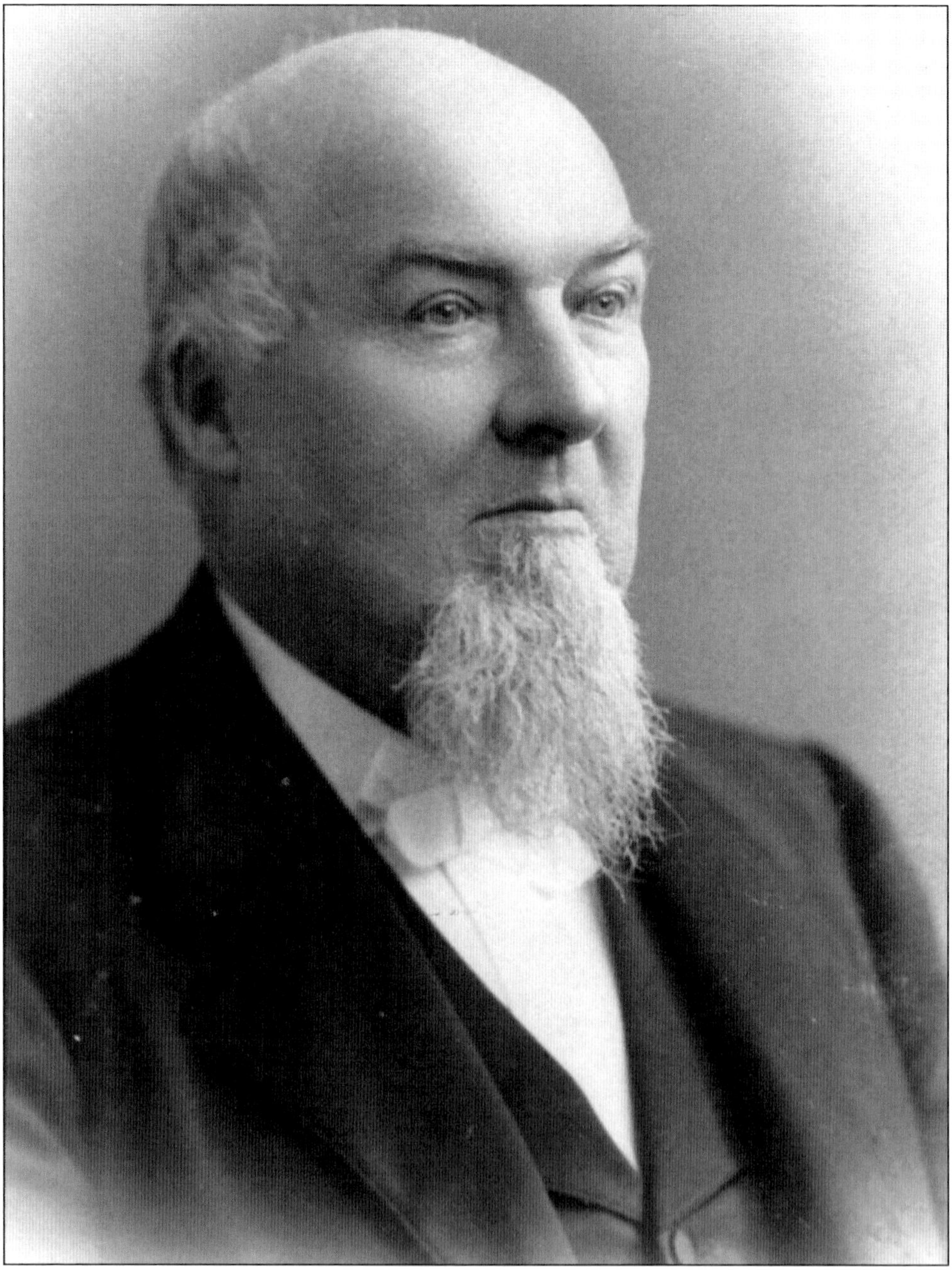

JACOB REESE. Jacob Reese worked with his father in the steel mills in the Pittsburgh area. He studied chemistry and metallurgy and eventually became well known for the design of factories and inventions within the steel industry. In 1885, he moved to Philadelphia and eventually found his way to Sharon Hill (then known as Darby) in 1890. Reese was semiretired when he lived in Sharon Hill. He purchased a three-story Oakford house on Bartlett Avenue near Chester Pike believed to be the oldest house in Sharon Hill. With this house came land from Cherry Street to Calcon Hook Road and from Chester Pike to Poplar Street. He commissioned the building of four houses, which are still standing today, along Chester Pike for his four sons. Reese Street was named for him.

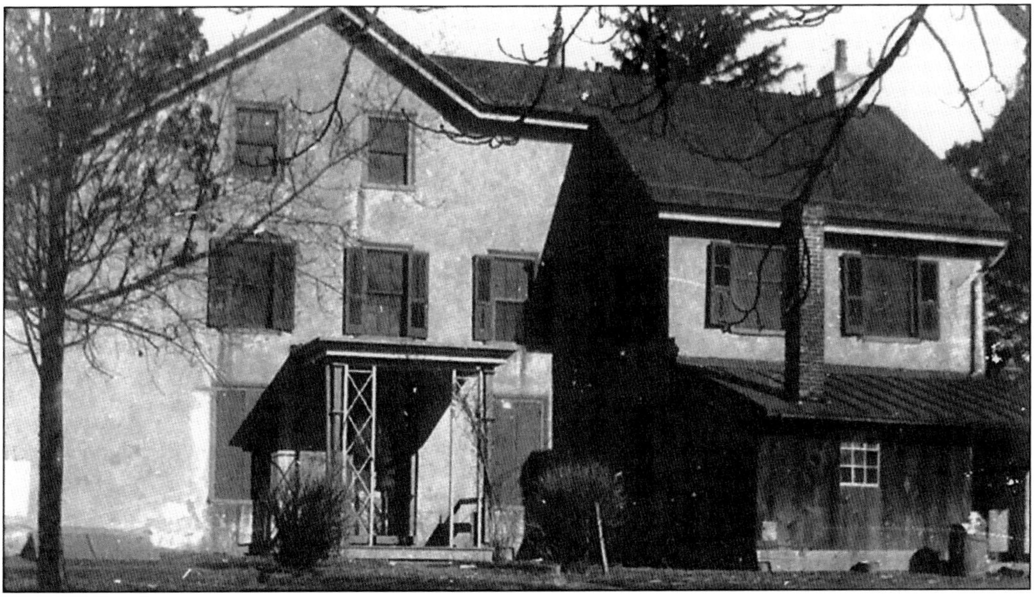

Oakford House, c. 1850. In 1788, Benjamin Oakford established a tanning yard on the north side of King's Highway (now Chester Pike). In 1838, John Oakford operated the plant until 1848 when it passed out of existence. In 1856, the Oakford farm located at 311 Bartlett Avenue was owned by Elizabeth and Hannah Oakford. They sold the property to Charles Lloyd. The walls are 18 inches thick in some places. The beams on the top floor have wooden pegs, and almost every room has a fireplace.

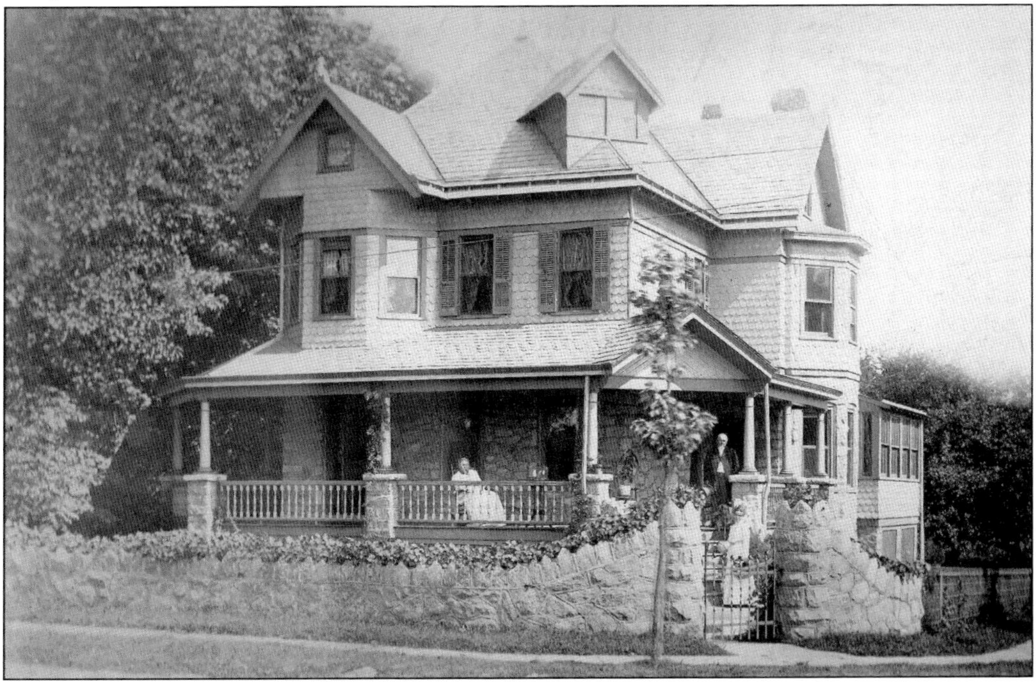

The Jacob Reese House, c. 1870. Jacob Reese built a house for each of his four sons, George, Walter, Harvey, and Frank. The houses were located at 411, 503, 511, and 527 Chester Pike. The homes are all three stories with open porches and large yards.

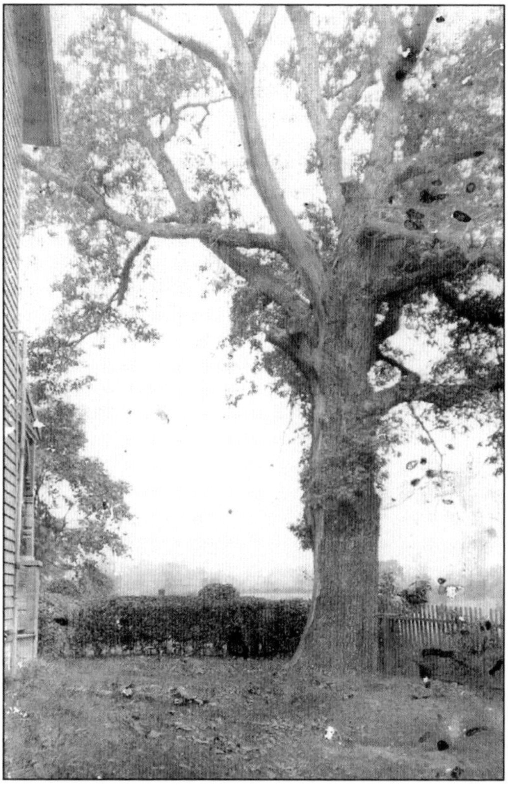

Oak Tree, 1876. This 18th-century tree was located at 709 Bonsall Avenue. Legend has it that Gen. George Washington and his men camped around this big old tree. Washington and his troops traveled the Chester Pike north of this site on the way to Philadelphia and from the Battle of the Brandywine. At the time of the Revolutionary War, Sharon Hill was farmland. (Courtesy of Joseph Walker Jr.)

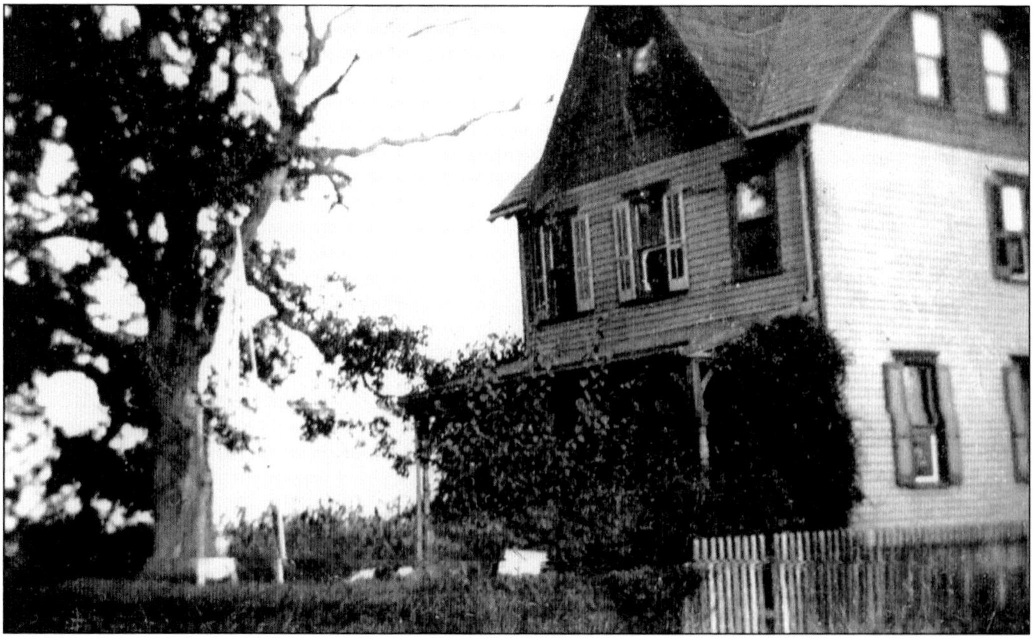

David Farran Home, 1896. This house was located at 709 Bonsall Avenue. Residents on Bonsall Avenue were part of a group of property owners that petitioned the court to secede from Darby Township and become part of Sharon Hill. The annexation occurred in 1922. (Courtesy of Joseph Walker Jr.)

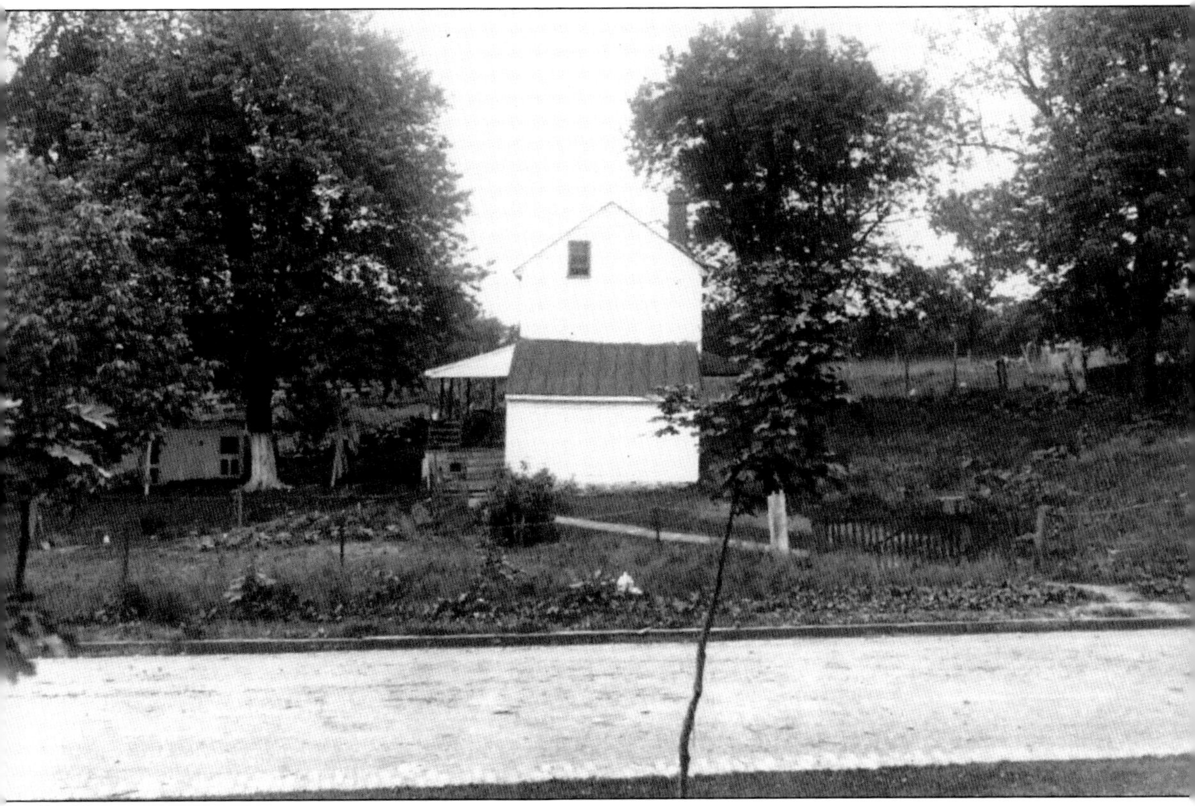

OLD FARMHOUSE, C. 1900. This farm was located at Spring Street and Clifton Avenue. Farmers who had dairy cattle usually took their cows to the south end of town to graze. When the railroad came through, farmers used the cow tunnels that were built for them to allow the cows to cross safely to and from the grazing fields.

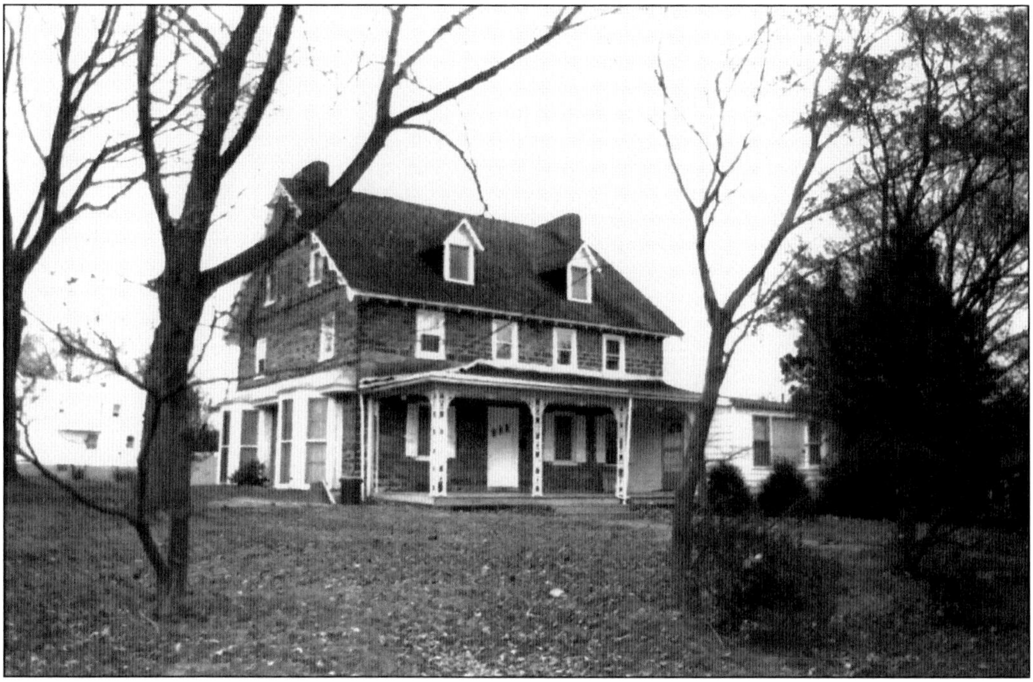

SPARKS HOUSE, c. 1872. Due to its proximity to the railroad at Poplar Street and Eggleston Circle, much of the Victorian gingerbread on the Sparks house had to be removed during the 1950s and 1960s due to the high maintenance caused by the dirt output of the steam engines on the Pennsylvania Railroad. Soot was a constant irritant until the railroad went electric.

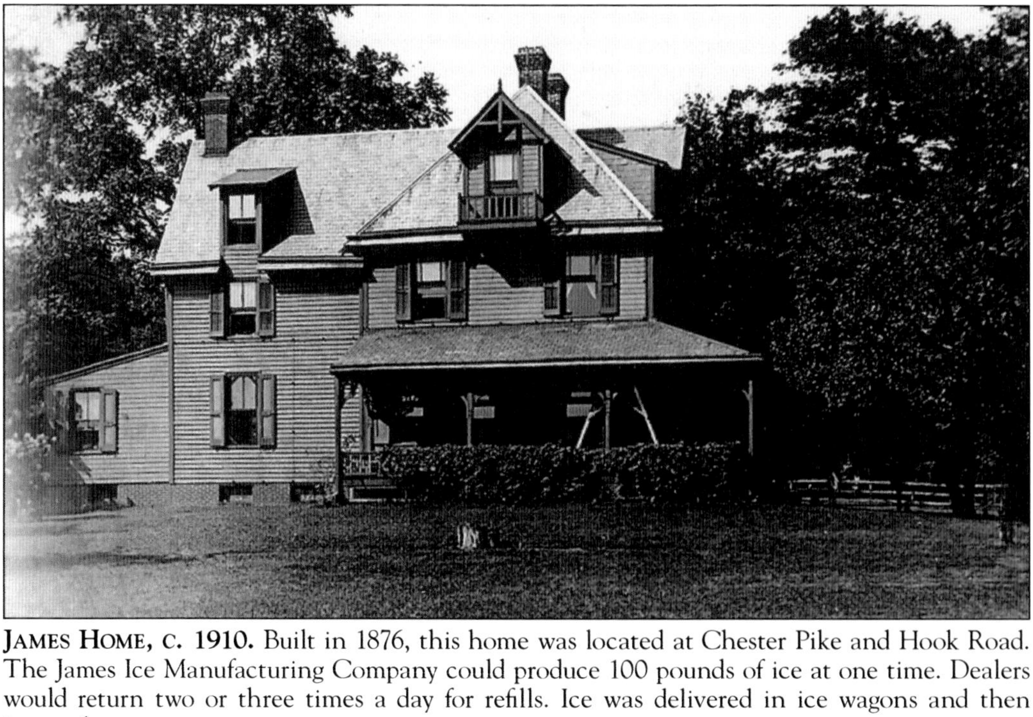

JAMES HOME, c. 1910. Built in 1876, this home was located at Chester Pike and Hook Road. The James Ice Manufacturing Company could produce 100 pounds of ice at one time. Dealers would return two or three times a day for refills. Ice was delivered in ice wagons and then ice trucks.

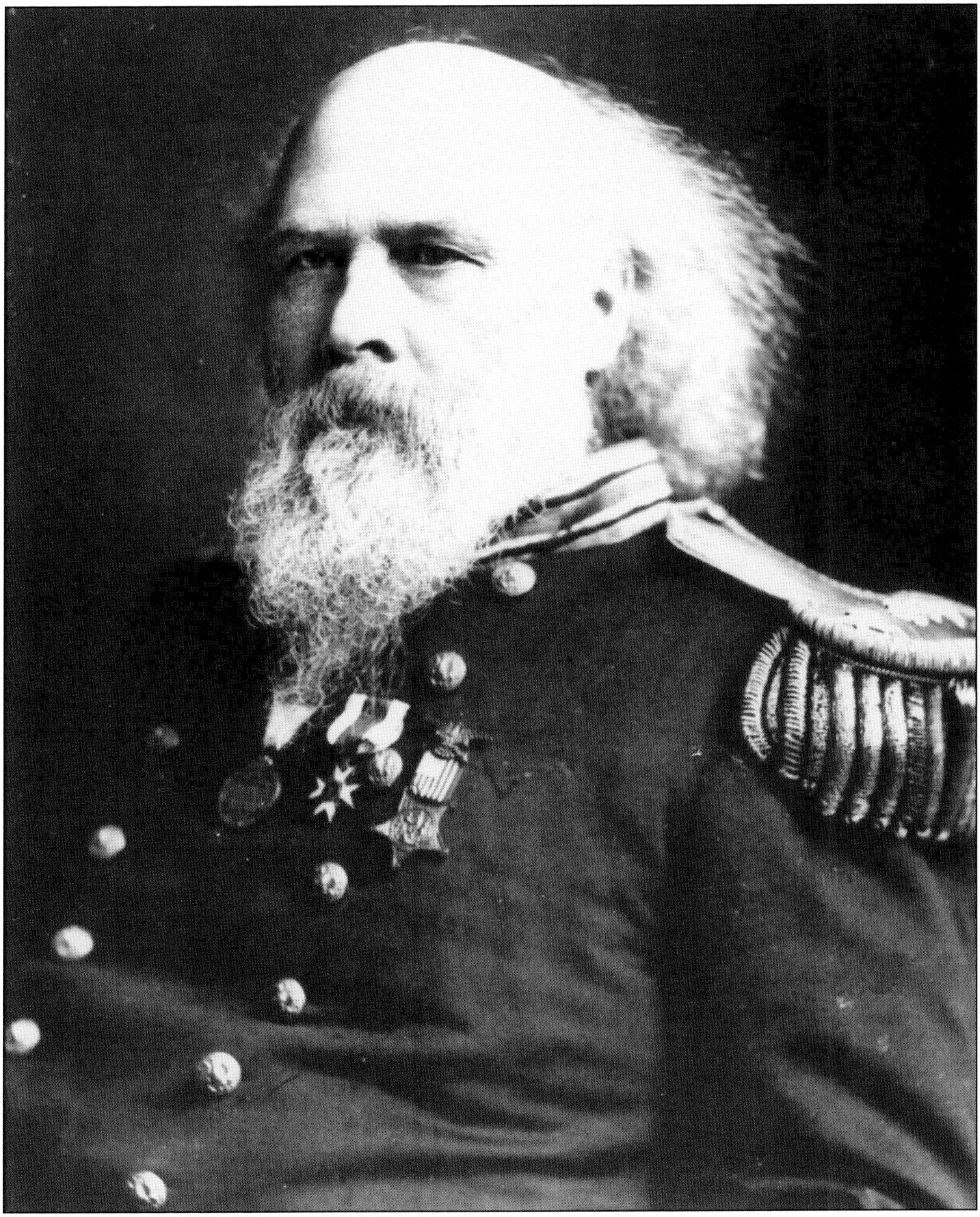

ADM. GEORGE W. MELVILLE. George W. Melville, a naval engineer and an Arctic explorer, was well known for his ventures in the Arctic region, and he served as an engineer on three different ships: the *Tigress*, the *Jeanette*, and the *Thetis*. His most dangerous mission occurred in 1879 on the ship the *Jeanette* commanded by George W. DeLong. On an expedition to the polar regions the ship was crushed by ice. Melville was in command of the only boat of men who survived. His hardships on the Lena River in the far north of Siberia are described in his book *In the Lena Delta* (1884).

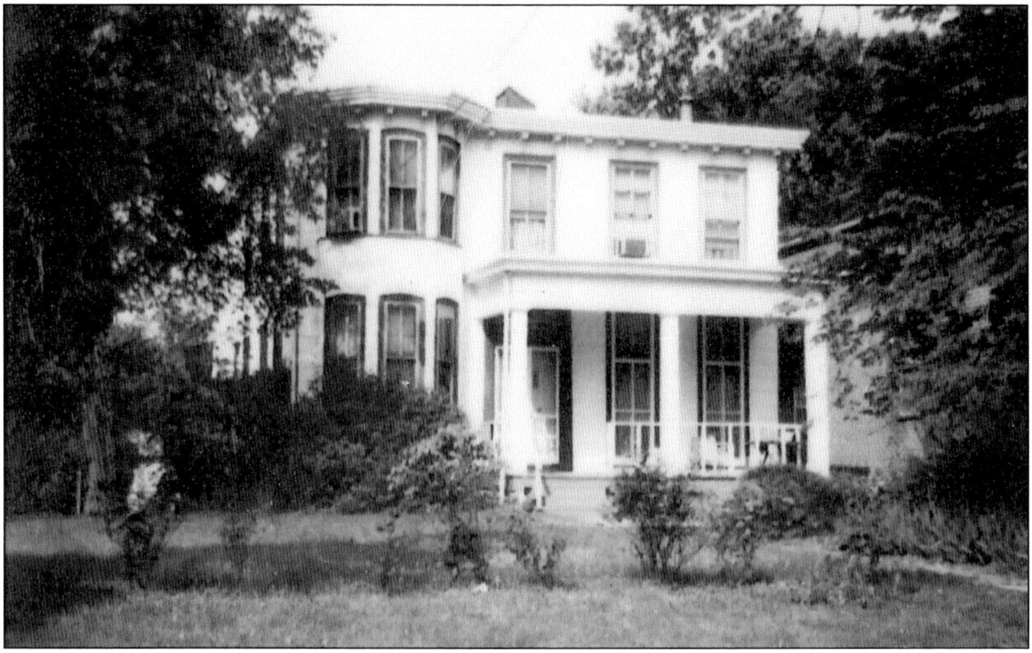

MELVILLE HOME, 1873. Adm. George W. Melville built this home at 326 Sharon Avenue in 1873. He purchased the land for $600. In 1882, Sharon Hill welcomed Melville home after his harrowing polar voyage. The streets were lit with colored lanterns, and there was a two-hour reception at his home to celebrate his safe homecoming.

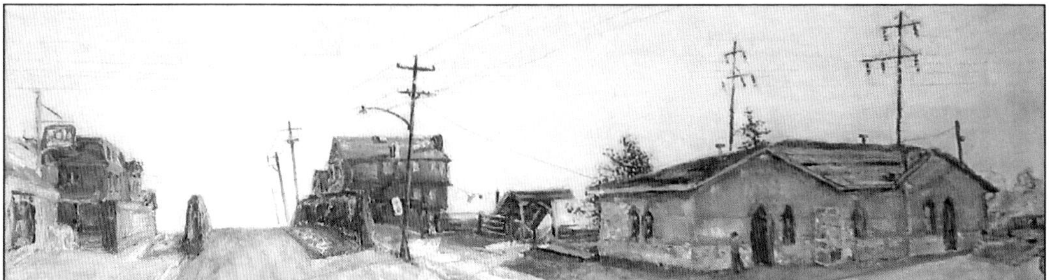

JACK LEEDS'S PAINTING, 1940S. Jack Leeds captured a unique scene of the train station landscape in his oil painting. His portrayal of the area is a rare view of the site looking southwest on Sharon Avenue. The stores on the left, the old bridge, the homes on the right along with the covered stairway to the tracks, and the 1872 historic station are reminiscent of the late-19th-century era of the town. Jack Leeds was a descendant of Jacob Reese.

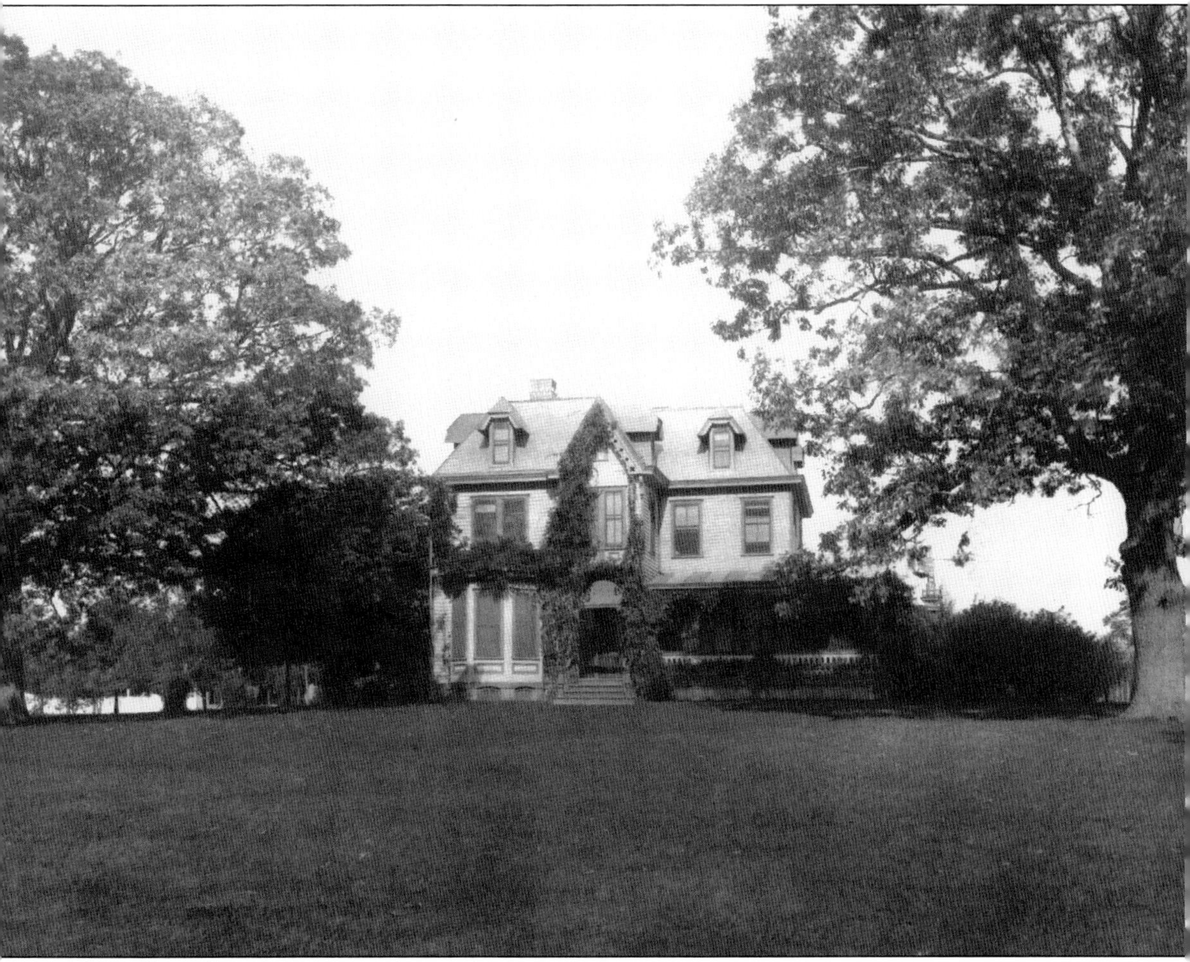

TWIN OAKS, 1884. Purchased from Clement Biddle in 1884 by William Hazelton Folwell, a manufacturer of textiles in Philadelphia, the home known as Twin Oaks consisted of 16 acres and ran from the northwest corner of Clifton Avenue and Chester Pike to the Baltimore and Ohio Railroad. Flowers, bushes, and trees of all species graced the property. The spacious grounds were also home to horses, donkeys, cows, chickens, and peacocks. Fresh vegetables were grown on the farm. The house had 11 bedrooms plus downstairs rooms that included a school room where the Folwell children began their early education. The Folwells resided in the house until 1909. (Courtesy of the Print and Picture Collection, Free Library of Philadelphia.)

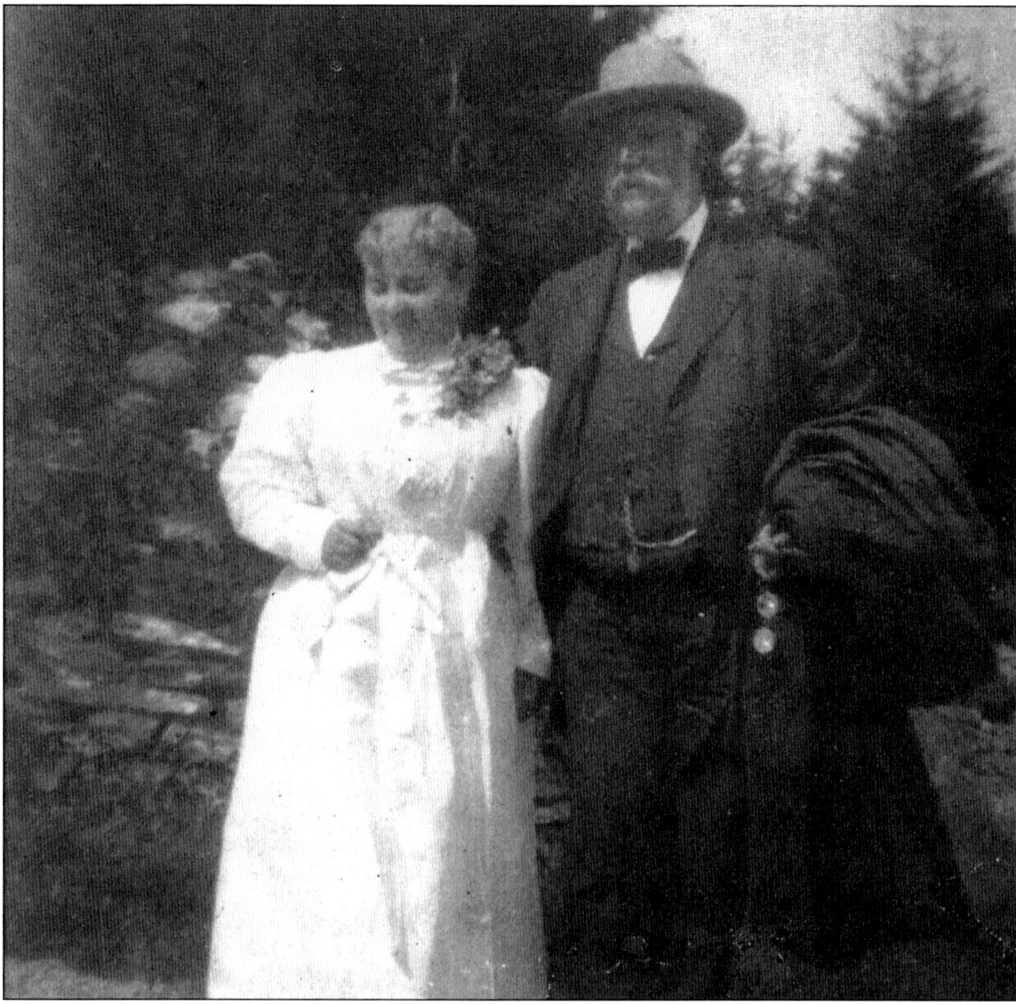

MARY ROBERTS PIERSOL FOLWELL AND WILLIAM HAZELTON FOLWELL, C. 1898. The Folwells were Quakers. Their two youngest children attended Friends Select Seminary in Philadelphia going by train each day. William was a manufacturer of textiles in Philadelphia and part owner with his brother, Nathan, of Folwell Brothers and Company Collingwood Mills. (Courtesy of Maida Barton Follini.)

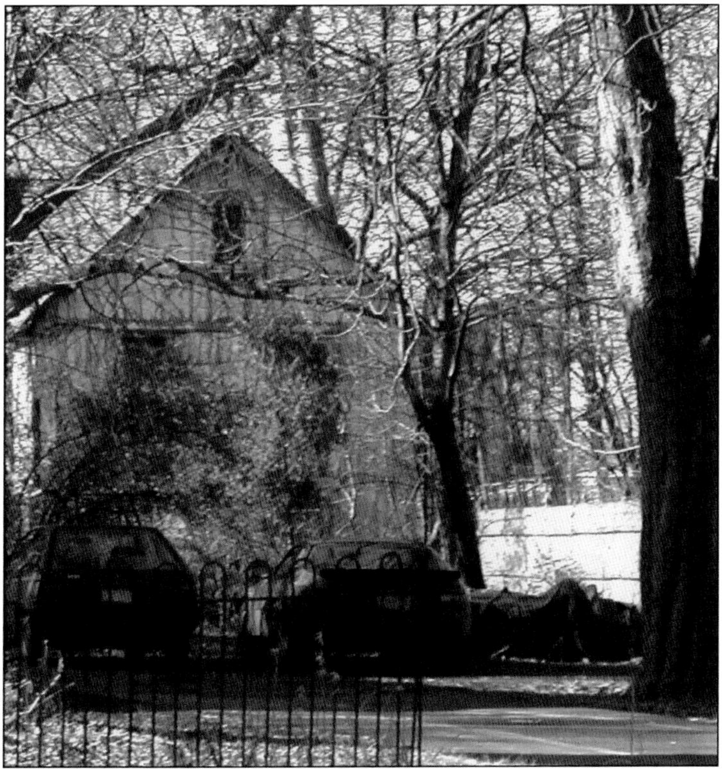

CARRIAGE HOUSE, C. 1880. Many gentlemen had a span of horses. After the railroad opened, it was common to see horse-drawn carriages from the mansions taking ladies in their finery to the station. This house is located at 318 Sharon Avenue. (Courtesy of Delaware County Planning Department.)

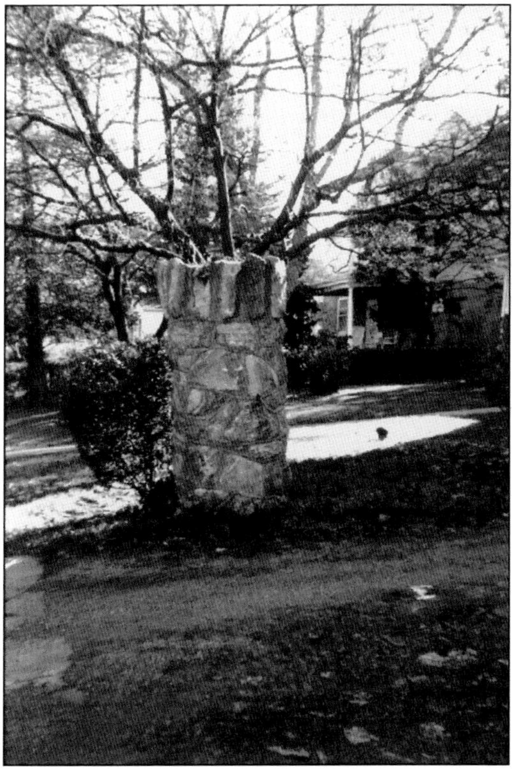

STONE GATEPOST, C. 1890. Gateposts such as the one seen here at 308 Oak Avenue are seen throughout the roads in Sharon Hill as many Victorians used the fieldstone pillars to adorn their entrances. (Courtesy of Dorothy Grover.)

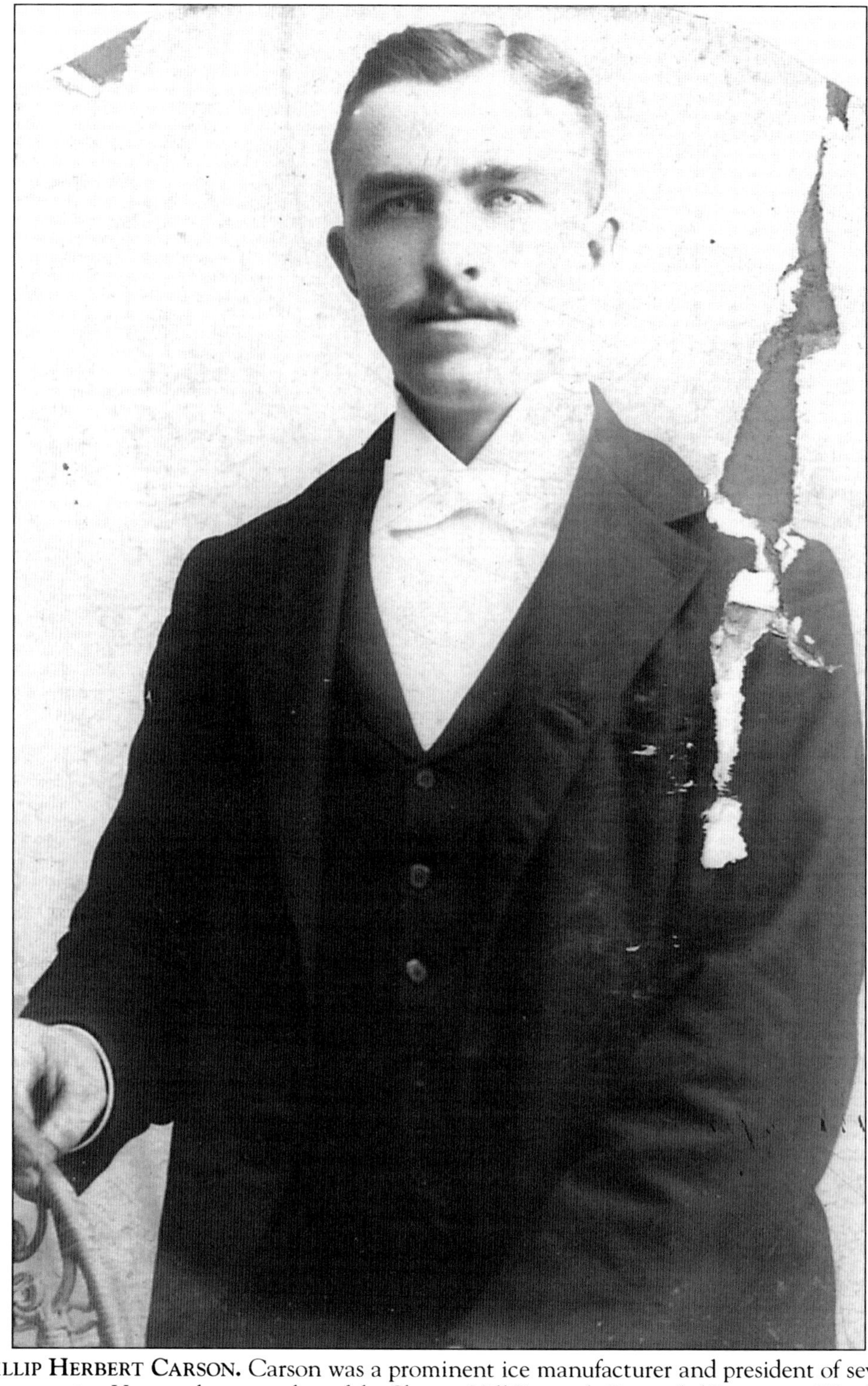

Phillip Herbert Carson. Carson was a prominent ice manufacturer and president of several ice companies. He was also a member of the Sharon Hill Borough Council. (Courtesy of Kimberly Carson McGowan.)

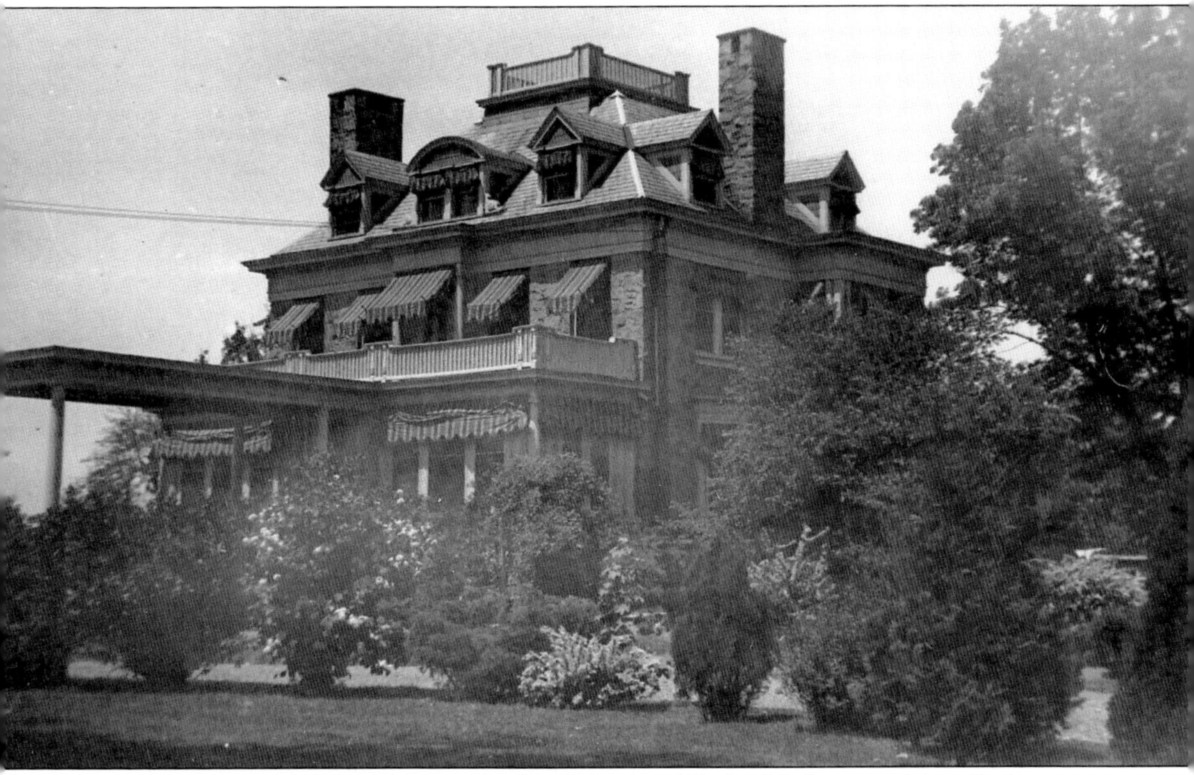

CARSON MANSION, C. 1878. This was the family home of Phillip Herbert and Mary Catherine Kennedy Carson. The three-story, gray-stone house was located on the north side of Chester Pike between the Red Arrow trolley line and Folcroft Avenue. The land was purchased by Food Fair supermarket in 1953, and the mansion was scheduled to be razed but was destroyed by fire. (Courtesy of Kimberly Carson McGowan.)

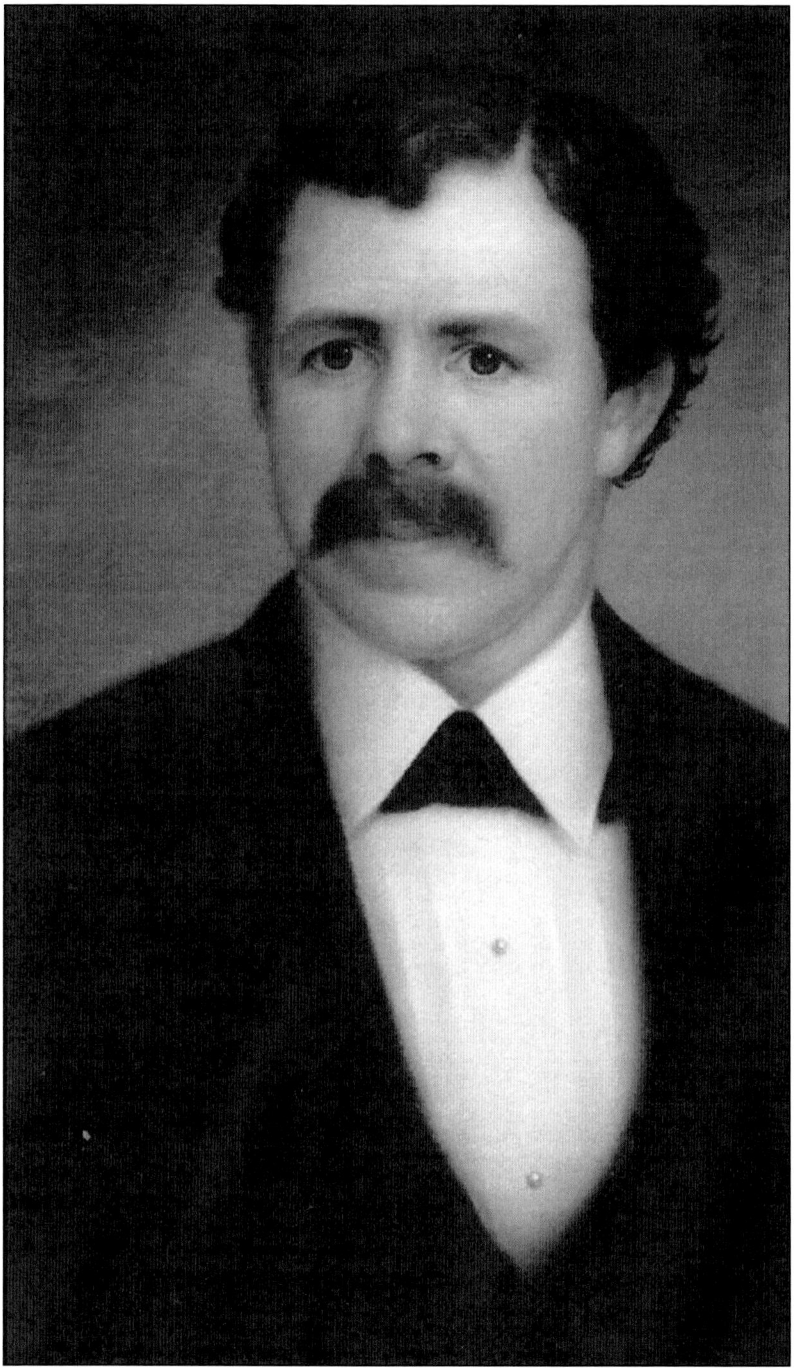

JOHN MULDOON. John Muldoon and his wife, Mary, moved from Philadelphia to Sharon Hill in 1880 to a beautiful home known as Evergreen Mansion near Clifton Avenue and Chester Pike. John Muldoon built houses at 202 and 206 Sharon Avenue. He was a successful dry goods merchant in Philadelphia. He played a major role in the development of Sharon Hill and organizing it into a borough. He served on the borough council in 1891. (Courtesy of Kimberly Carson McGowan.)

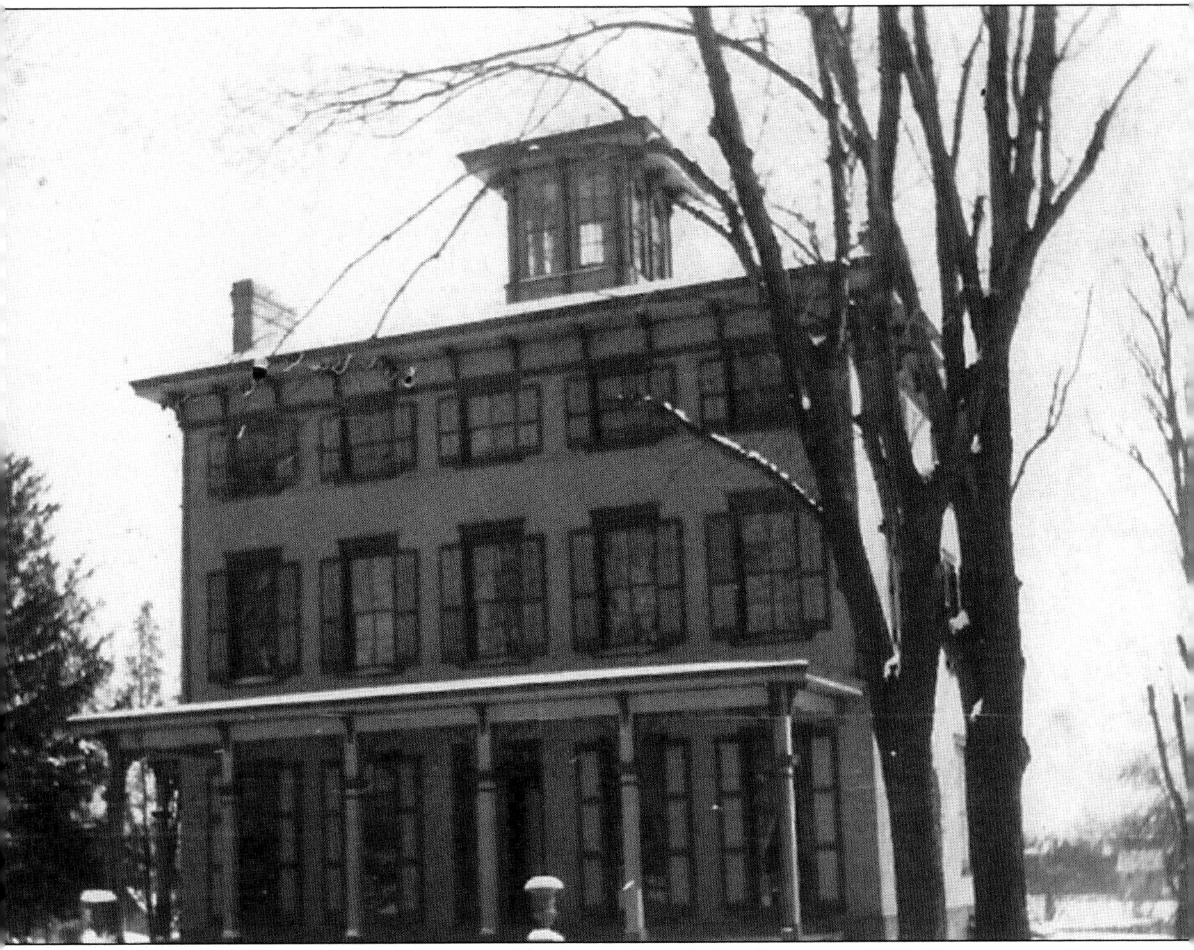

Muldoon Mansion, c. 1869. John Muldoon purchased this home in 1908. It was owned by Capt. Joseph McMakin in 1869. Captain McMakin and his wife, Martha, purchased the property from Rachael Jackson in 1860. The house, like several others in the town, had a cupola and was located at Clifton Avenue and Chester Pike.

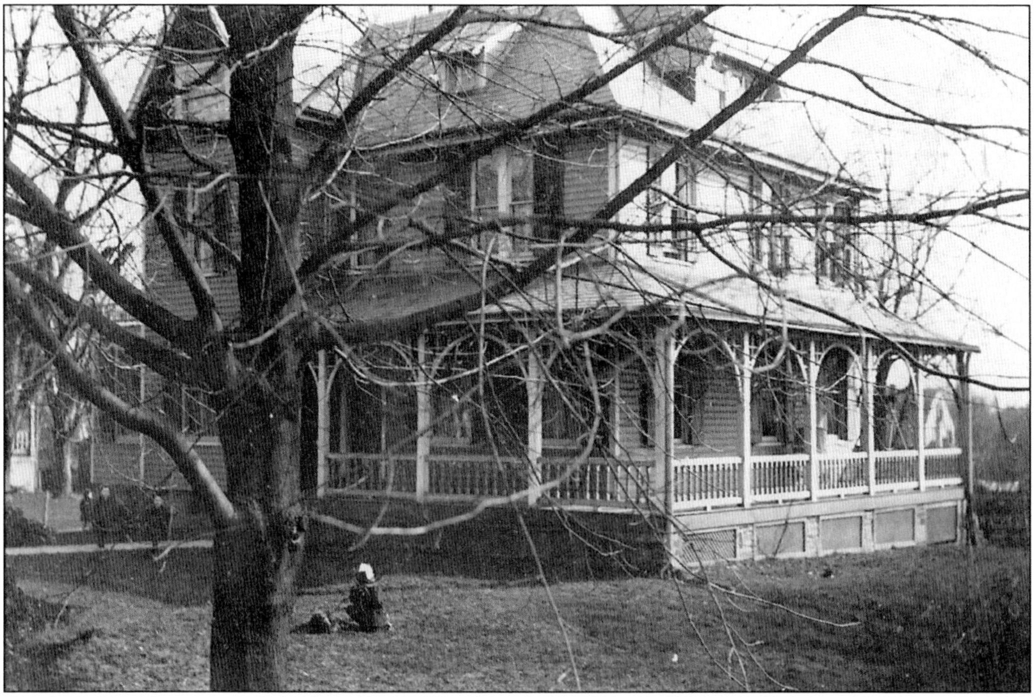

HAUCK HOME, C. 1906. Descendants of John Muldoon occupied this house at 106 Chester Pike near Felton Avenue.

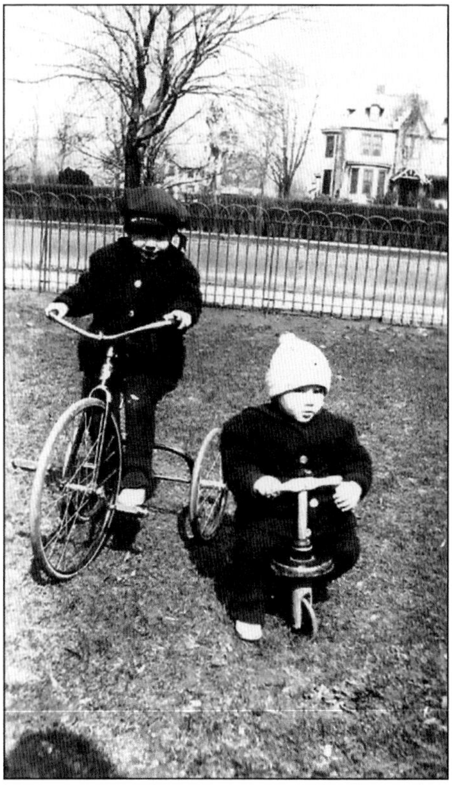

TWO YOUNG BOYS, 1924. Smed and Jude enjoy riding their tricycles in a front yard in Sharon Hill. The Folwell home appears in the background. (Courtesy of Kimberly Carson McGowan.)

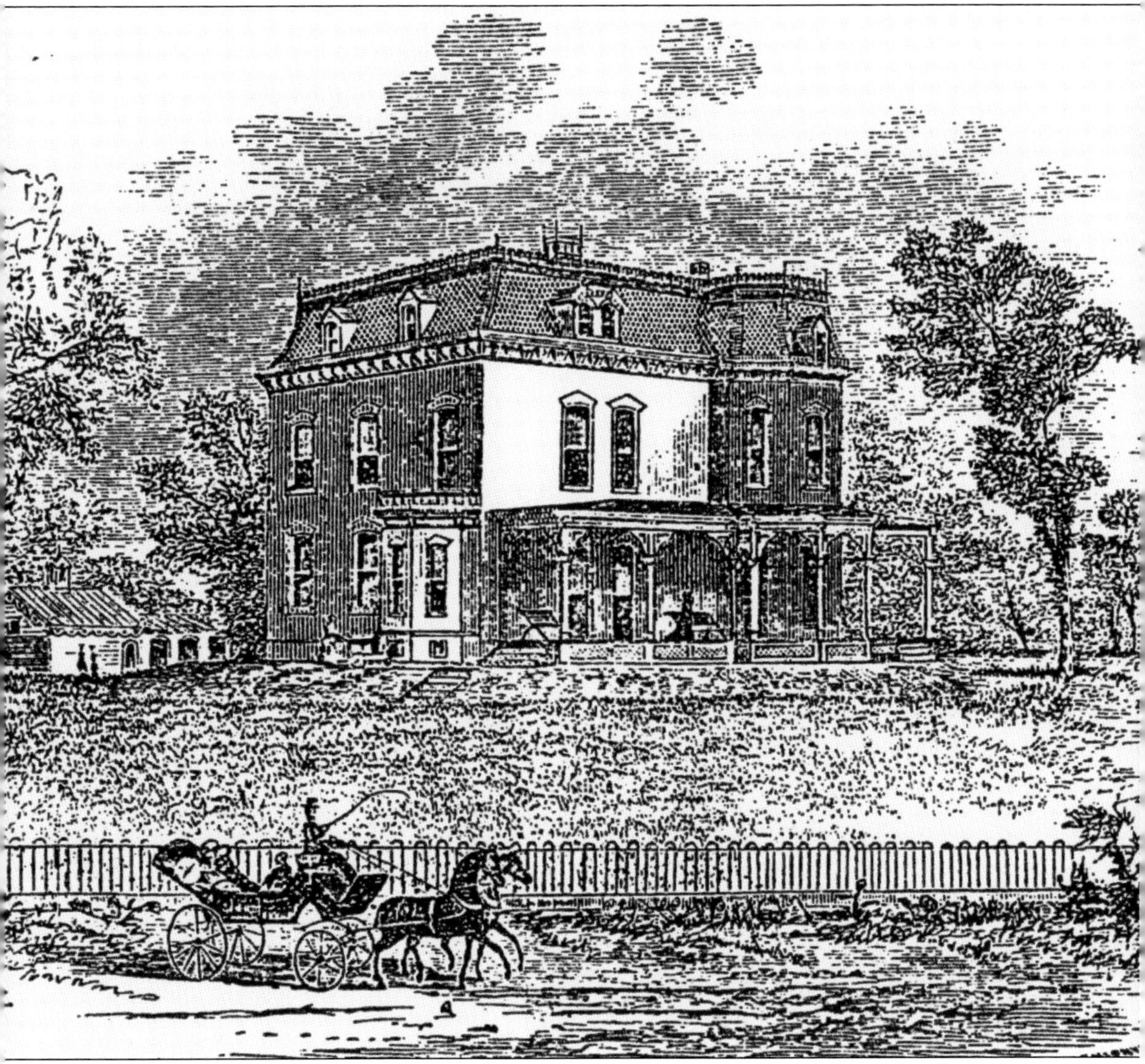

CHARLES LAFFERTY ESTATE, 1870S. This house was located on Calcon Hook Road and Chester Pike in what is now the area of the athletic field and elementary school. Charles Lafferty had a horsecar business in Philadelphia. His grounds were noted for their large barns and beautiful gardens. Buildings in Philadelphia could be seen from the cupola of his home.

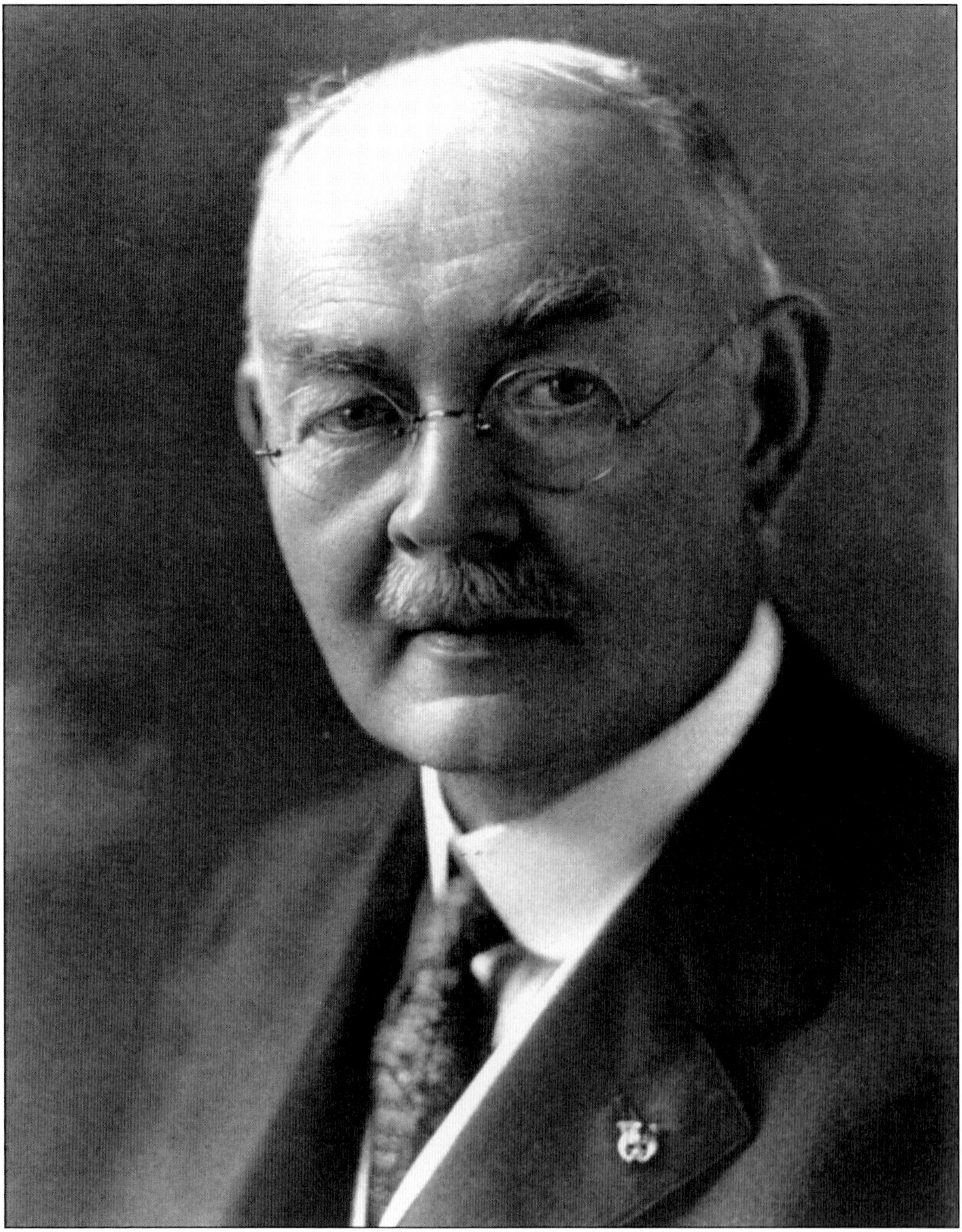

GEORGE MCKENSIE DUNLAP. George McKensie Dunlap was the founder of the American Stores Company. He lived in a Victorian mansion approximately where the Acme supermarket and shopping center now stand. After his death, his son George Dunlap Jr. built houses on Barker Avenue, Ridley Avenue, Kenney Avenue, Burnside Avenue, and Marshall Road. The Acme Market officially opened on December 9, 1959. The 24-lane bowling alley called Sharon Hill Lanes opened in an adjoining building.

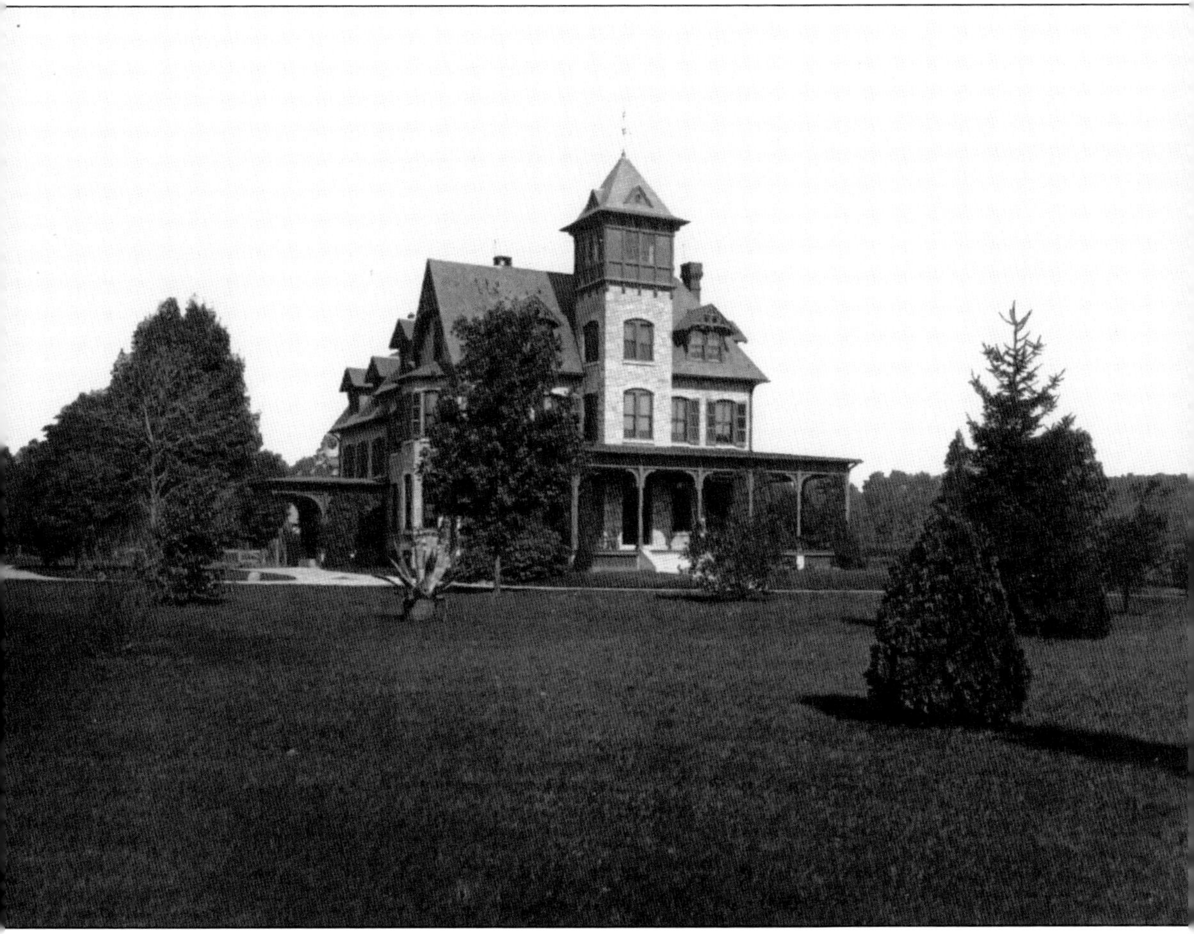

EDGEWOOD MANSION, 1870S. This stone mansion was owned by Samuel Bunting, who was an auctioneer in Philadelphia with the firm S. J. and S. Bunting. The cost to build the mansion was $25,000. It was located at Chester Pike and Sharon Avenue. The Acme Market complex now occupies the Buntings' land. (Courtesy of the Print and Picture Collection, Free Library of Philadelphia.)

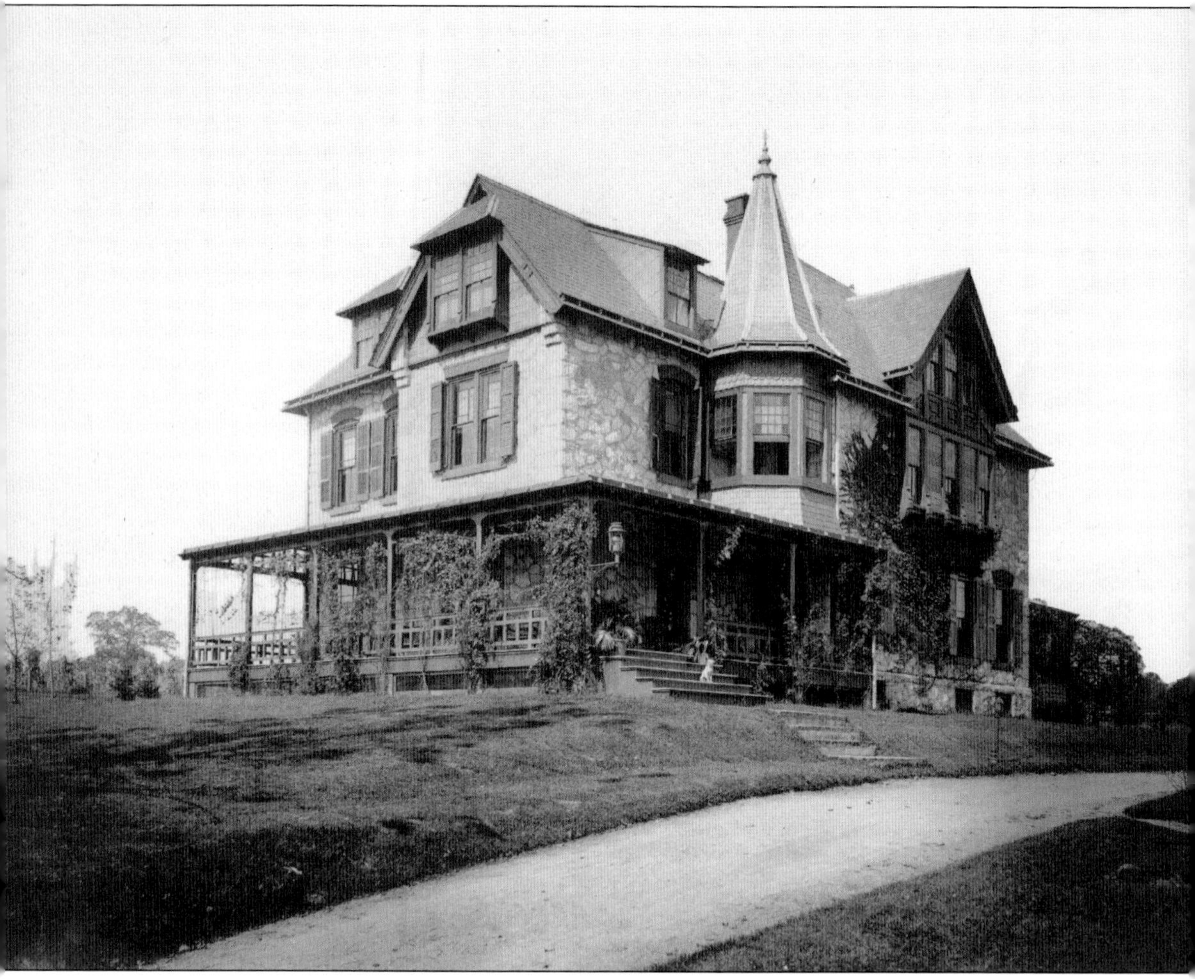

THE HEIGHTS, 1870S. The mansion known as the Heights is listed in the files of the Free Library of Philadelphia as the residence of Joseph S. Bunting in Sharon Hill. The Bunting family had properties in Darby Borough and the Sharon Hill area, which was part of Darby Borough until 1890. Joseph Bunting's property shown on old maps was near the Darby Creek on the Darby side. Whether Bunting considered his property to be in Sharon Hill or owned a property in Sharon Hill is not known. It is being shared as a point of historical interest. (Courtesy of the Print and Picture Department, Free Library of Philadelphia.)

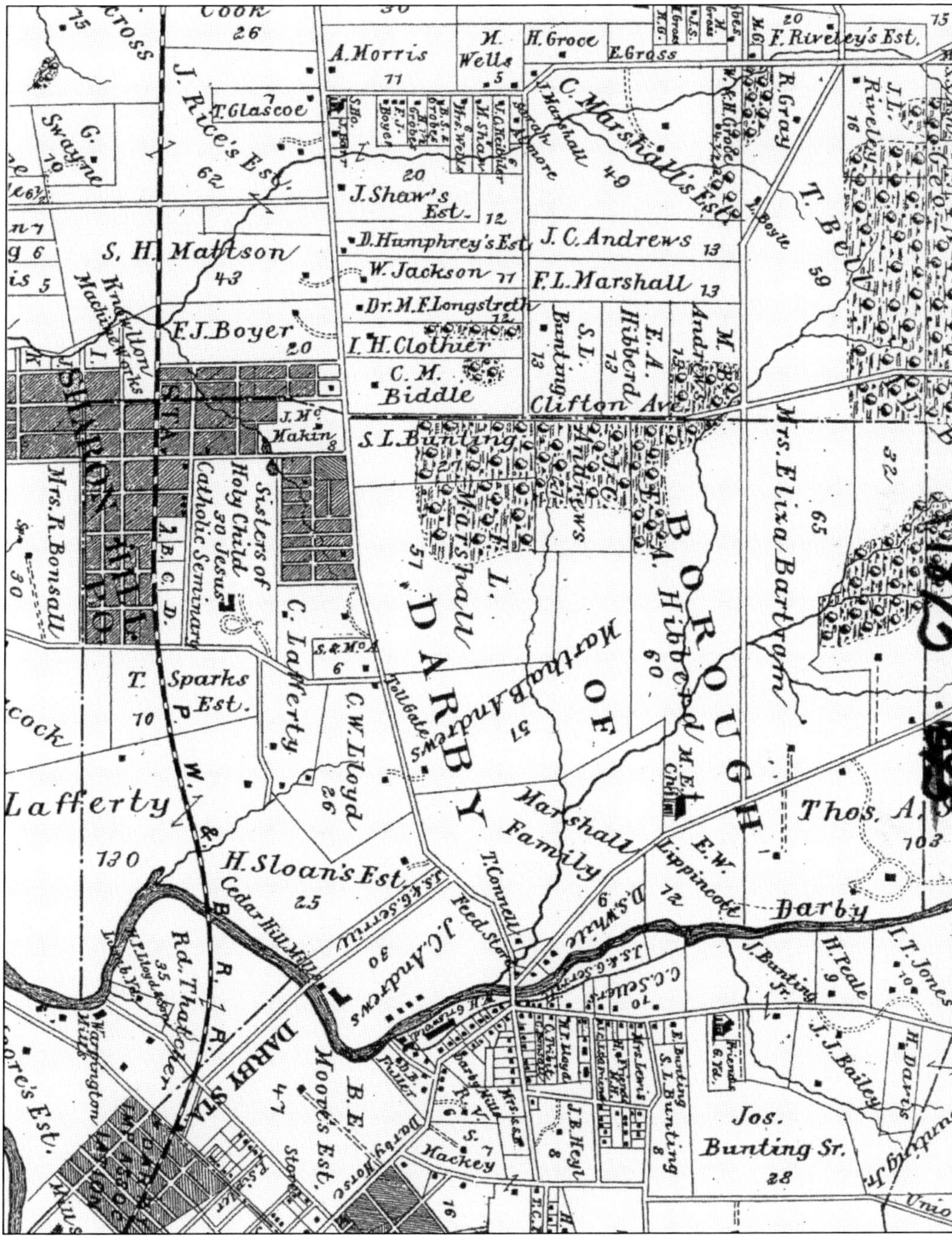

SHARON HILL MAP, 1875. The location of the residences and properties of the early settlers can be found on this 1875 map. It shows east–west designations with the Philadelphia, Wilmington and Baltimore Railroad on the south. Chester Pike with its tollgate to the north goes through the village. At this time Sharon Hill was part of Darby.

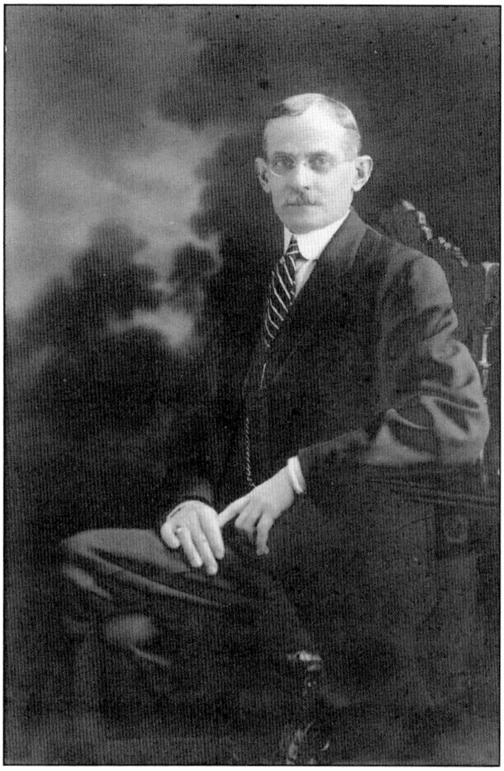

JOHN HAROLD DONOHUE, 1890S. John Donohue assisted his father and others in a butcher shop in Philadelphia. When he came to Sharon Hill in 1895, he continued in the meat business. In 1905, he established his own grocery store at Sharon Avenue below the railroad. (Courtesy of Henrietta Donohue.)

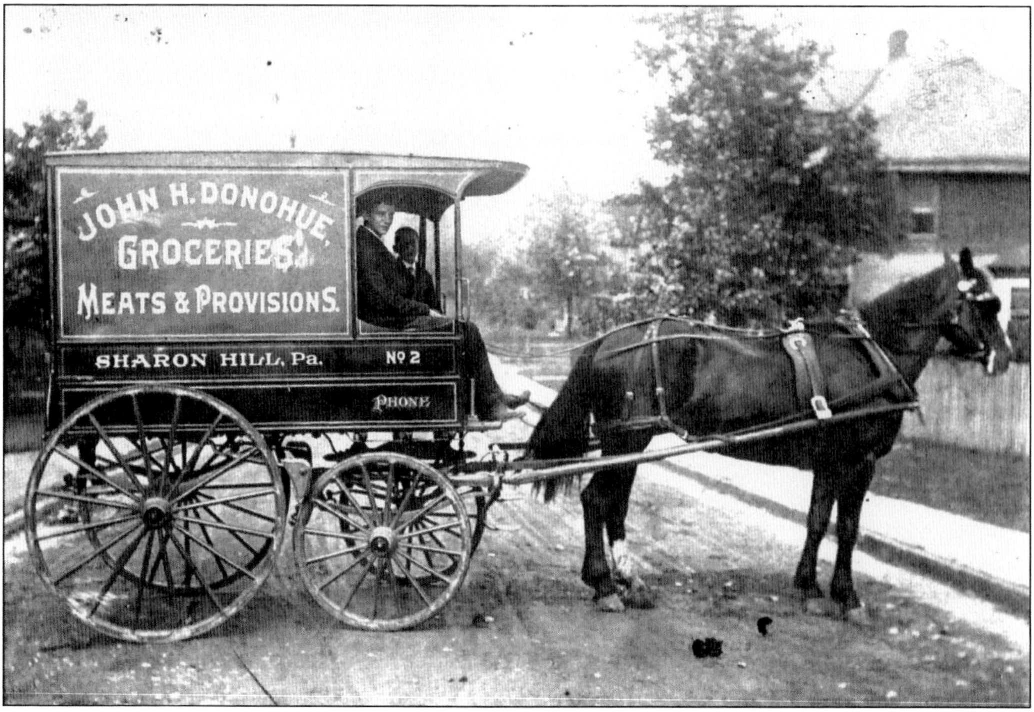

DELIVERY WAGON, C. 1906. Pictured on Elmwood Avenue is the Donohue Grocery wagon delivering meat and provisions to Sharon Hill residents. (Courtesy of Henrietta Donohue.)

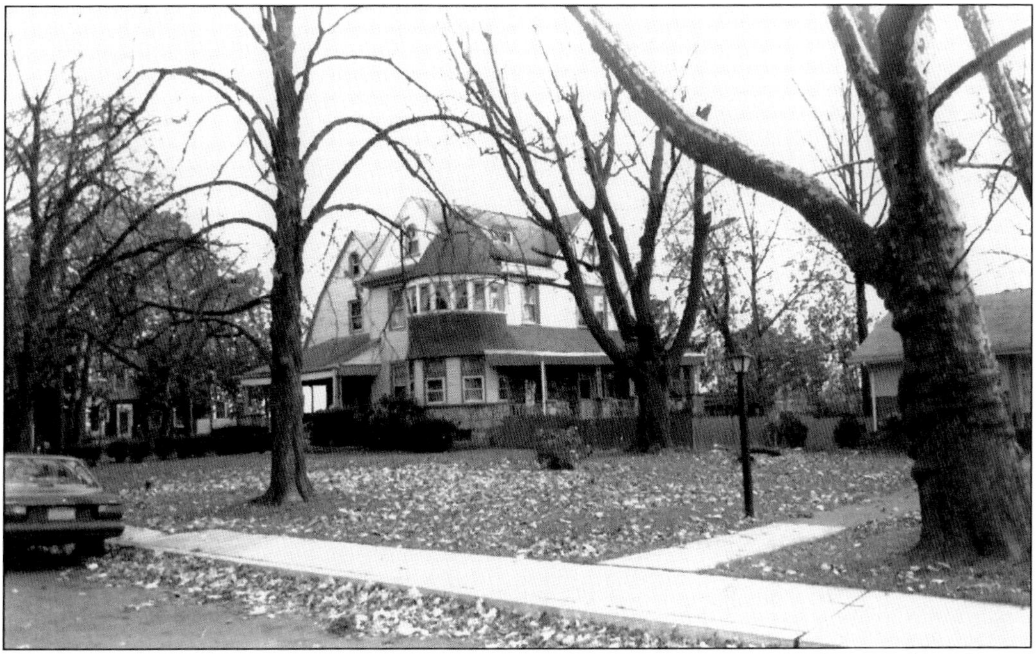

THE DALTON HOME, 1987. Located at 753 Woodland Terrace was the home of Dr. David Dalton. It was known as the Pines. Dr. Dalton was a pharmacist and one of the early surgeons at Taylor Hospital in nearby Ridley Park. He served on the borough's first planning commission in 1935. His daughter, Margaret, taught music in the Sharon Hill school system.

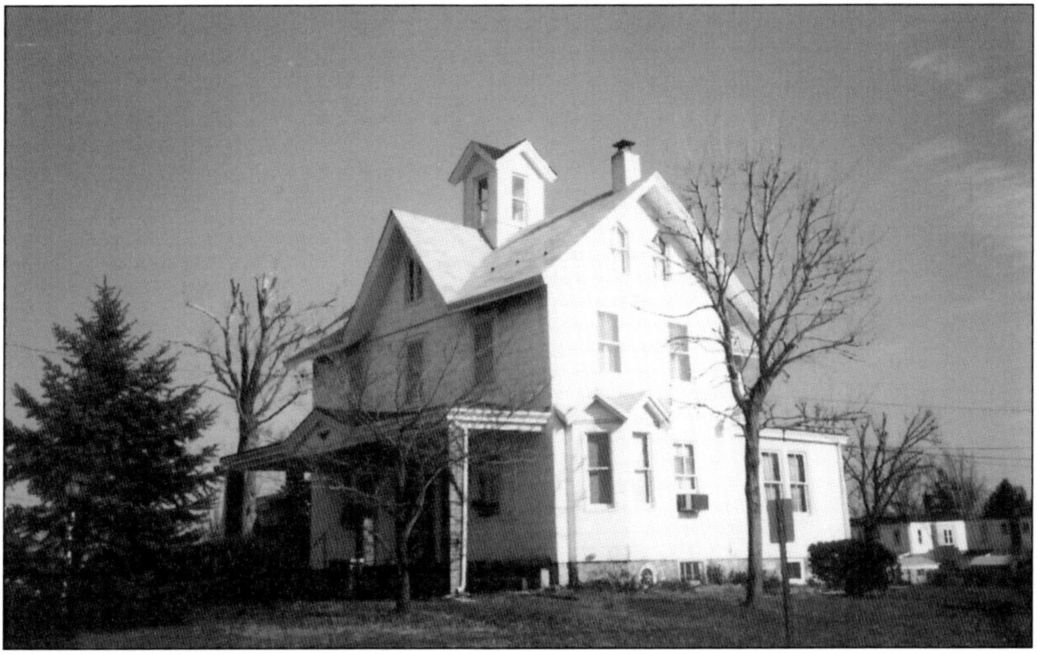

PARET HOME, 1897. Located at 921 Chester Pike, this building has a cupola or widow's walk above the third floor. Sailing and shipping vessels on the Delaware River could be seen from this vantage point. It is called a widow's walk because wives would go there to look to watch for the safe return of their seafaring husbands.

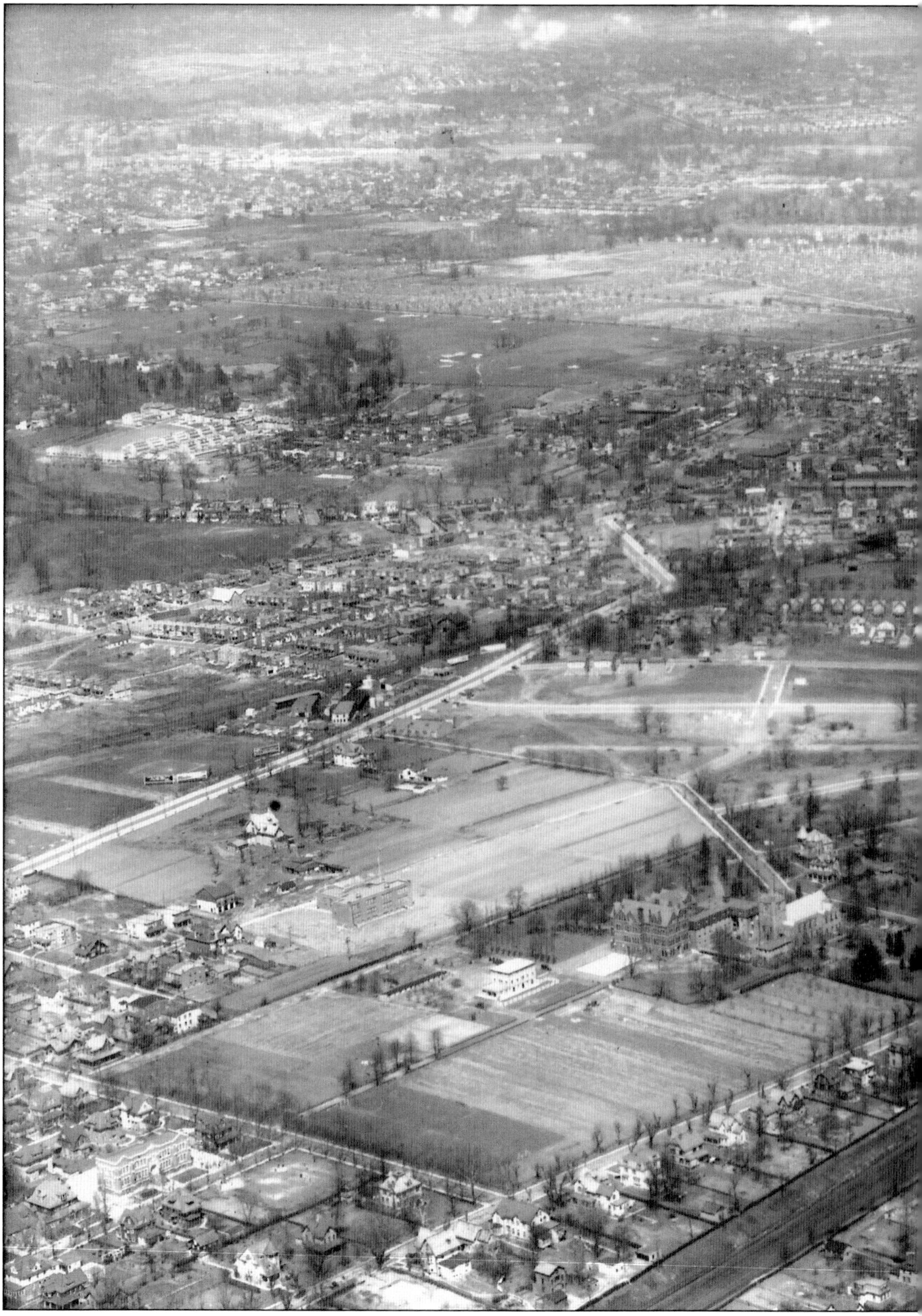

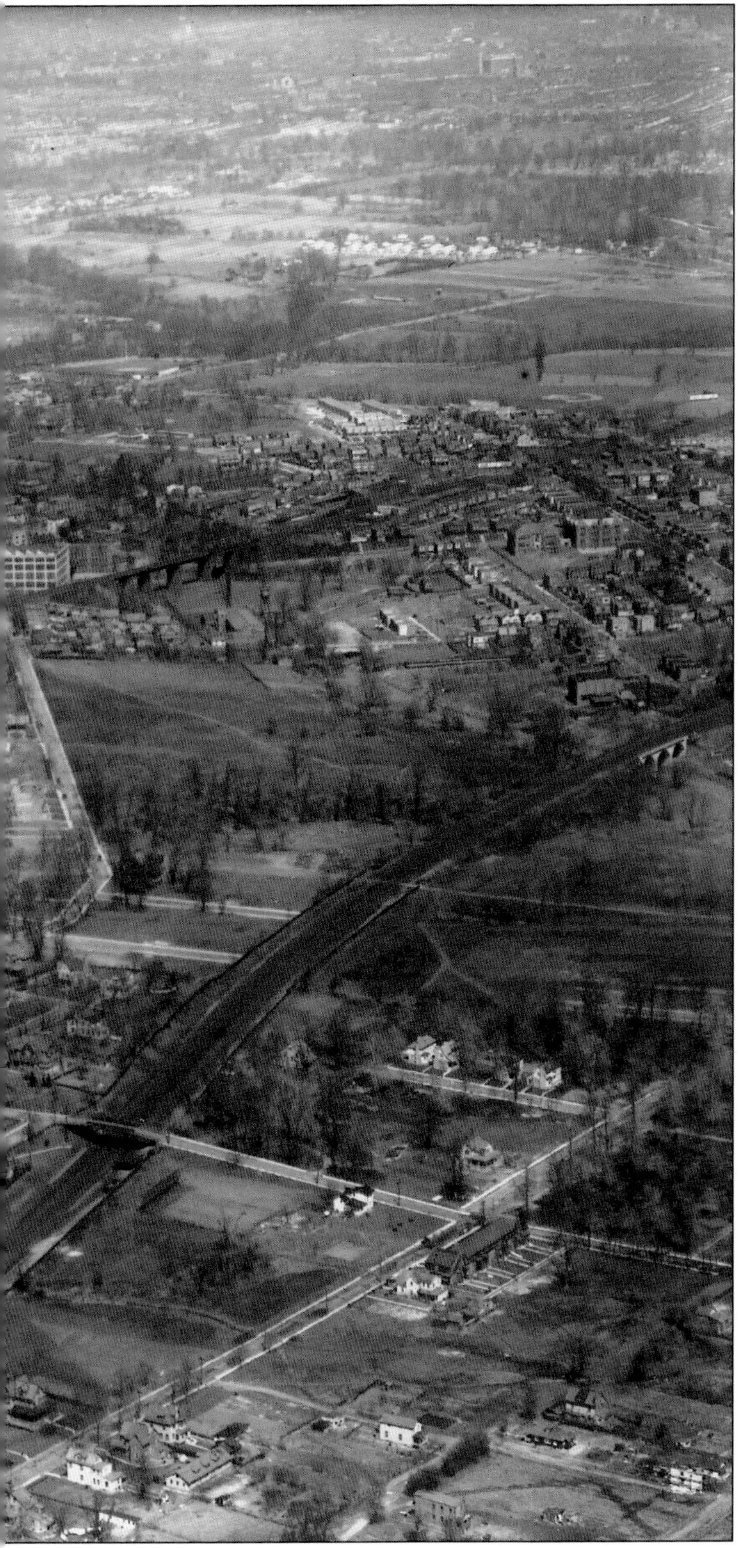

AERIAL VIEW OF SHARON HILL, 1926. This view of Sharon Hill shows the Pennsylvania Railroad lines going east to Philadelphia and west to Wilmington, Baltimore, and Washington, D.C. On the north side is a row of 1890s residences on Woodland Avenue. To the south are residences bordering Elmwood Avenue. Calcon Hook Road is shown going north past the Holy Child Academy and the Sharon Hill High School on the left and a district of 1890s residences on the right at Woodland Terrace and Oak Avenue. Continuing north the road passes the Lafferty Estate, James Ice Company, and Lewis's gas station and garage at Chester Pike. This was the location of toll gate No. 6. The lower left side of the view shows Holy Spirit Elementary School on School Street, Maple Avenue, Barker Avenue, and Coates Street. Going east along Chester Pike is the Jacob Reese estate.

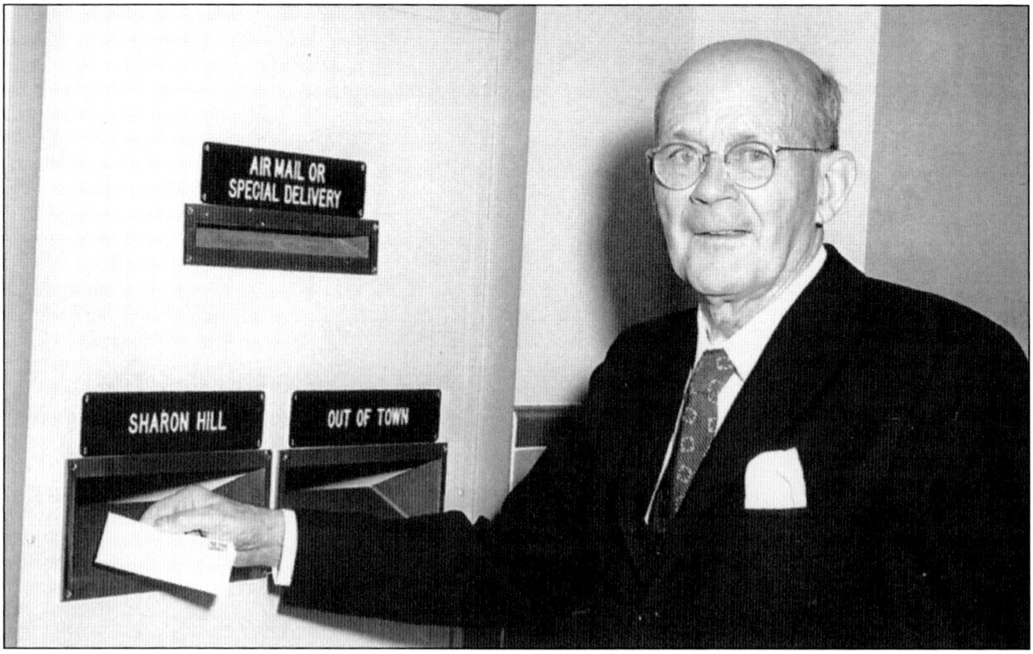

GEORGE GOODWIN. Octavius Goodwin, father of George Goodwin, purchased the Rose Tool Company in the 1890s. George succeeded him and ran the company well with the production of fine quality tools. His daughter, Gertrude, eventually became the president of the company. Shown in the picture is George at the opening of the Sharon Hill Post Office on Chester Pike.

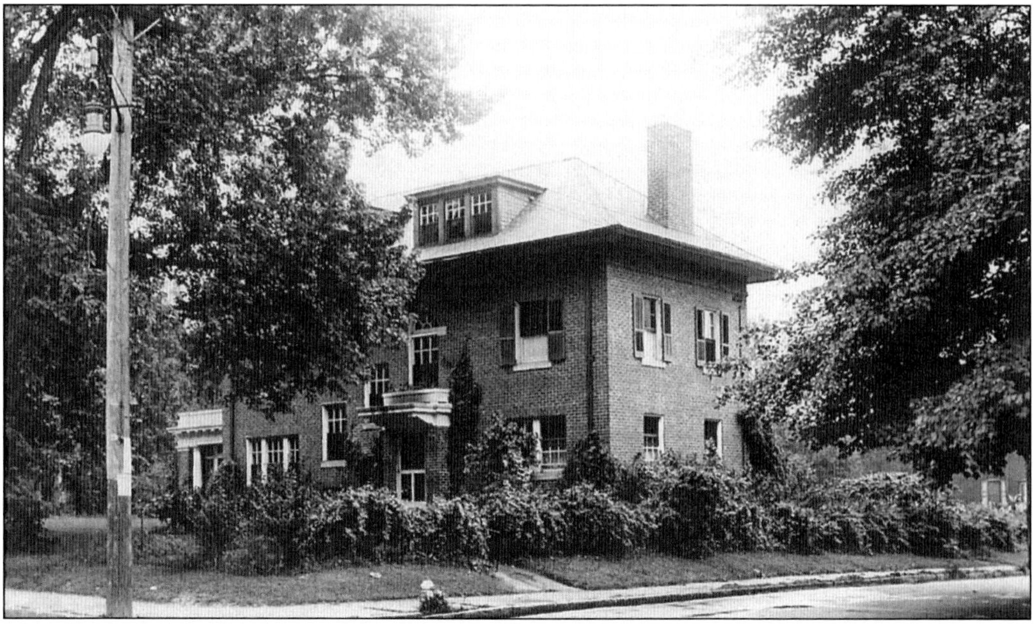

GOODWIN HOME, 1920. This house was owned by the George Goodwin family until 1998. George Goodwin owned and operated the Rose Tool Company on Elmwood Avenue. The house is unique in that it is completely fireproof. What appears to be wood trim on the brick exterior of the house is actually cement. The basement ceiling is made of steel. The architect was Frank Keisker, who designed the home in 1912.

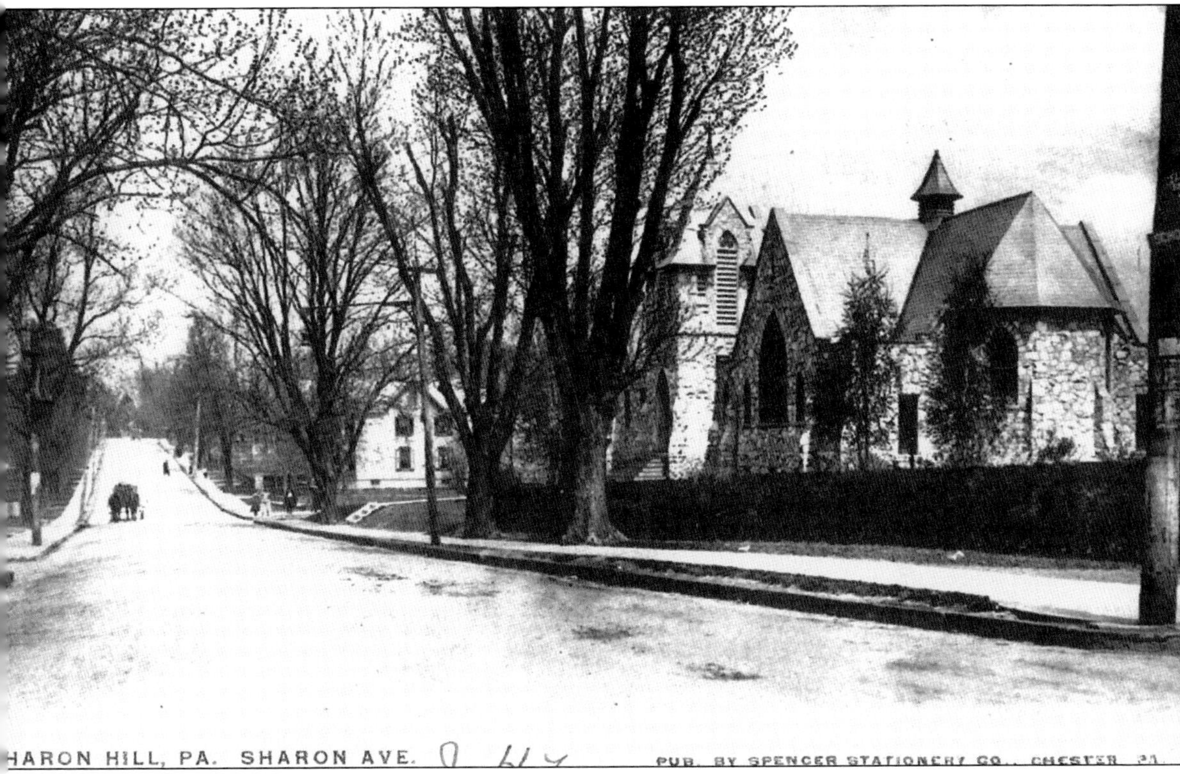

SHARON AVENUE, 1907. Shown on the east side of Sharon Avenue in this 1907 postcard is the Methodist Episcopal church.

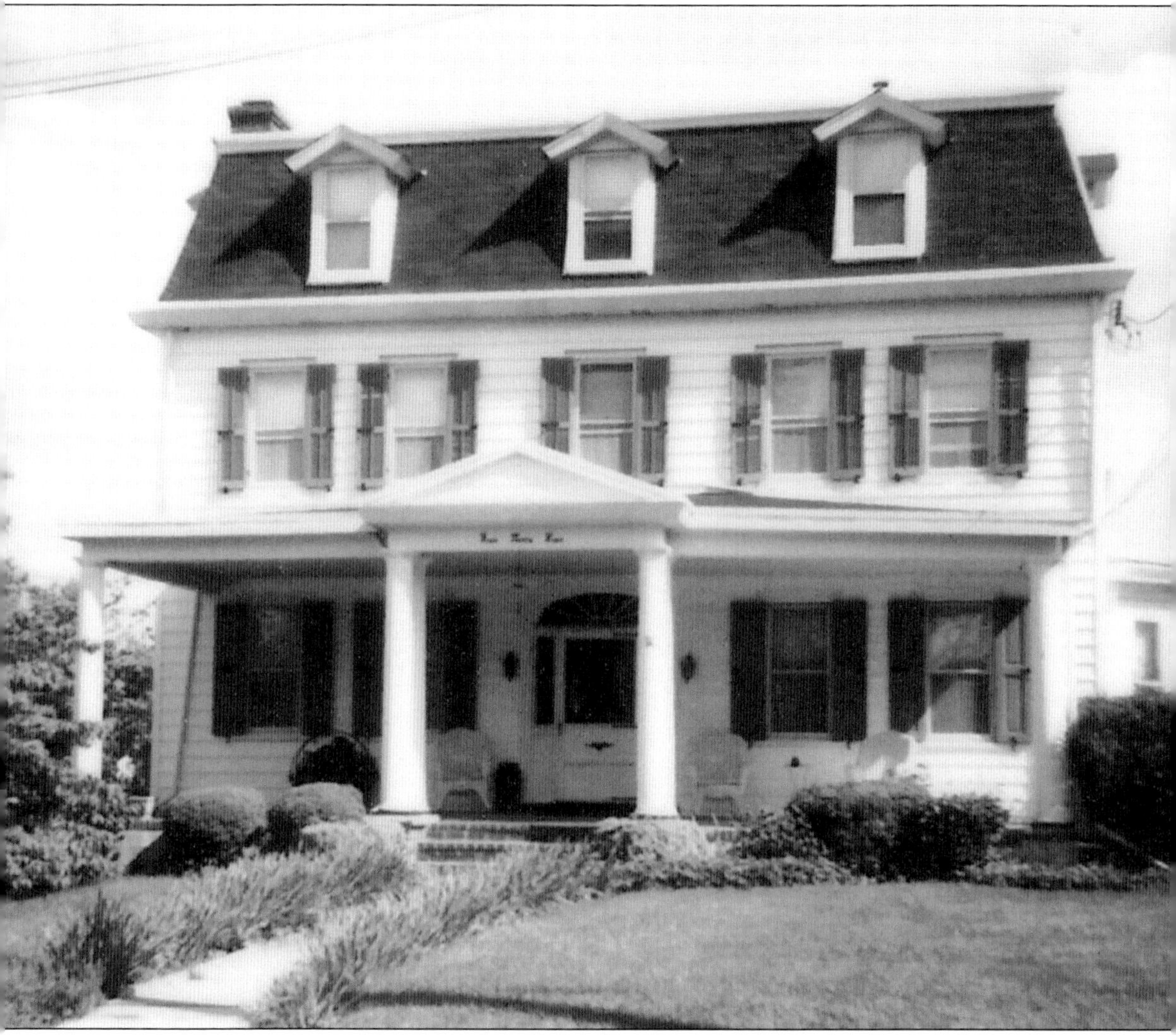

No. 939 Woodland Avenue, 1880s. This home was originally owned by Thomas Garvin. Garvin was a state representative, Sharon Hill's first treasurer, and chief burgess of the council. In 1891, Garvin Boulevard in Sharon Hill was named for him. The Sisters of the Holy Child converted the building into a convent for the teaching nuns at Holy Spirit in 1972; at present it is a privately owned home.

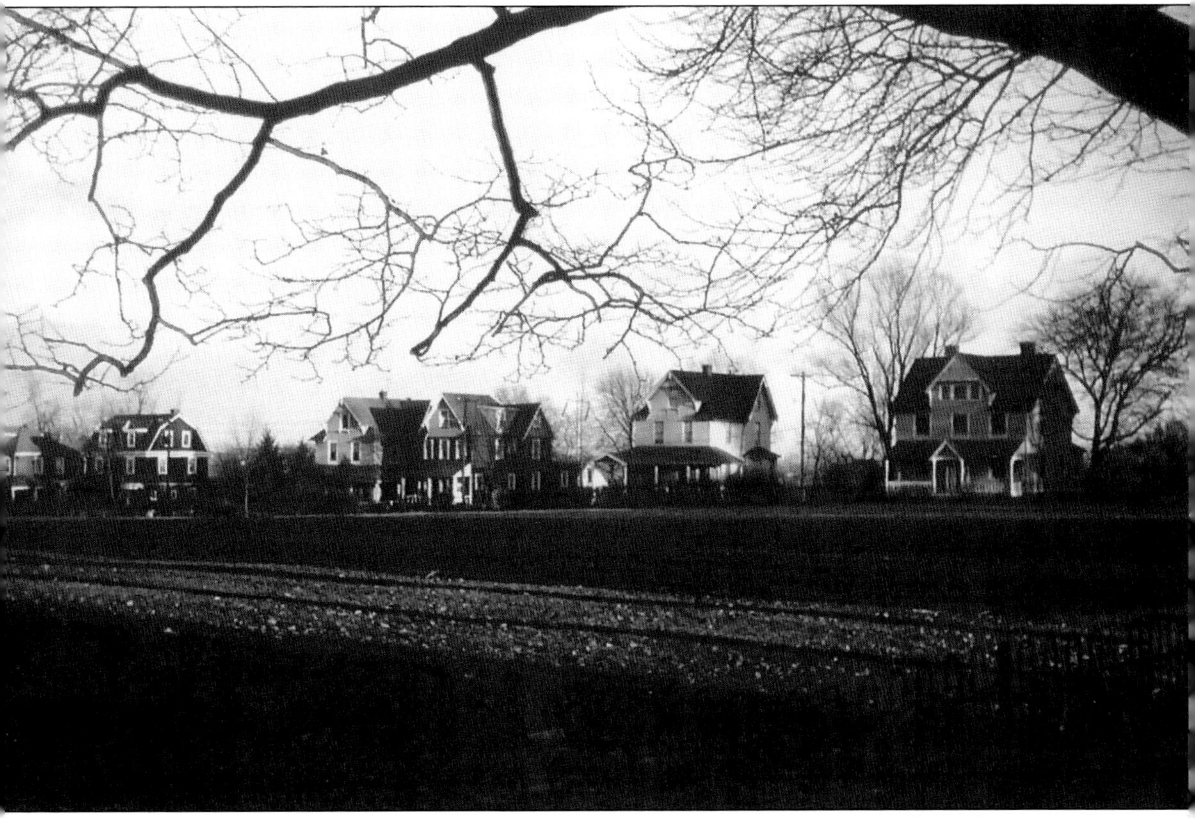

WOODLAND AVENUE, 1950S. The large Victorian homes pictured here originally had water to their homes furnished by a pump. Private wells were in the backyard. Some houses still retain the path that led to the outhouse. The second-largest ginkgo tree in Pennsylvania is located at 819 Woodland Avenue.

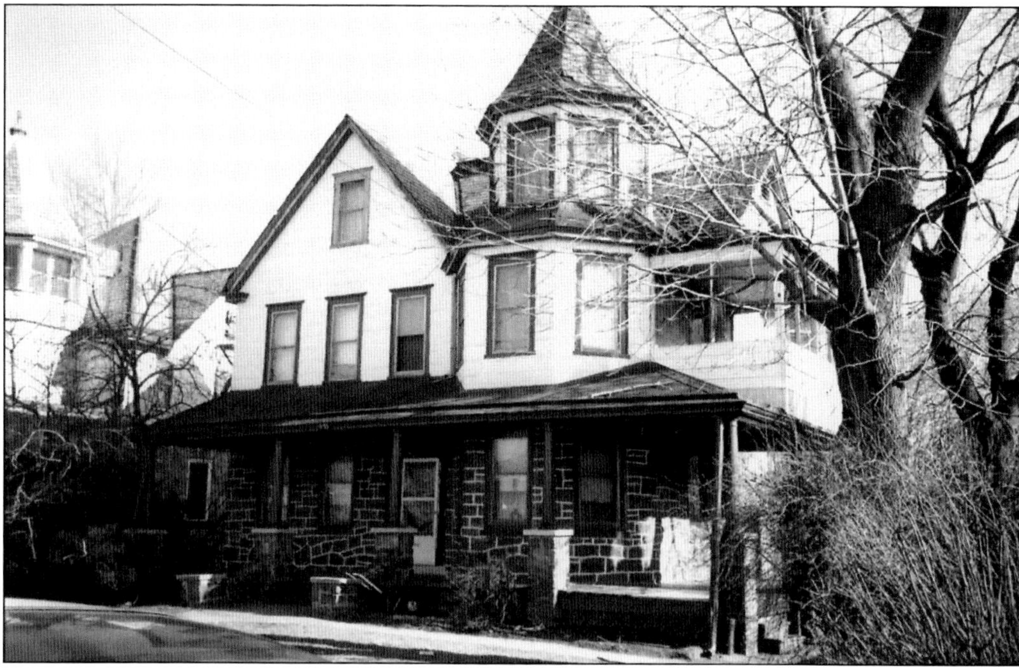

THE EMERSON HOME, C. 1889. This home was located on Chester Pike next to the Venus Beauty School. It was formerly owned by Dr. Ruth Goyne and sold to Venus Beauty School. It was demolished in 1986.

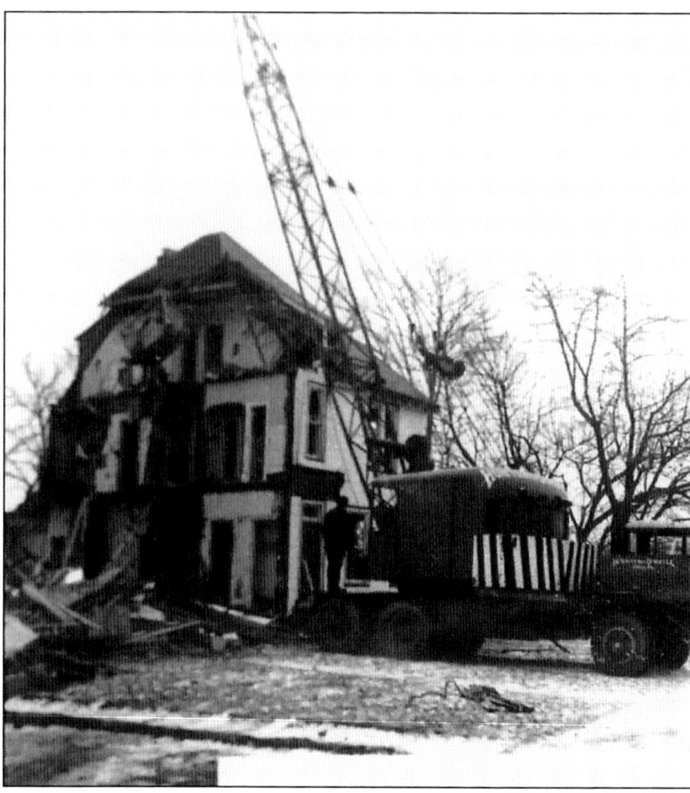

SOUTHERN HOTEL, 1934. Many buildings have been constructed, demolished, and rebuilt on this choice piece of real estate on the corner of Chester Pike and Clifton Avenue. Among them was the Southern Hotel, opened in 1934. Having housed a taproom for two years, it closed in 1936 after the town voted to prohibit the sale of alcoholic beverages. It was later demolished to make room for another enterprise.

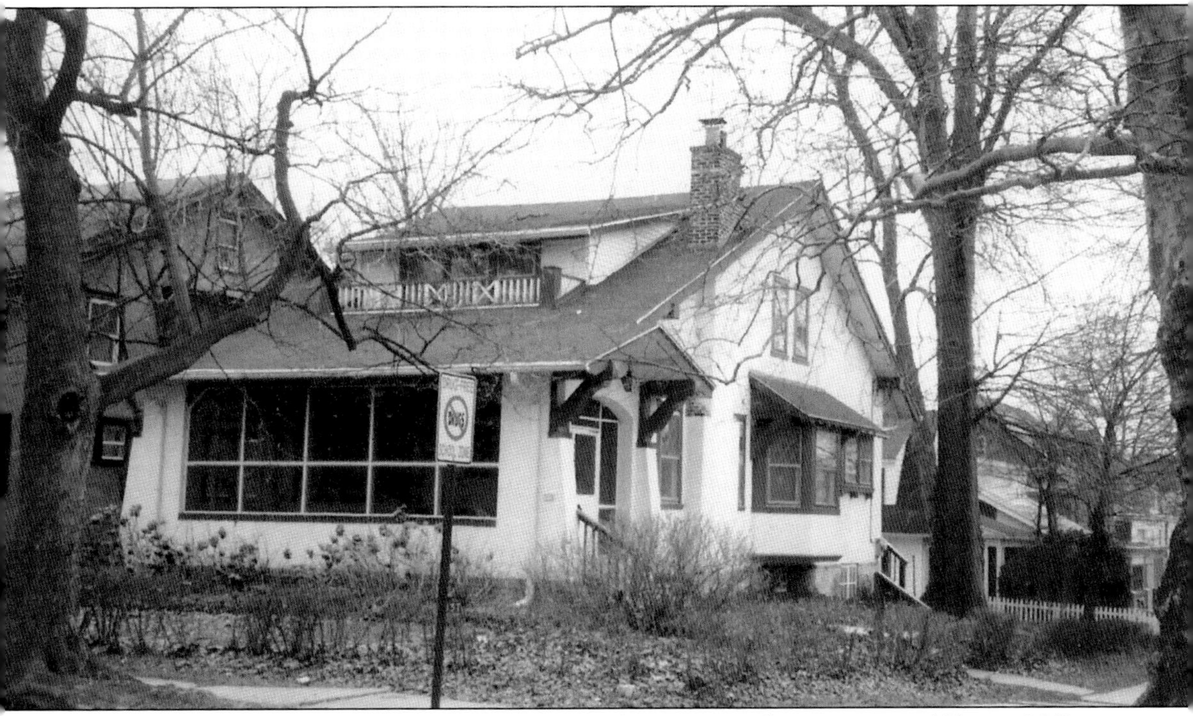

THE DOUGLASS HOUSE, C. 2000. William G. Douglass was noted as a pioneer of Sharon Hill. He was a prime mover in the organization of the borough and civic movement. Douglass became chief burgess of the town and was later elected the first assessor of Sharon Hill. He was a leader in the actions that led to the borough's separation from Darby. As a self-made man, with little formal education, Douglass achieved much in his lifetime. The Methodist Episcopal church on Sharon Avenue was another of Douglass's projects. He was instrumental in the building of the church and held the position of treasurer of the church for many years. He was also the treasurer of the Sharon Building and Loan Association.

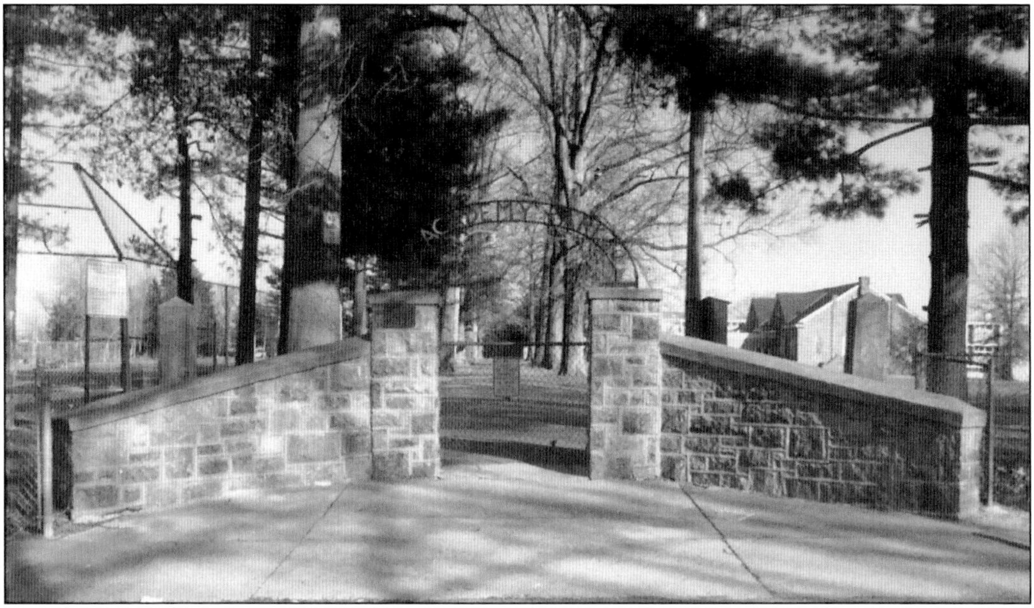

ACADEMY PARK ARCH, 1927. This beautiful archway is a combination of the old and new. The entrance to the park was made by local masonry contractor Clayton Valerio. He used the stone from the dismantled chapel that was part of the Holy Child Academy. The construction represented the efforts of three generations of the Valerio family, grandfather Clayton, his son Vito, and grandson Vito Jr. (Courtesy of Michael Finnegan.)

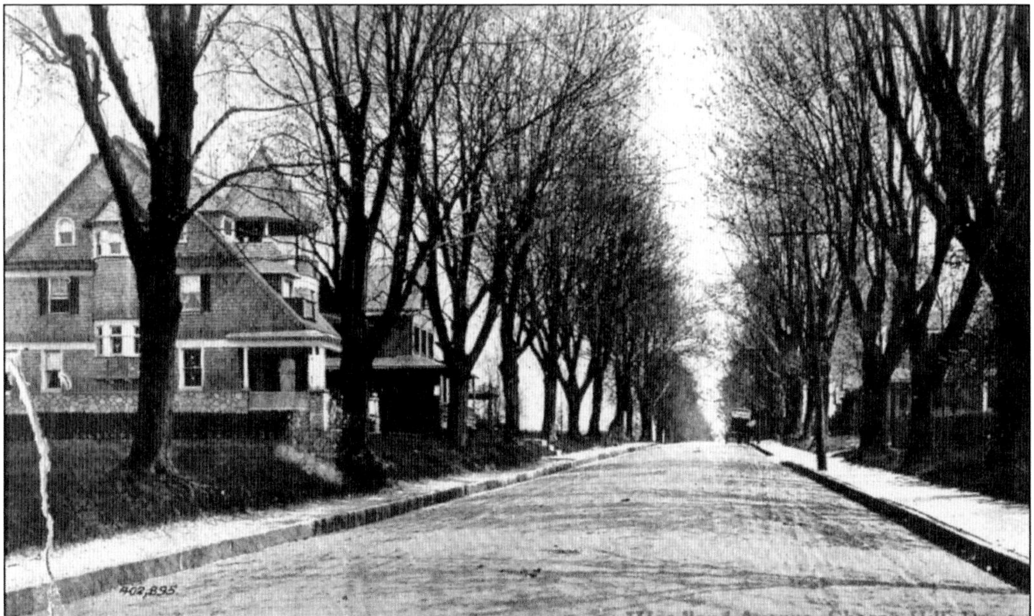

WOODLAND AVENUE, 1908. This view of Woodland Avenue is looking east toward Calcon Hook Road. It was a tree-lined street of large Victorian homes built in the 1880s.

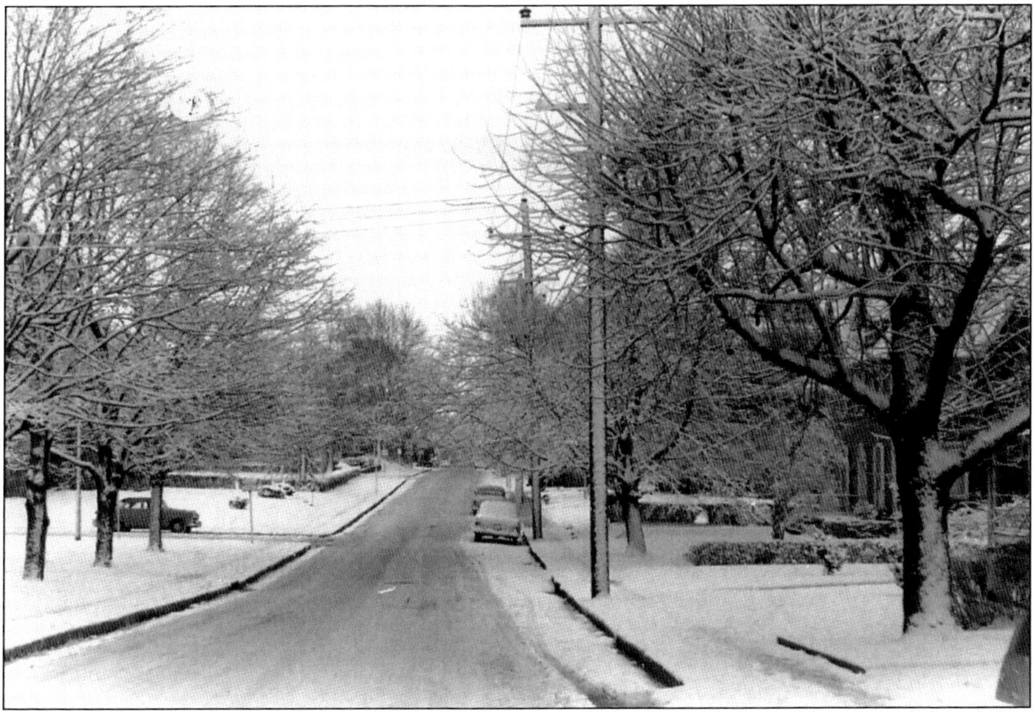

SHARON AVENUE, 1950S. A snowy scene like this one on Sharon Avenue in the 1950s is typical of the three-lined streets and roads of old Victorian homes. (Courtesy of Clara Hagarty.)

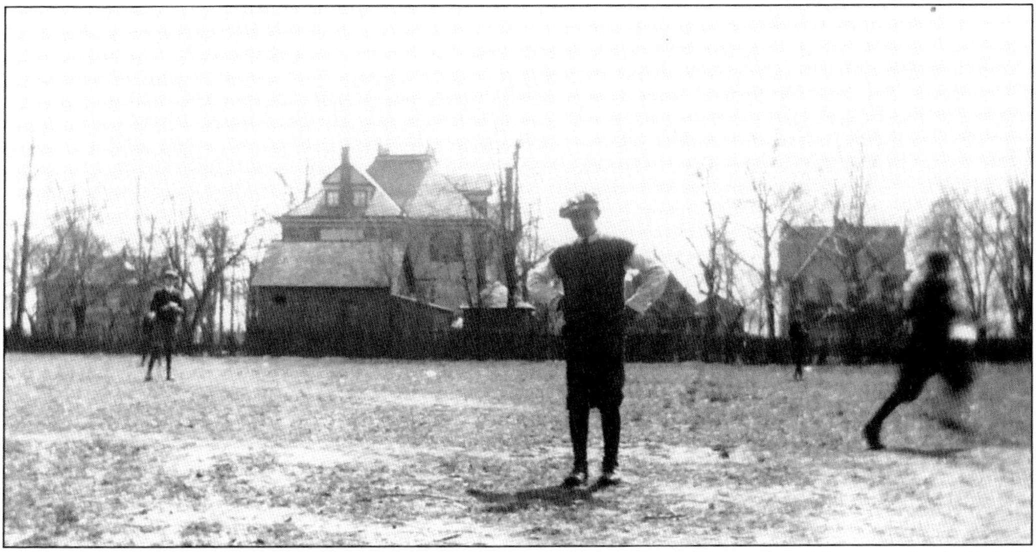

BOYS ON THE BALL FIELD, 1924. These boys are having some after-school fun on the ball field facing the residences on Woodland Avenue. (Courtesy of Holy Spirit Church.)

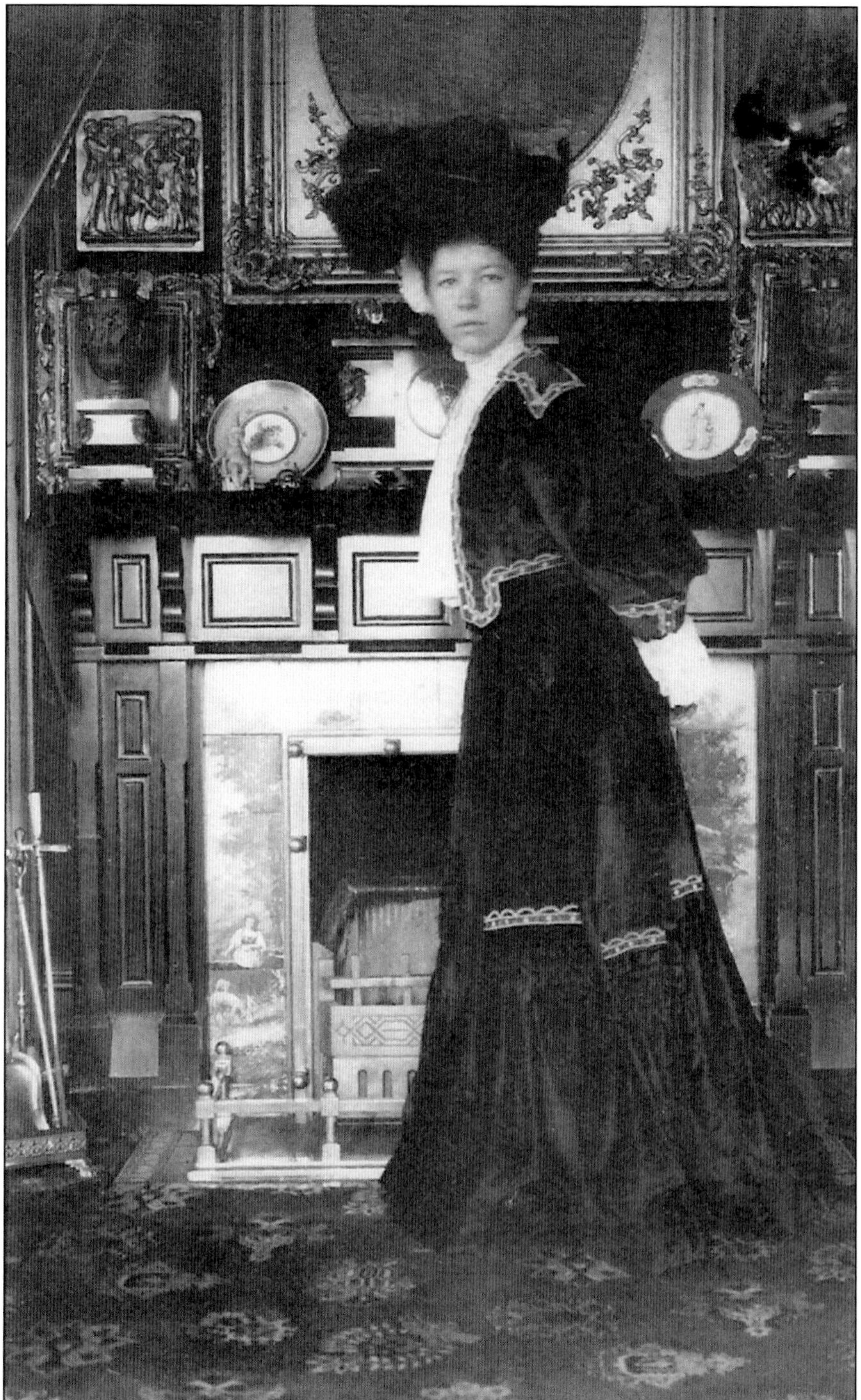

EDITH GRACE FOLWELL, 1906. This picture, taken inside Twin Oaks, depicts both the Victorian dress and Victorian interiors of the time. On September 23, 1909, Edith Grace Folwell married Thomas Charlton Hudson at the Methodist Episcopal church. The reception was held at Twin Oaks. (Courtesy of Maida Barton Follini.)

Three

CHURCHES AND EDUCATION

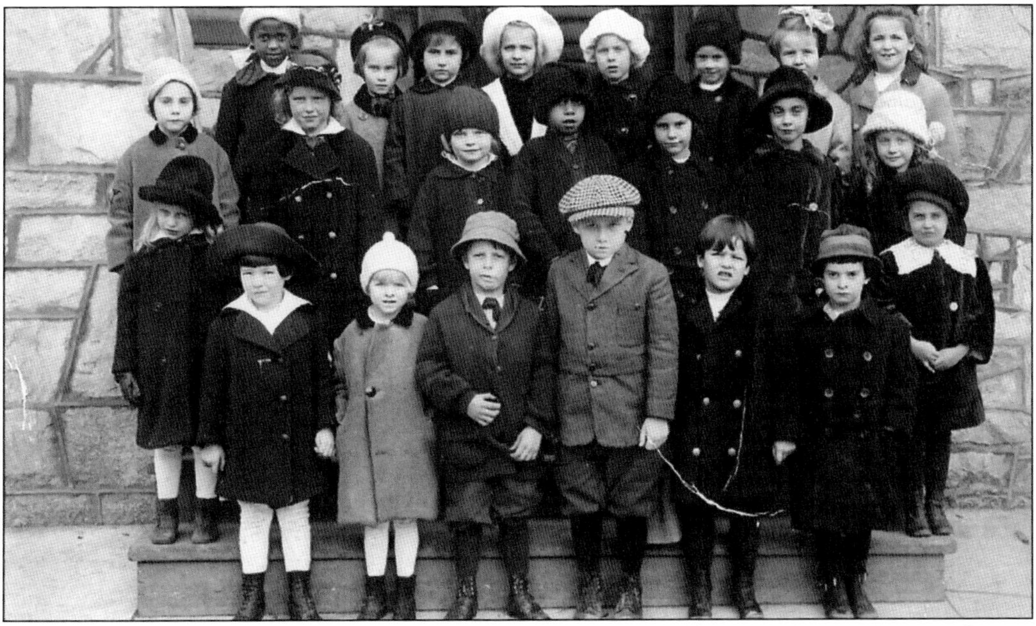

SHARON HILL GRADE SCHOOL, 1916. These first-grade children in the 1915–1916 class at Sharon Hill Grammar School at Sharon and Maple Avenues pose for a postcard photograph on the front steps of the school.

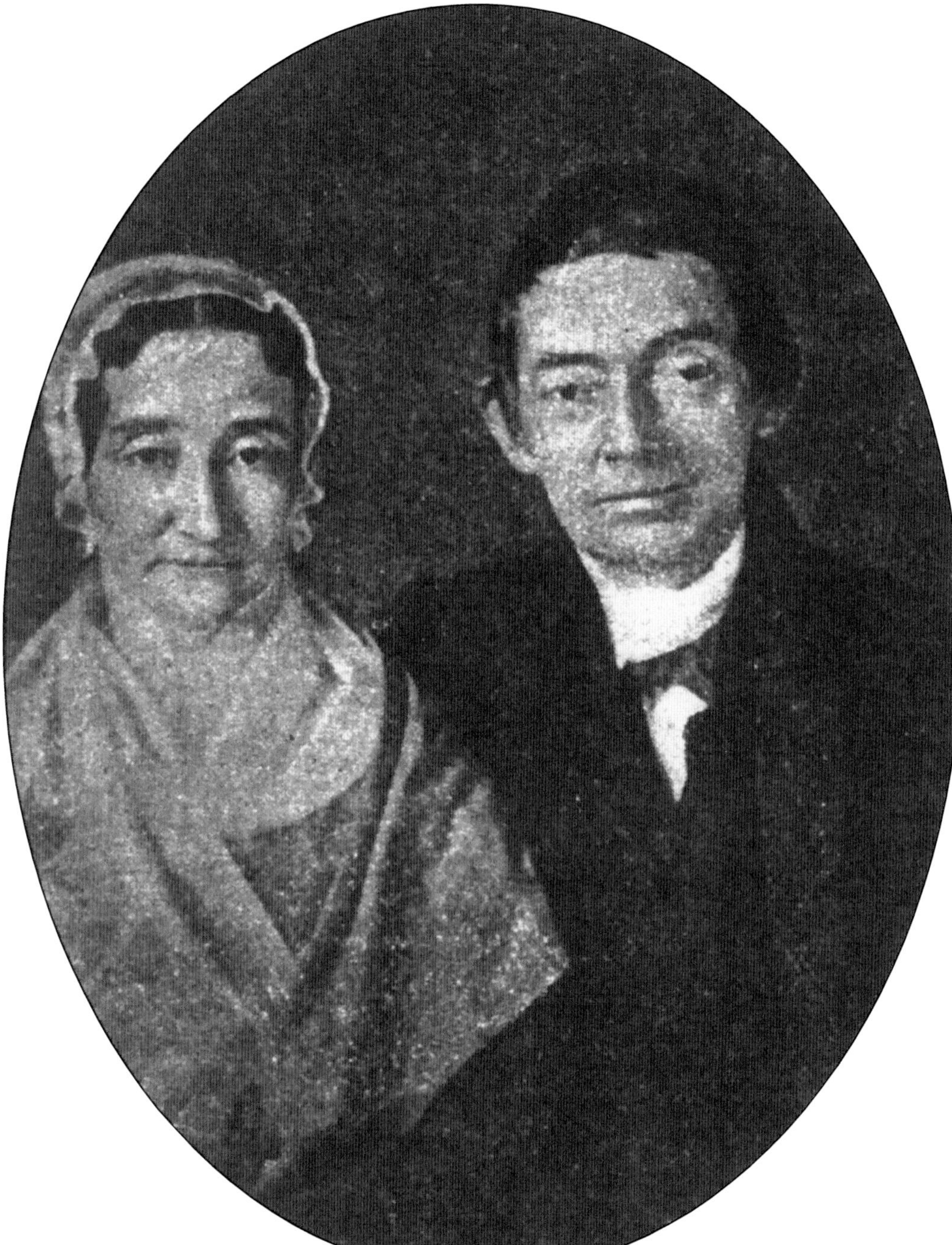

JOHN AND RACHAEL JACKSON, 1830S. John and Rachael Jackson were Quakers. John was a preacher, scholar, writer, astronomer, and land surveyor. He preached frequently at the Friends Meeting House in Darby. In 1835, he founded the Sharon Female Seminary for Quaker Girls. Rachael Jackson continued the school after his death. John Jackson was an abolitionist and played a major role in the Underground Railroad. (Courtesy of Delaware County Historical Society.)

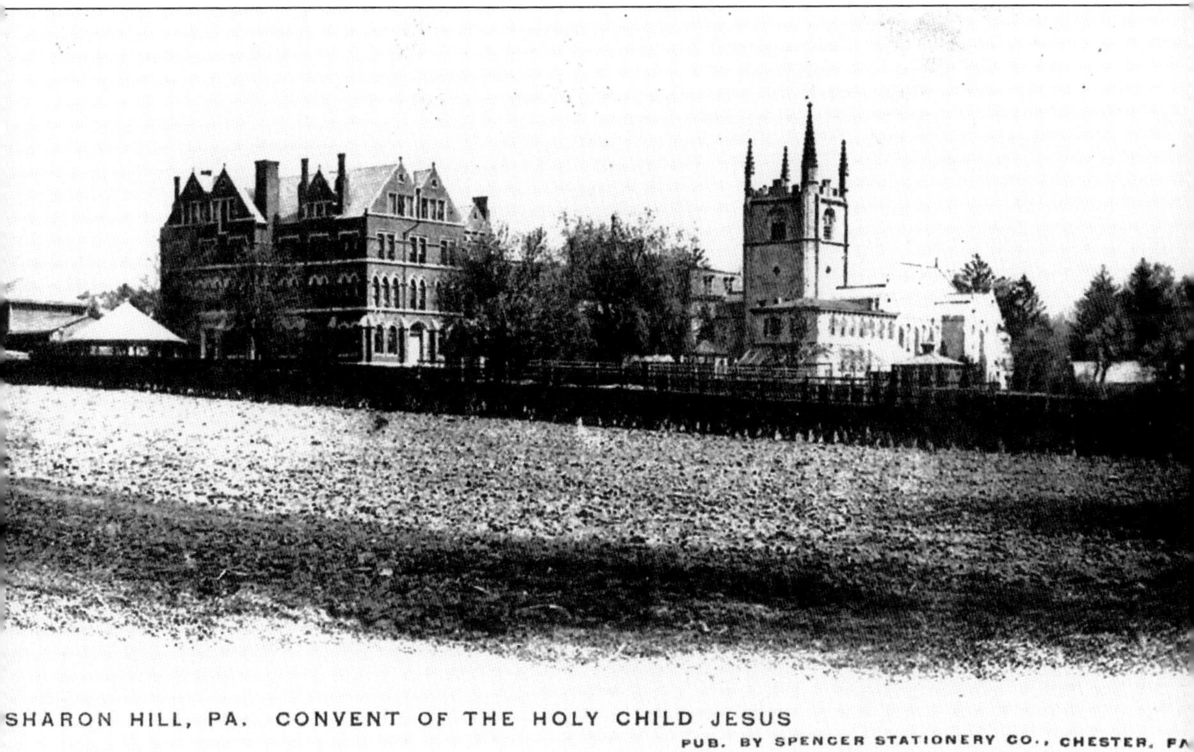

HOLY CHILD ACADEMY, 1864. Halliday Jackson, a Quaker, whose ancestors came from Ireland in the early 1700s, purchased about 26 acres in 1803 and called his estate Sharon. His son John Jackson founded the Sharon Female Seminary for Quaker Girls. In 1864, Rev. Charles Carter, a Catholic clergyman, bought the school and property and it became known as Holy Child Academy. The Sisters of the Holy Child established a boarding school for girls, which was renowned for its academic excellence. The four-storied redbrick building was constructed in 1890 and the gray-stone Gothic chapel in 1899. The academy closed its doors in 1978. The property was sold to Sharon Hill in 1979, and in 1984, the Academy Park High School was built. The stone gymnasium of the academy was retained and still stands today.

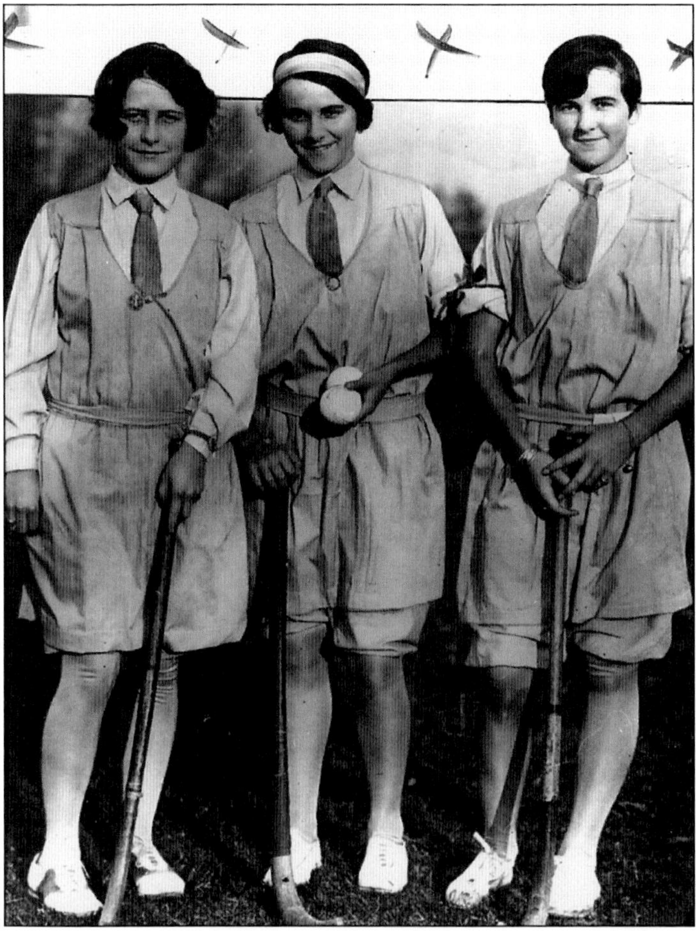

The Hauck Sisters, c. 1920. Mary (left), Helen (center), and Frances Hauck were members of the Sharon Hill Academy's hockey team. The students are shown here after their defeat of Darlington. (Courtesy of Kimberly Carson McGowan.)

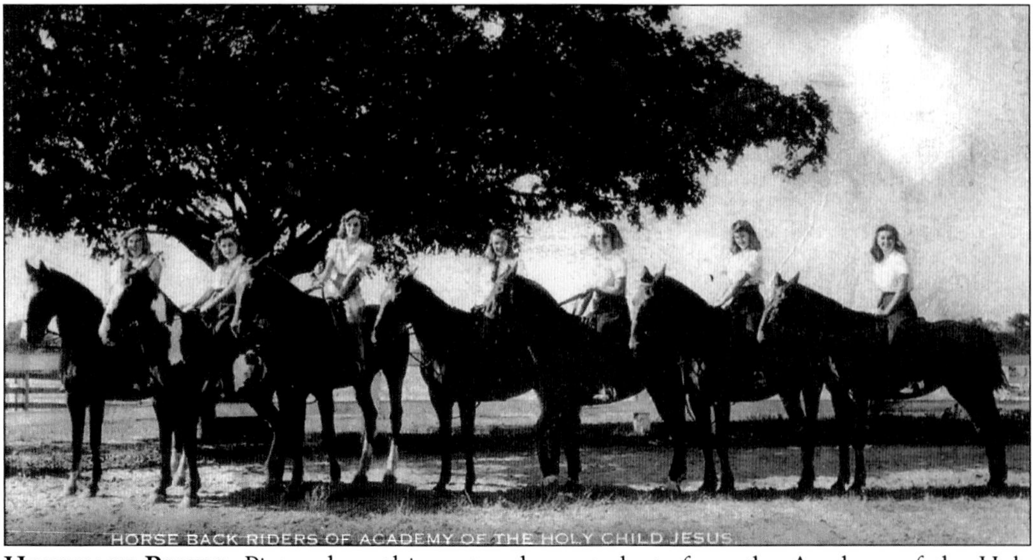

Horseback Riders. Pictured on this postcard are students from the Academy of the Holy Child Jesus. Horseback riding was a favorite with the girls at the school.

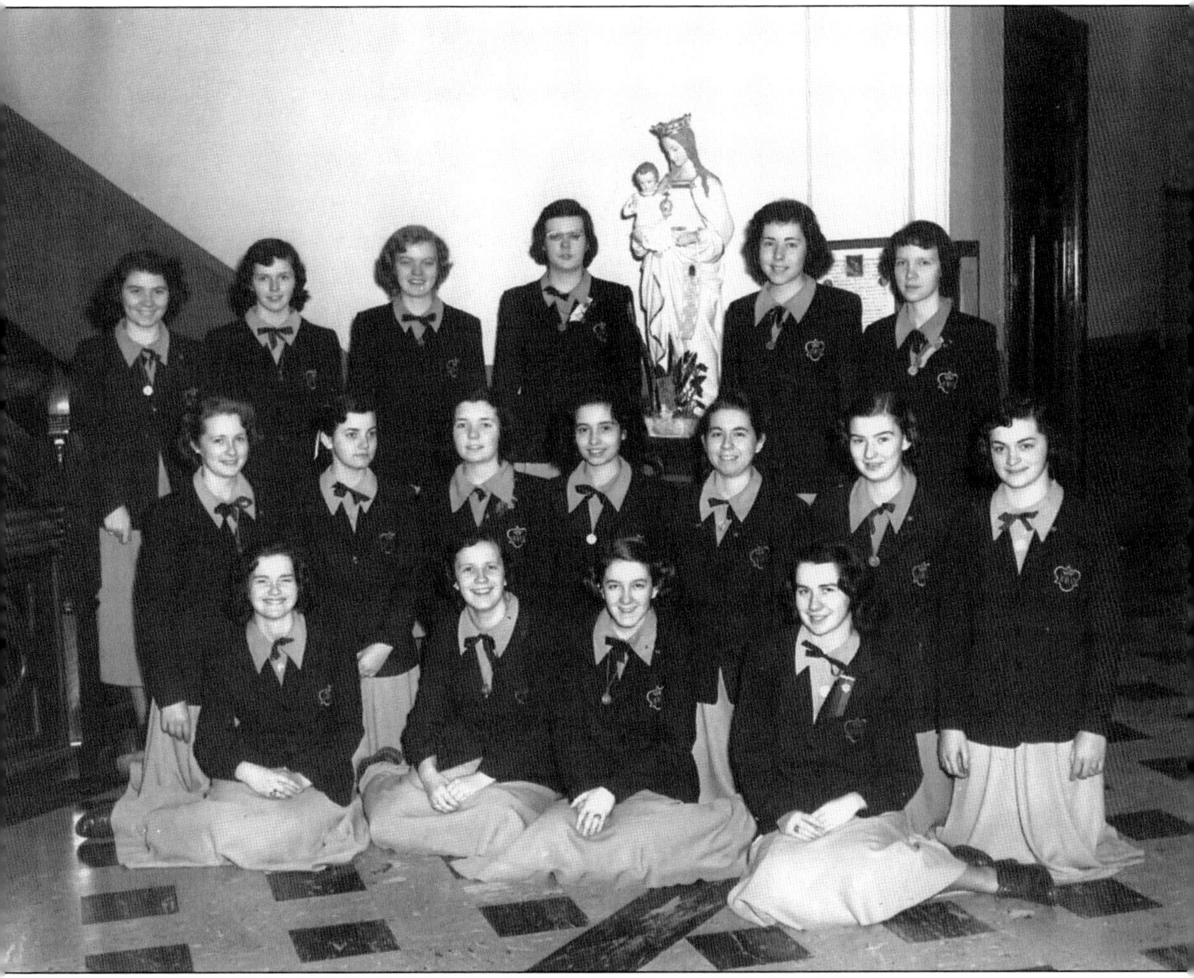

HOLY CHILD ACADEMY SODALITY, 1952. Shown inside the Sharon Academy are members of the sodality. The students in this group enriched their spiritual lives through prayer and charitable works. They assisted at fund-raisers and visited local charitable organizations that benefited children with their needs. (Courtesy of Kimberly Carson McGowan.)

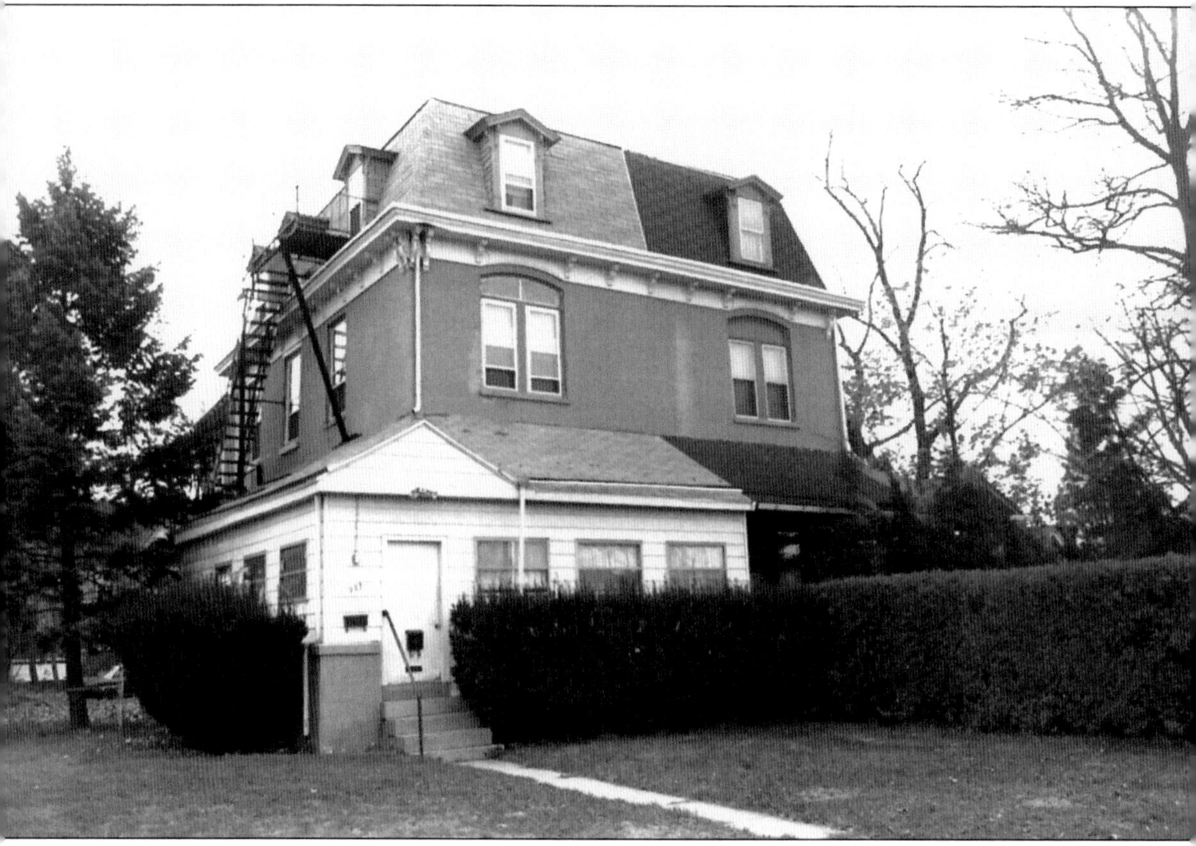

SHARON HILL ELEMENTARY SCHOOL, 1886. Located at Chester Pike and Ridley Avenue, this building was constructed in 1879. A second story was added in 1886. The building became the home of the first schoolhouse after the borough was incorporated in 1890. The school housed 40 pupils who were taught the three Rs, oral grammar, U.S. history, physiology, and hygiene. A teacher's salary was $40 per month. The school served the students until 1894. The building is now two houses at 933 and 935 Chester Pike.

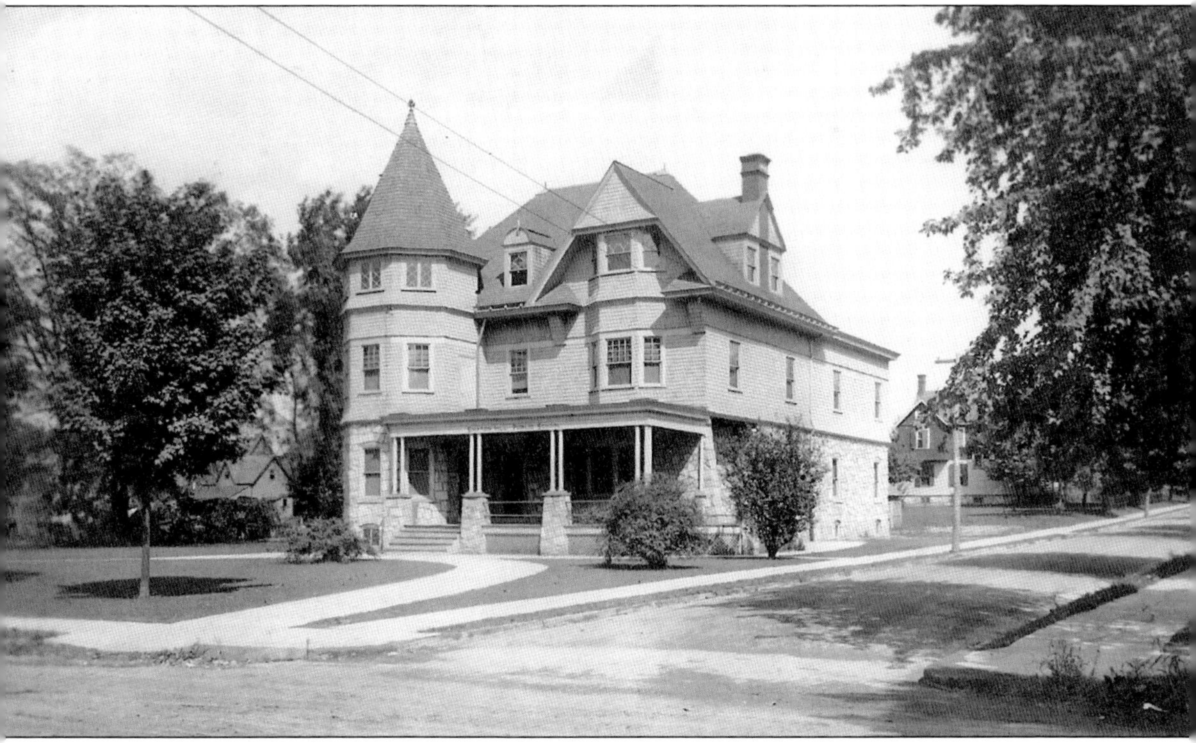

THE LYCEUM, 1906. Established in 1894, the lyceum was a club for meetings, lectures, reading, and instruction. A copy of the articles of incorporation dated July 30, 1894, indicates that six of the town's leading citizens of the era formed the corporation and proposed the name Sharon Hill Lyceum. Located on the corner of Maple and Sharon Avenues, the club existed for only a short time before the building was sold in 1896 to the Sharon Hill School District for $6,000 as a replacement for the first school. In 1925, a fire destroyed the second floor and a new school was constructed on Coates Street.

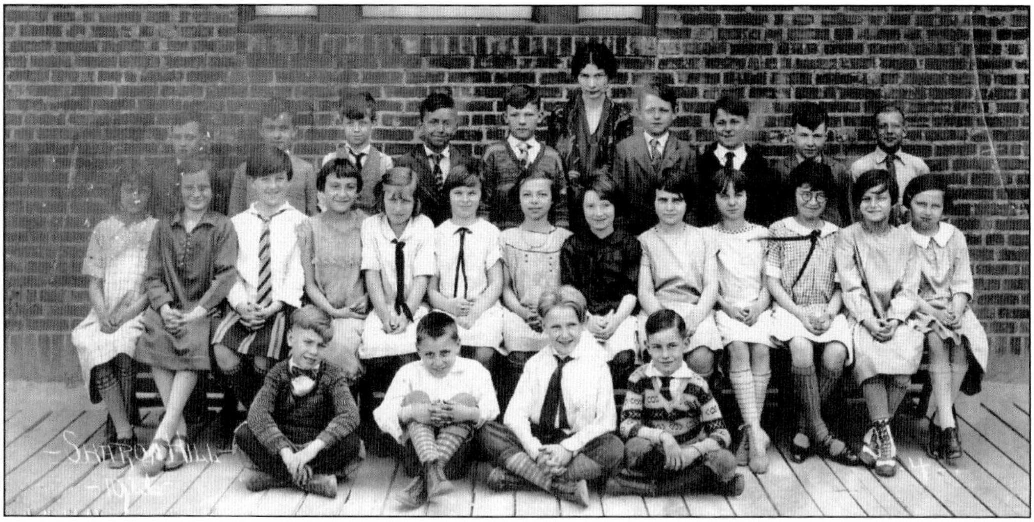

SHARON HILL PUBLIC SCHOOL, 1926. Pictured is Margaret Dalton's class in 1926. Dalton taught several generations of families in Sharon Hill.

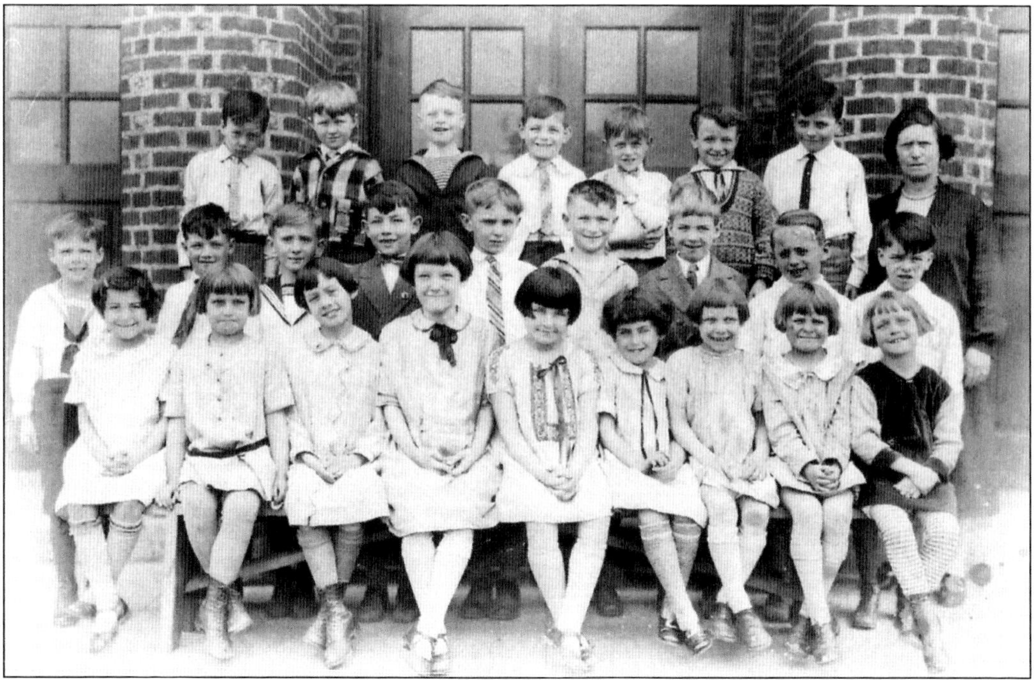

SHARON HILL SCHOOL, 1927. Anna Cromie's second-grade class is pictured at the new elementary school on Coates Street.

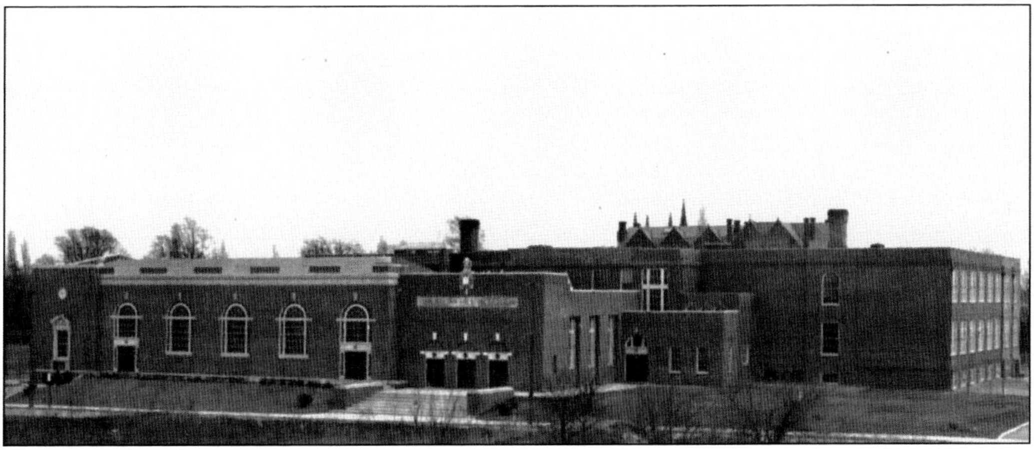

SHARON HILL HIGH SCHOOL, 1925. In October 1925, ground was purchased on Coates Street and a new school was built to house the students who had been displaced by the fire at the former school at Maple and Sharon Avenues. In 1929, a ninth grade was established, and the first high school graduating class was in 1933; accreditation occurred in 1934. Later years saw the addition of a gymnasium and an auditorium. In 1931, an athletic field was added. The final graduating class at this location was in 1982.

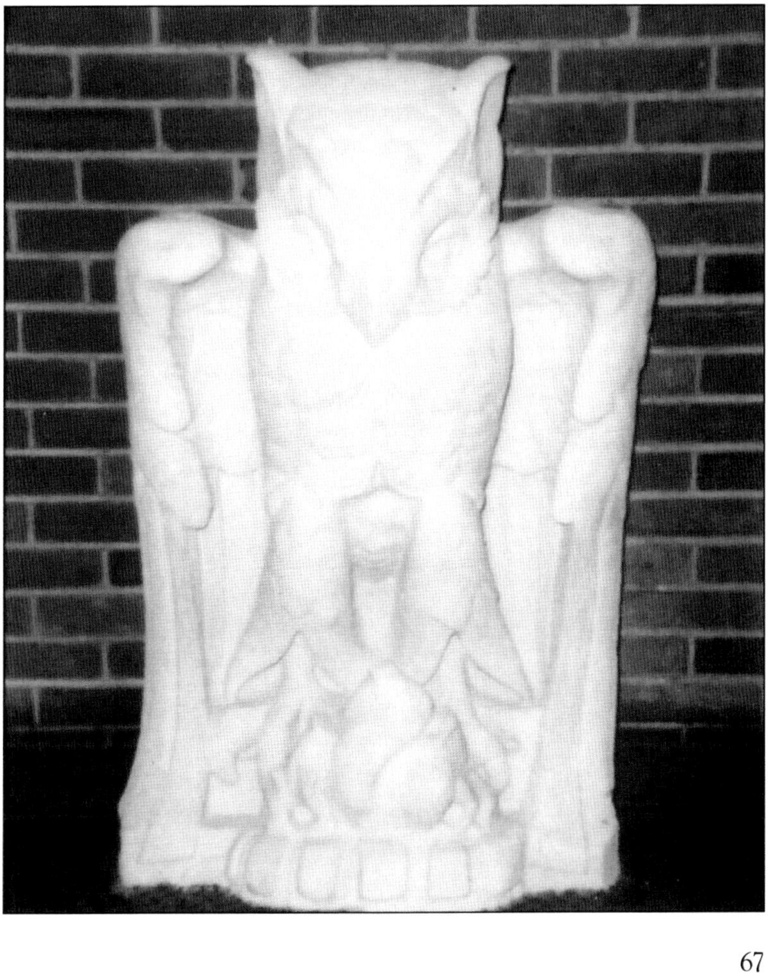

THE SHARON HILL HIGH SCHOOL OWL, C. 1982. The scholarly owl that watched over the high school for all its years was salvaged after the school demolition. Although damaged and appearing beyond repair, it was taken under the care and expertise of local stone worker Clayton Valerio, who restored the wise old owl's original looks. The owl was the official mascot of the school students and their activities.

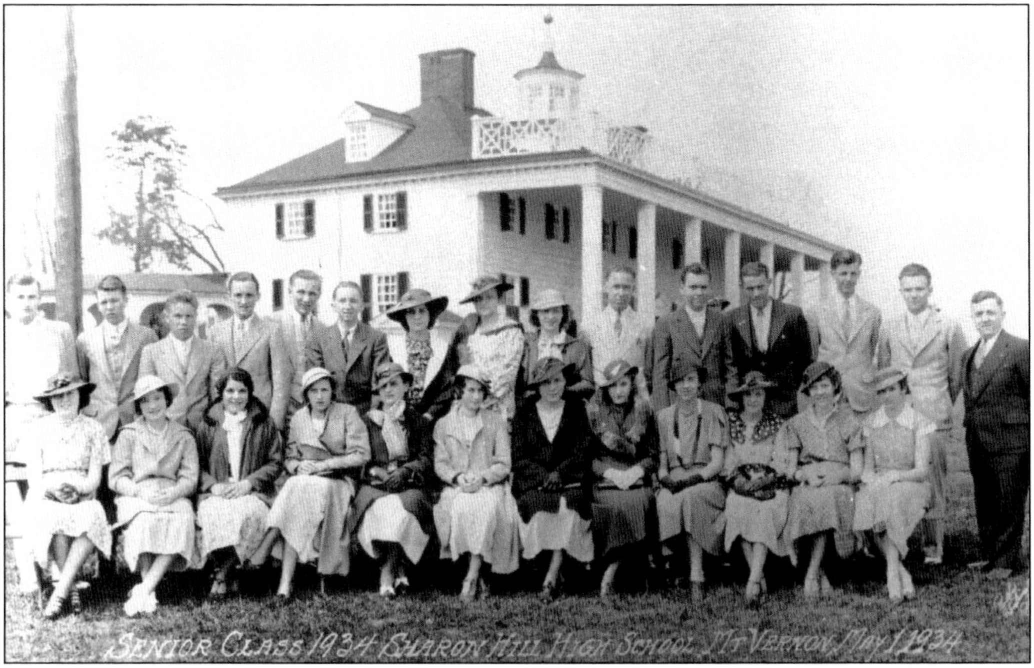

Senior Class Trip, 1934. Pictured are the chaperones and Sharon Hill High School seniors of the class of 1934 who visited Washington and Mount Vernon on their class trip on May 1, 1934.

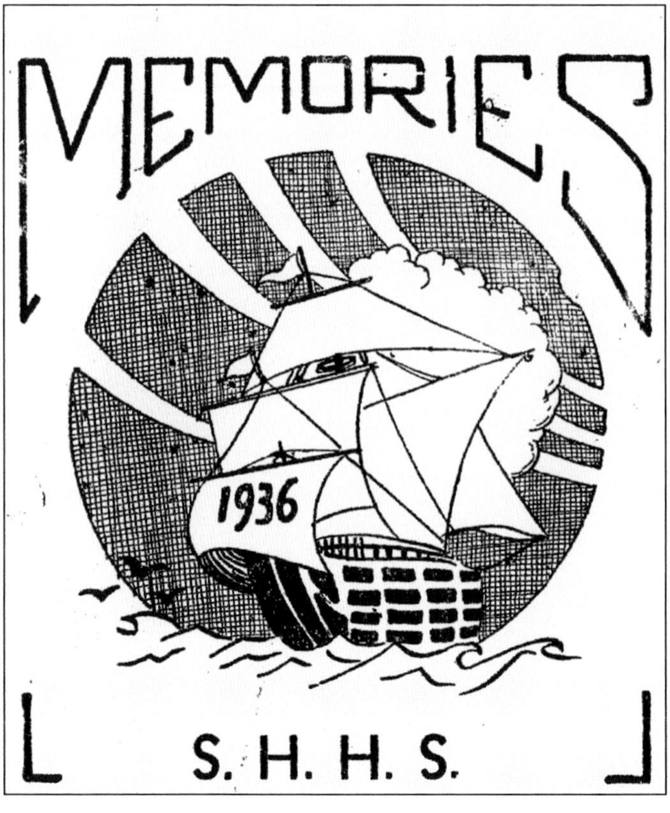

Memories Program Book, 1936. This memories book from Sharon Hill High School was used on May 22, 1936. It had a dance program and autograph and memories section. Listed are the names of 18 faculty members, 35 seniors, and 41 juniors.

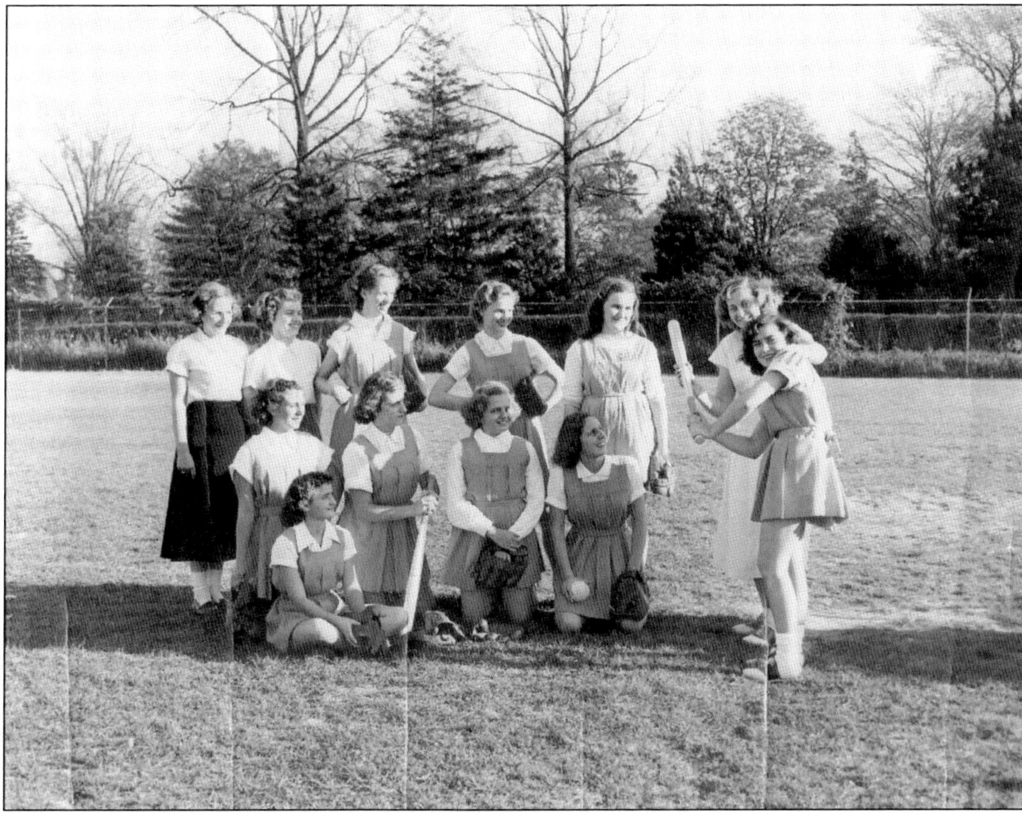

SHARON HILL HIGH SCHOOL SPORTS. Pictured above is Grace Knopf's 1950 gym class. The subject of this lesson is "how to play softball." The girls are paying strict attention and eagerly await their turn at bat. Below are the members of the 1937 Sharon Hill High School baseball team. The team had a successful season playing against the other local high schools.

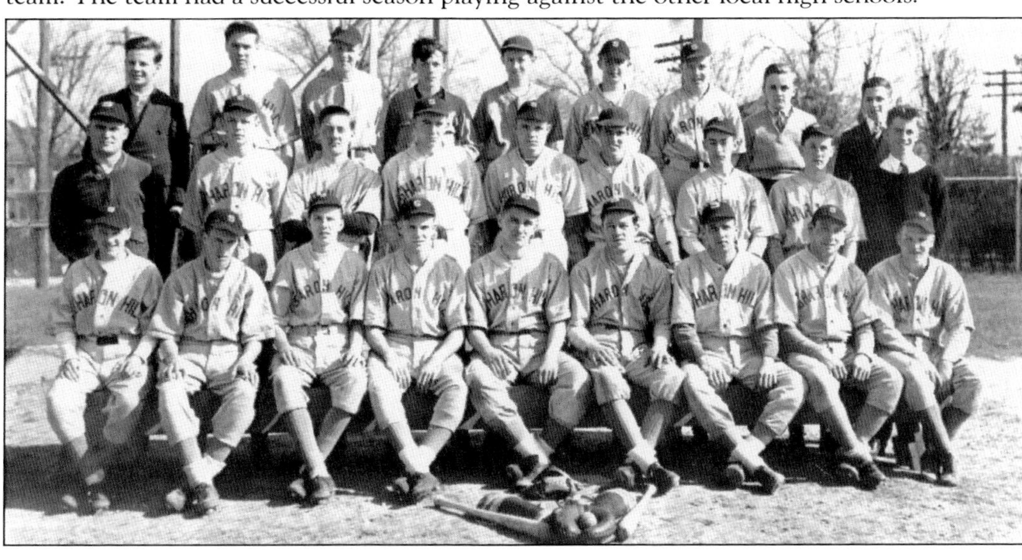

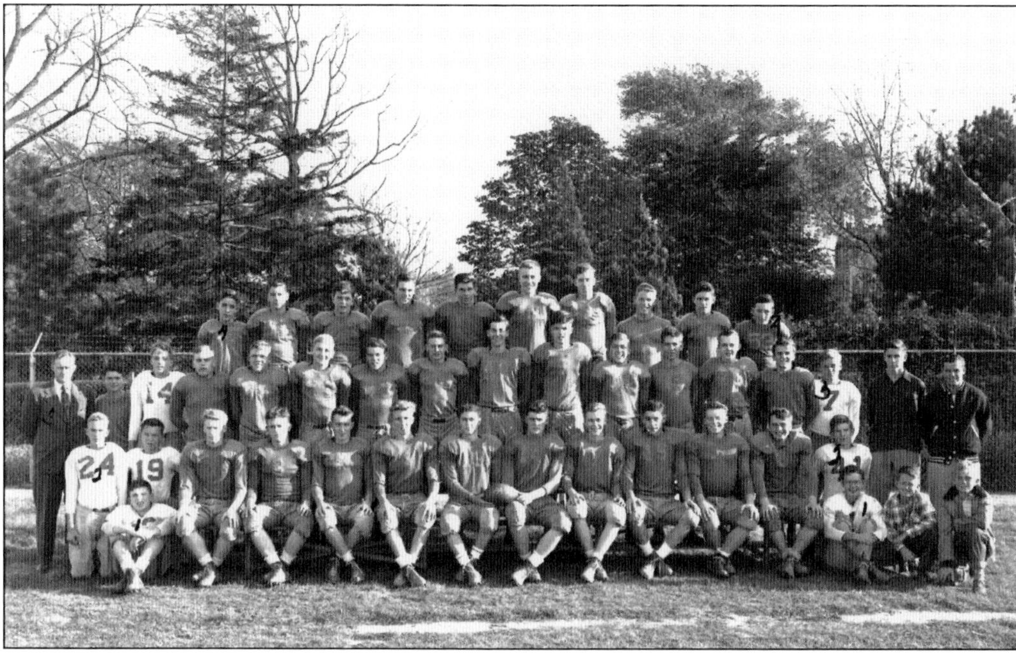

SHARON HILL HIGH SCHOOL FOOTBALL. Pictured above is the 1951 Sharon Hill High School football team. Despite the enrollment disadvantages they faced in playing most of the other schools in the area, a fierce determination and a rich athletic tradition made the Owls tough competitors. Shown below is the 1956 cheerleading squad. Like their predecessors they cheered for their team, win or lose.

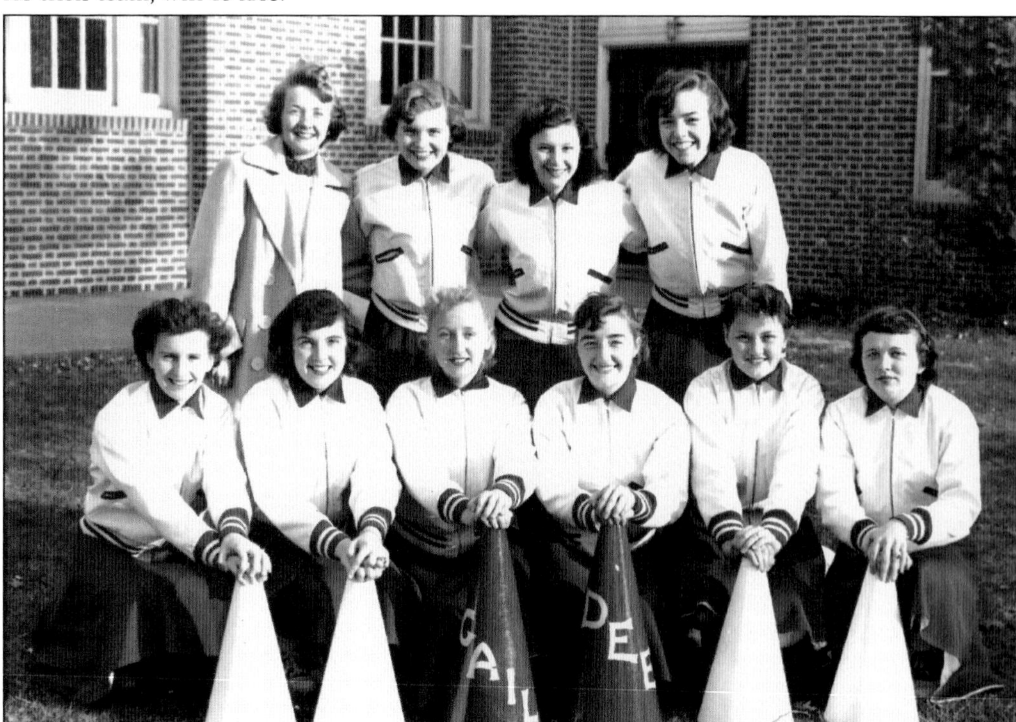

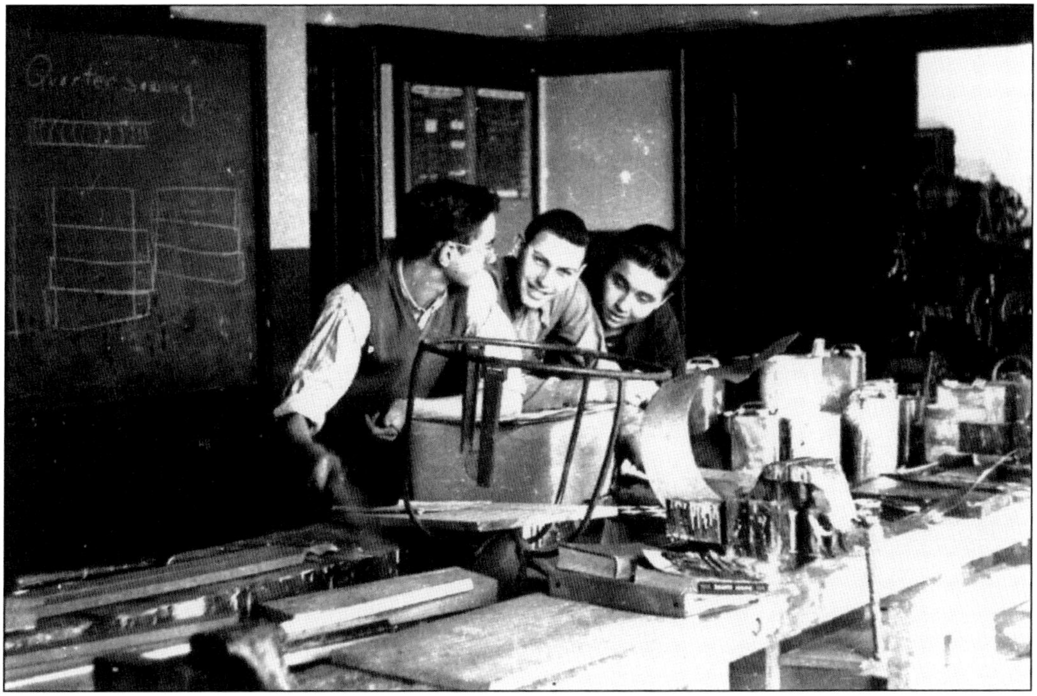

SHARON HILL HIGH SCHOOL SHOP CLASS, 1949. These seniors, from left to right, Warner Siegle, Walt Schriver, and Gordon Nuss, discuss their latest project in shop class. Shop was a way for the students to learn mechanical, metallurgical, and carpentry skills.

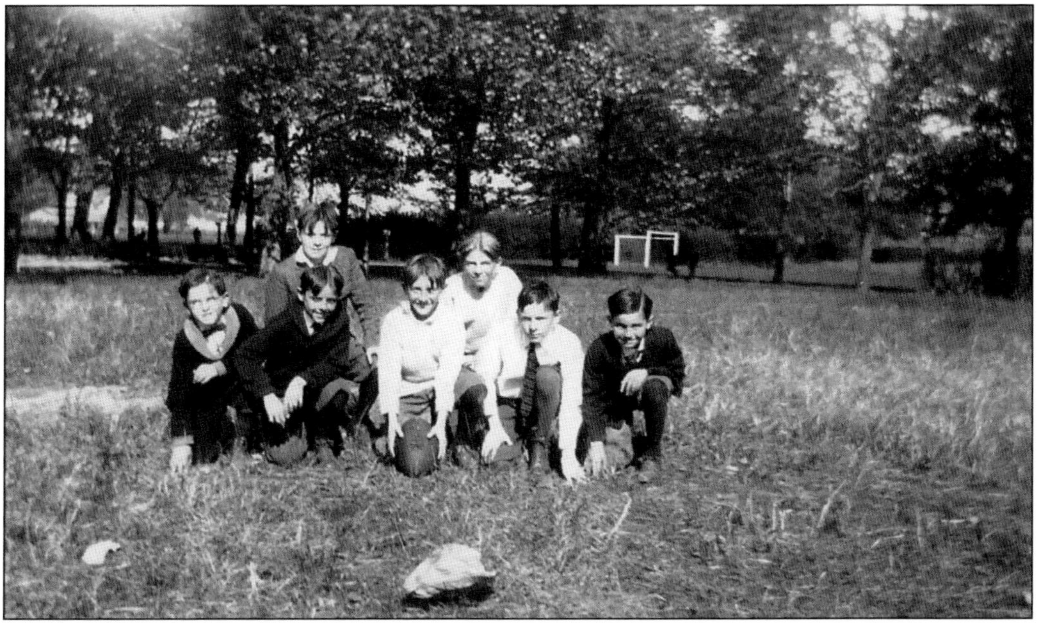

PRACTICING FOOTBALL, 1924. These young boys are anxious to begin a game of football on the field at School Street and Barker Avenue. The field is not far from their school, Holy Spirit. (Courtesy of Holy Spirit Church.)

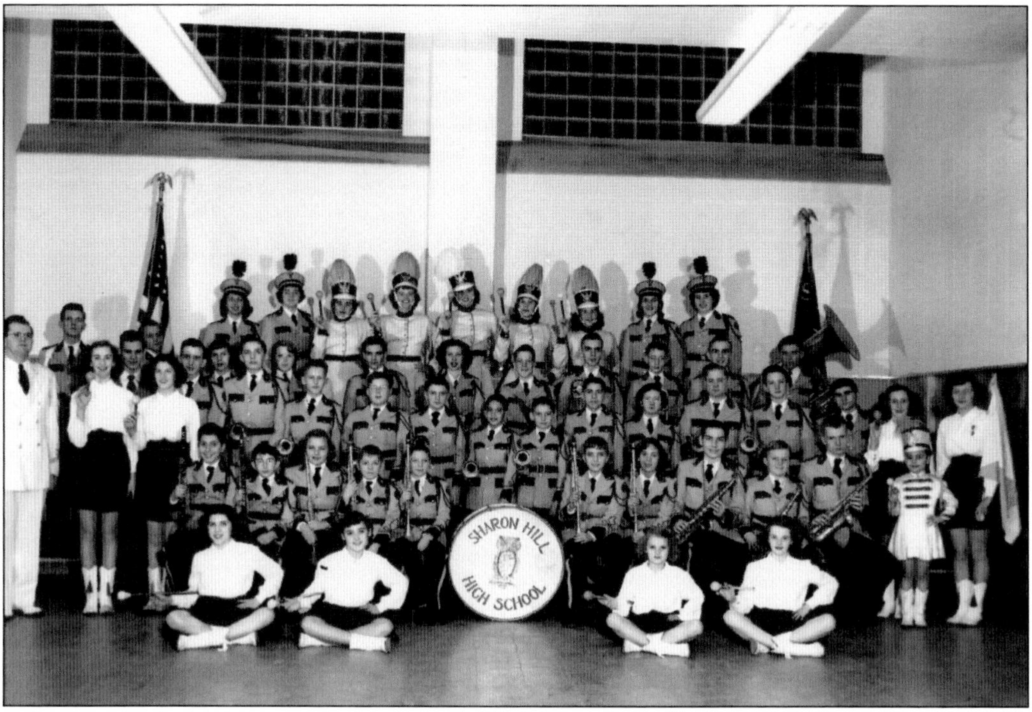

SHARON HILL HIGH SCHOOL MARCHING BAND, C. 1950. Here is the full complement of the band. Their halftime shows provided entertainment for the Sharon Hill High School football fans.

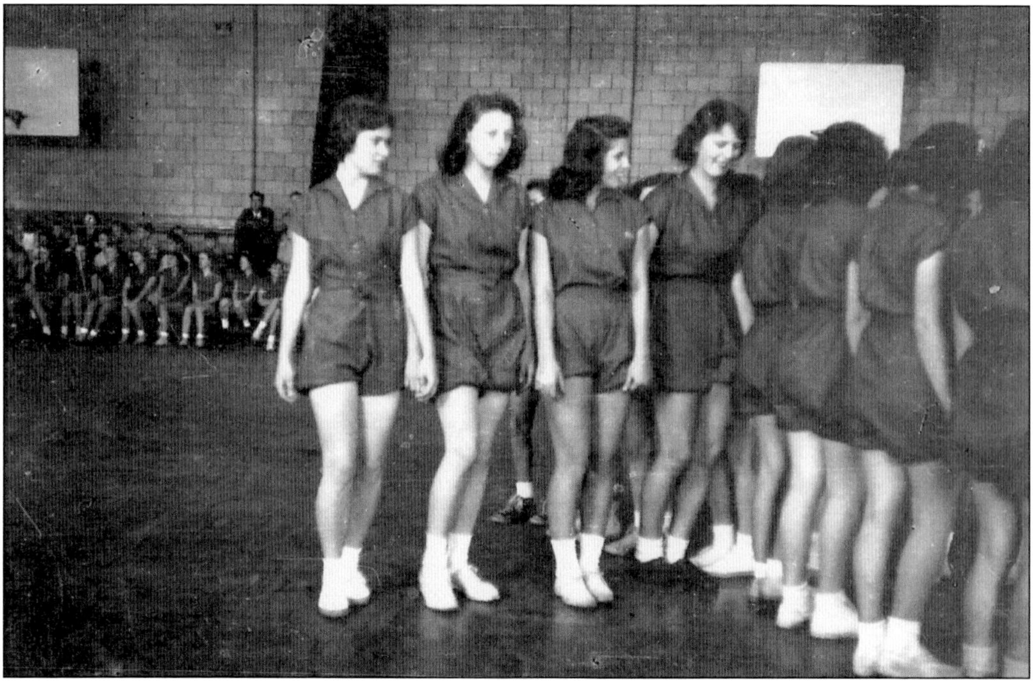

GYM CLASS, 1949. The gym class students are practicing their precision marching techniques to the delight of their classmates at Sharon Hill High School. (Courtesy of Robert A. Erb.)

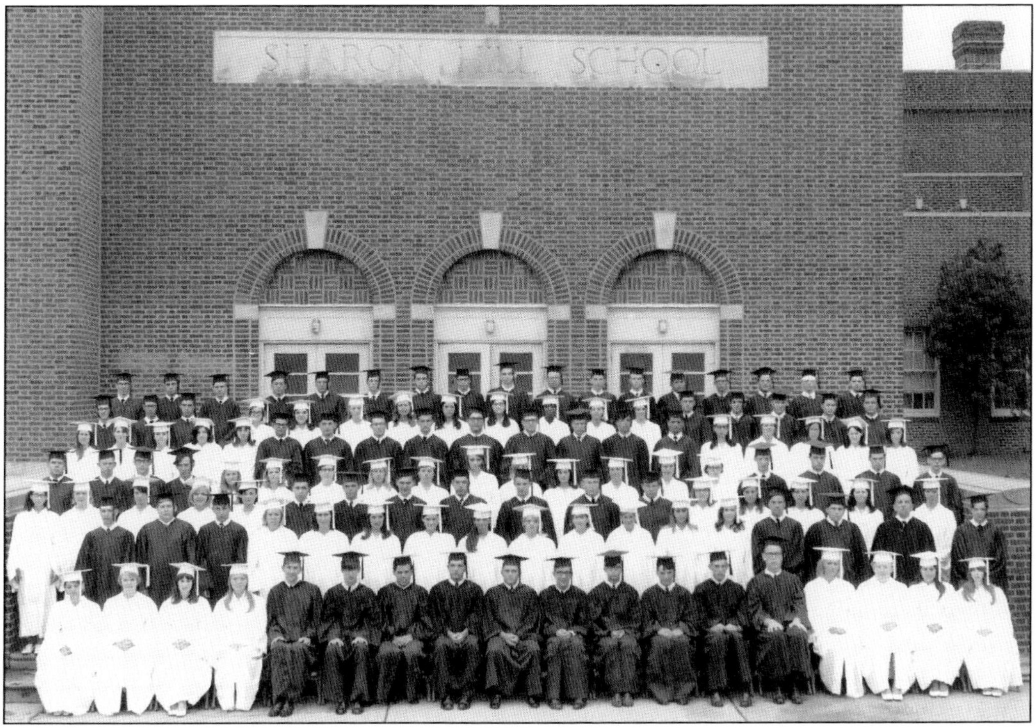

SHARON HILL HIGH SCHOOL, 1969. In accordance with school tradition, this graduating class was photographed in front of Sharon Hill High School. (Courtesy of Kathleen Fitzgerald Sharkey.)

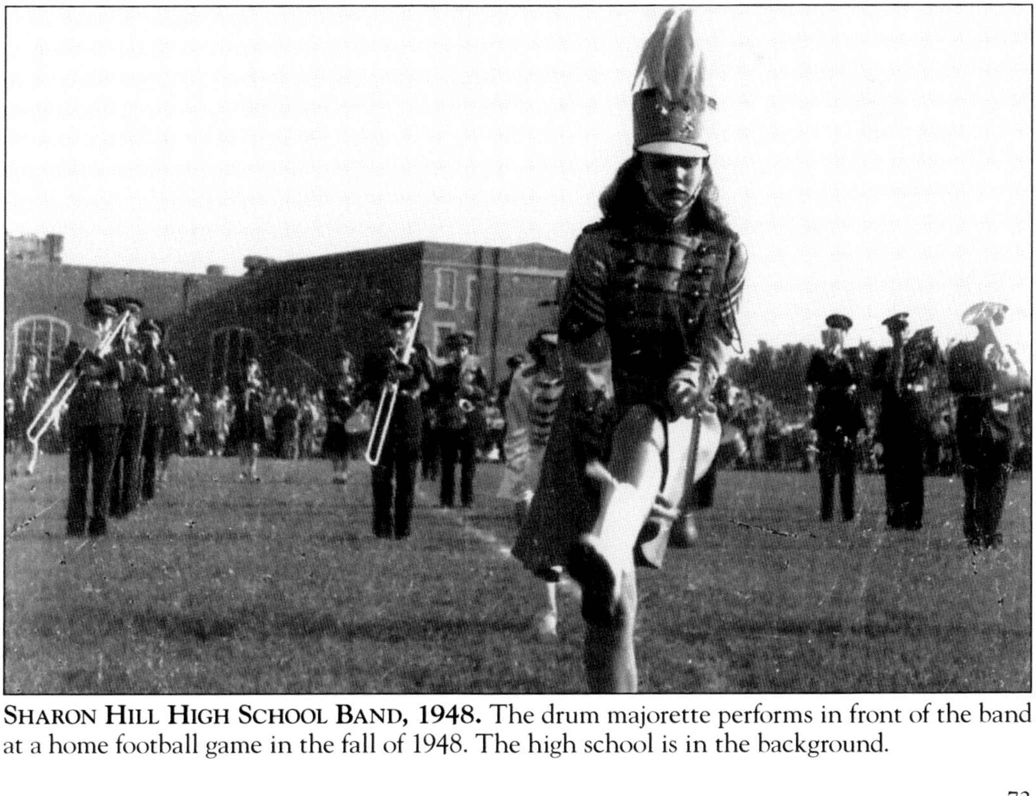

SHARON HILL HIGH SCHOOL BAND, 1948. The drum majorette performs in front of the band at a home football game in the fall of 1948. The high school is in the background.

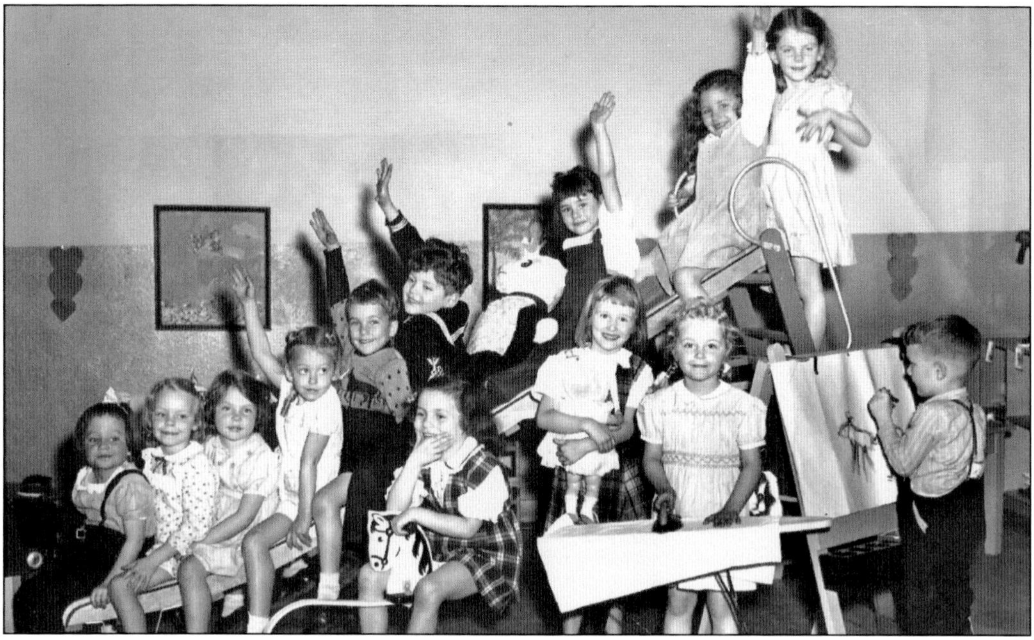

KINDERGARTEN CLASS, 1949. This is Hilda Hartzell's class having fun with activities. Although not shown in this photograph, Hilda Hartzell started the first kindergarten in Sharon Hill in 1940. Classes were held in the Tully Memorial Presbyterian Church Sunday school room. In 1952, her ideas for the design of kindergartens were used in the new elementary school.

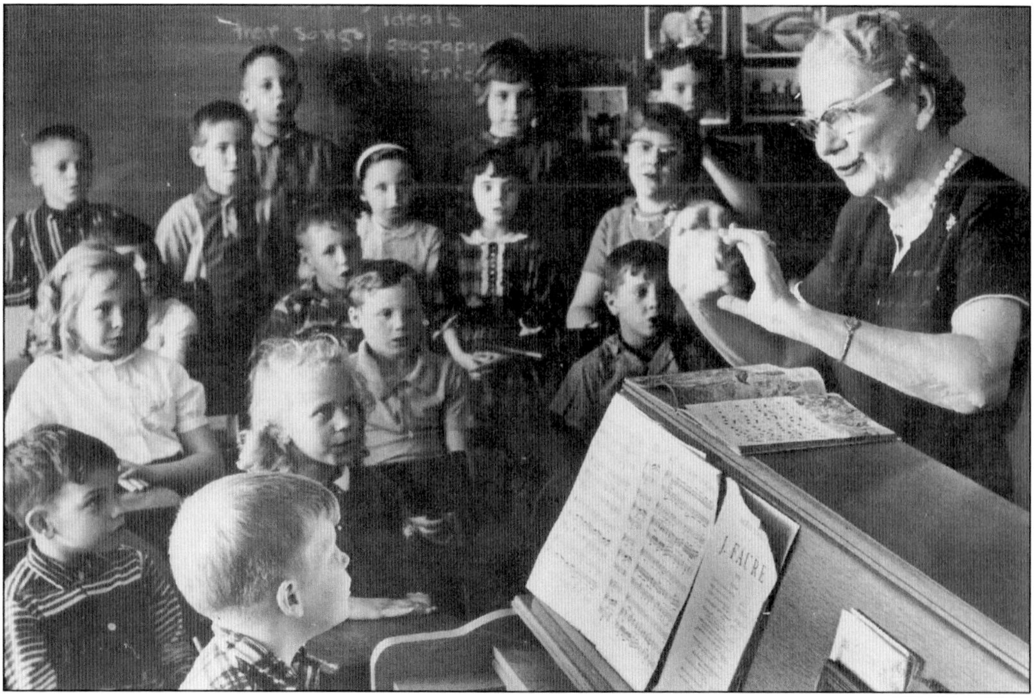

MUSIC CLASS, 1950S. Margaret Dalton, the daughter of Dr. David Dalton, is shown instructing the students in music. She was also a classroom teacher for many years, having taught students in the Sharon Hill grammar school on Maple Avenue and the Sharon Hill School on Coates Street.

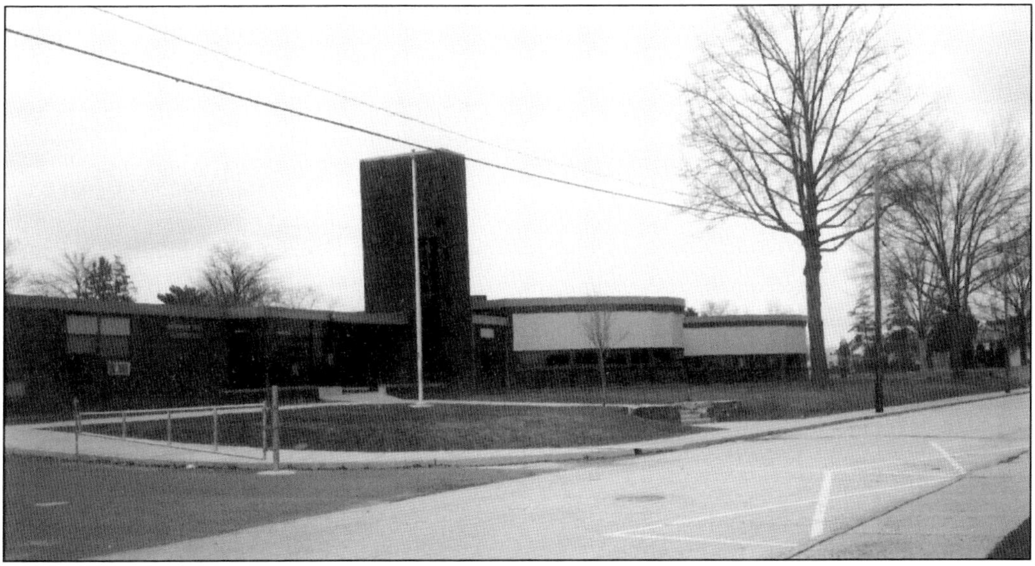

SHARON HILL ELEMENTARY SCHOOL, 1996. The main building located at Coates Street and Kenney Avenue contained six classrooms for grades one through six. The building also housed an administrative office, a health room, and a conference room. A kindergarten classroom was also included.

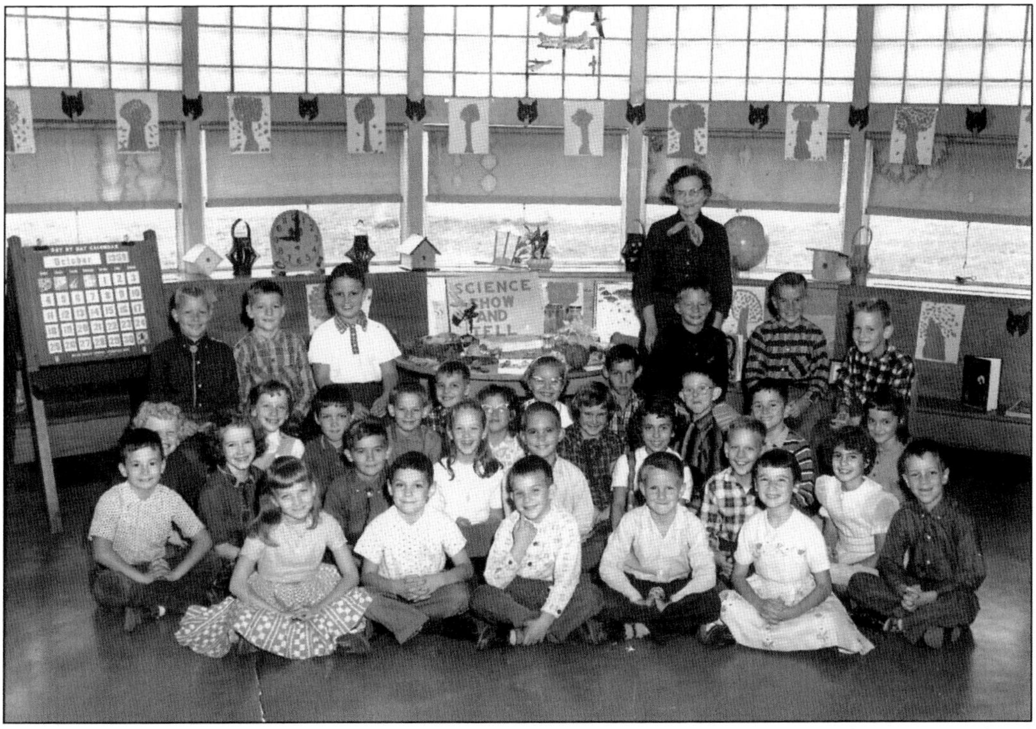

ELEMENTARY CLASS, 1959. The children in Miss Bielon's class at the new elementary school are enjoying the activities of their classroom. The new school provided much-needed space for additional academic programs.

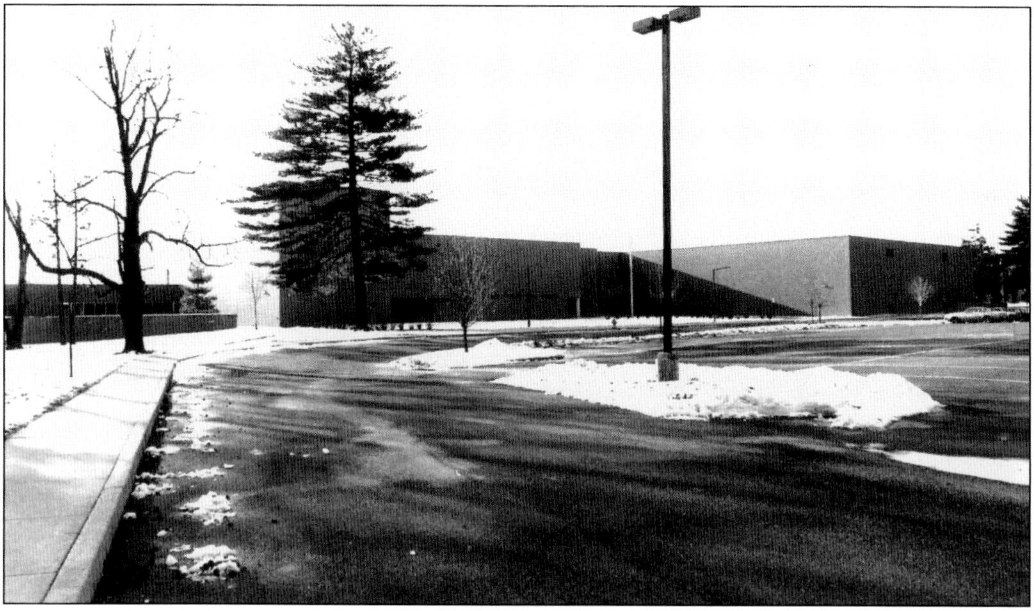

ACADEMY PARK HIGH SCHOOL, 1982. Grounds that formerly housed the Holy Child Academy were purchased when four school districts merged to form the Southeast Delco School District in 1982. The new school was named Academy Park High School. Before the new school was built, the seventh-, eighth-, and ninth-grade students held classes in one of the newer buildings of the former Holy Child Academy in what was known for a brief time as Central Junior High School.

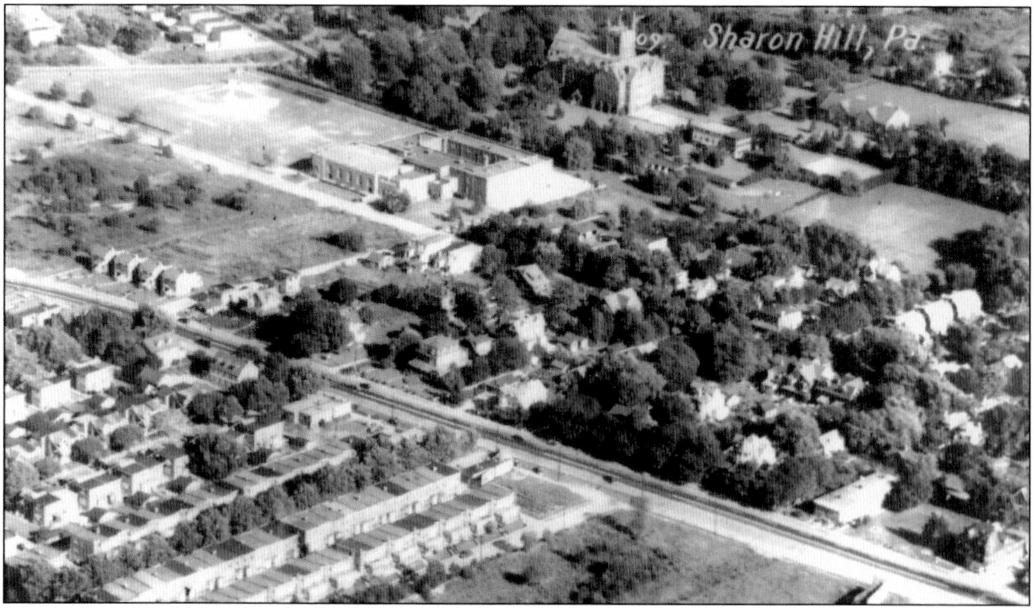

AERIAL VIEW OF SCHOOL LOCATIONS, 1939. In the top center looking south is the Holy Child Academy. The Sharon Hill High School with its new gymnasium is shown in the center located at Coates Street and Kenney Avenue. Going north to Chester Pike and then west to the next road, Ridley Avenue, is the first schoolhouse in Sharon Hill. The Bell Telephone building and Quinn's Grocery Store can be seen on the lower right.

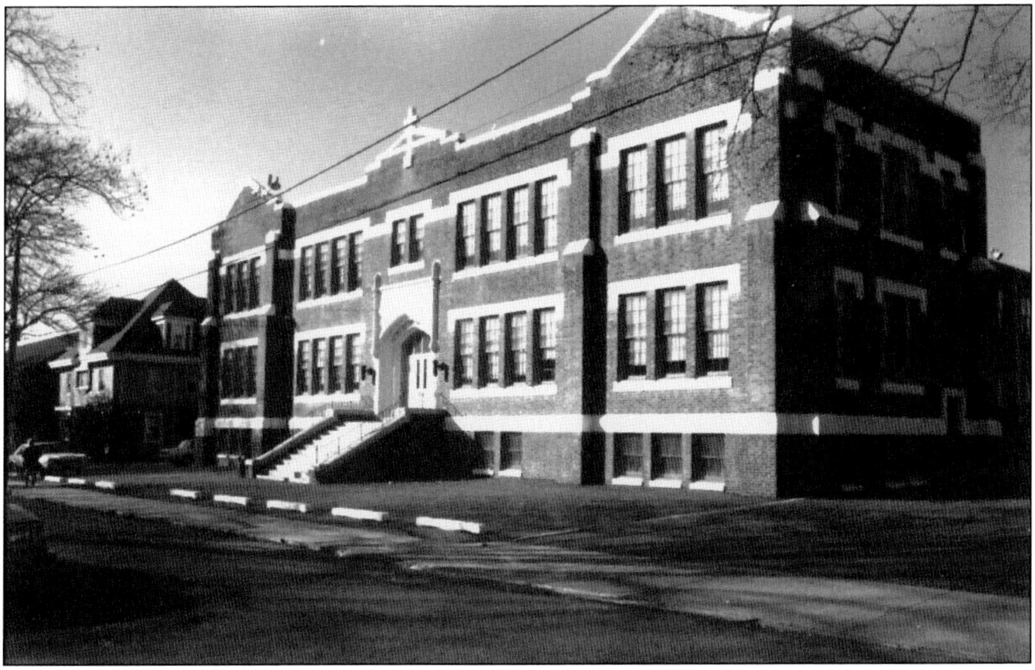

HOLY SPIRIT SCHOOL, 1917. Under the guidance of the Sisters of the Holy Child, who had fostered students since their arrival in 1881, Catholic students from grades one through eight began their elementary education at Holy Spirit in 1917 on School Street, now named Cardinal Foley Drive. An addition was built in 1949 to accommodate more students. Decreased enrollment and increased costs led to the school's closing in 2003. (Courtesy of Michael Finnegan.)

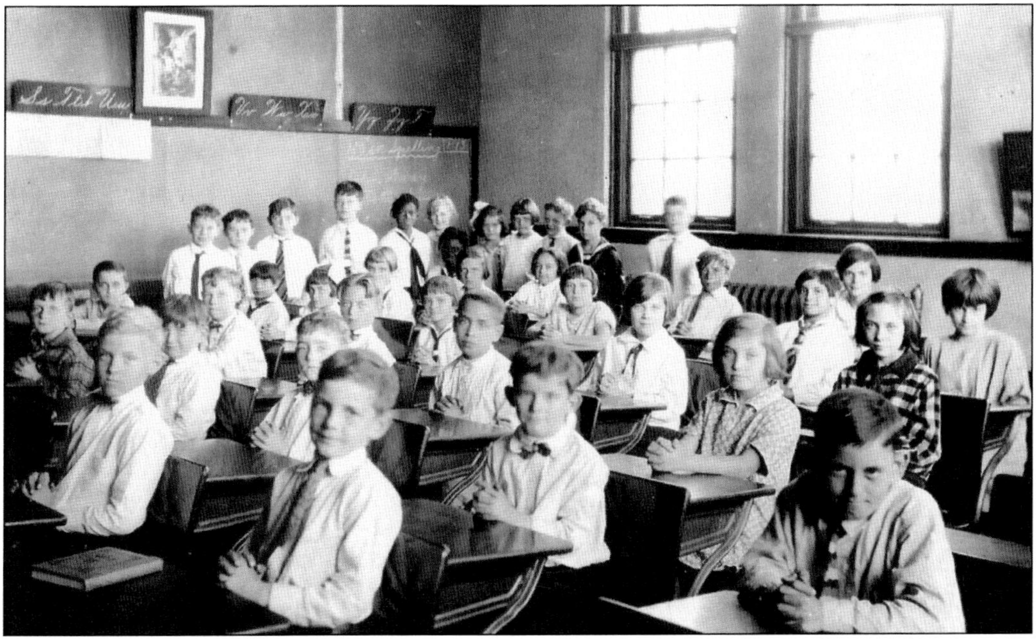

HOLY SPIRIT CLASS, 1928. The children in this elementary class pose for a picture portrait in 1928. Palmer Method handwriting cards can be seen above the blackboard. (Courtesy of Holy Spirit Church.)

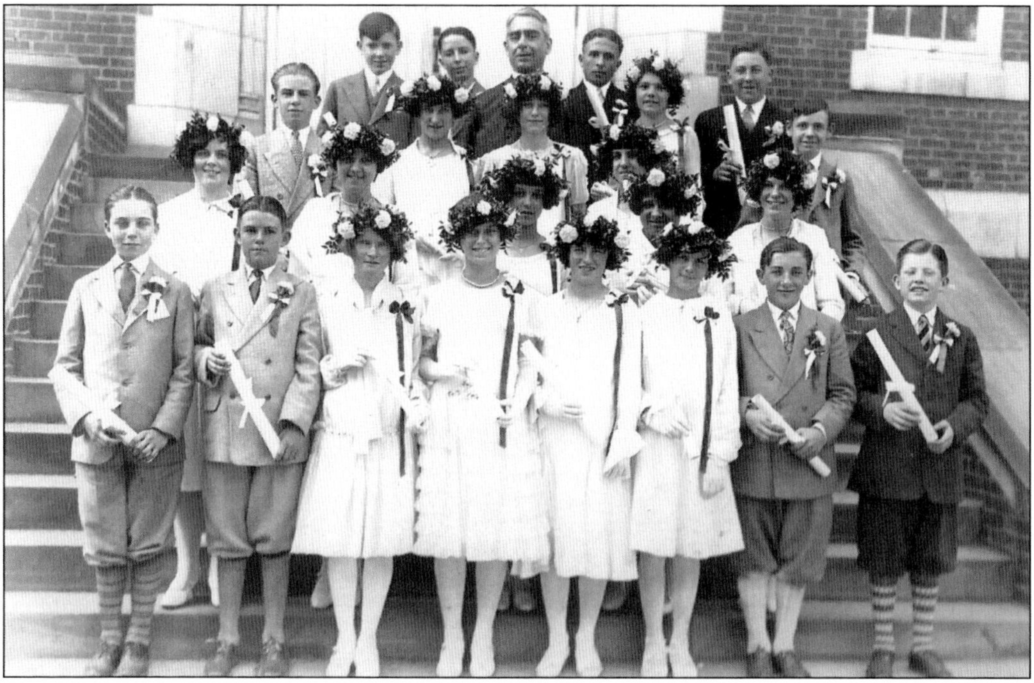

HOLY SPIRIT STUDENTS, 1920S. The eighth-grade graduation class of 1926 from Holy Spirit School is pictured above with its pastor Fr. Joseph Monville. Wearing the traditional garb of the day, the students seem happy to have their diplomas and are ready for high school. Pictured below is the First Holy Communion class on May 22, 1927. The children are photographed in front of Holy Spirit School located at Sharon Avenue and School Street. (Courtesy of Holy Spirit Church.)

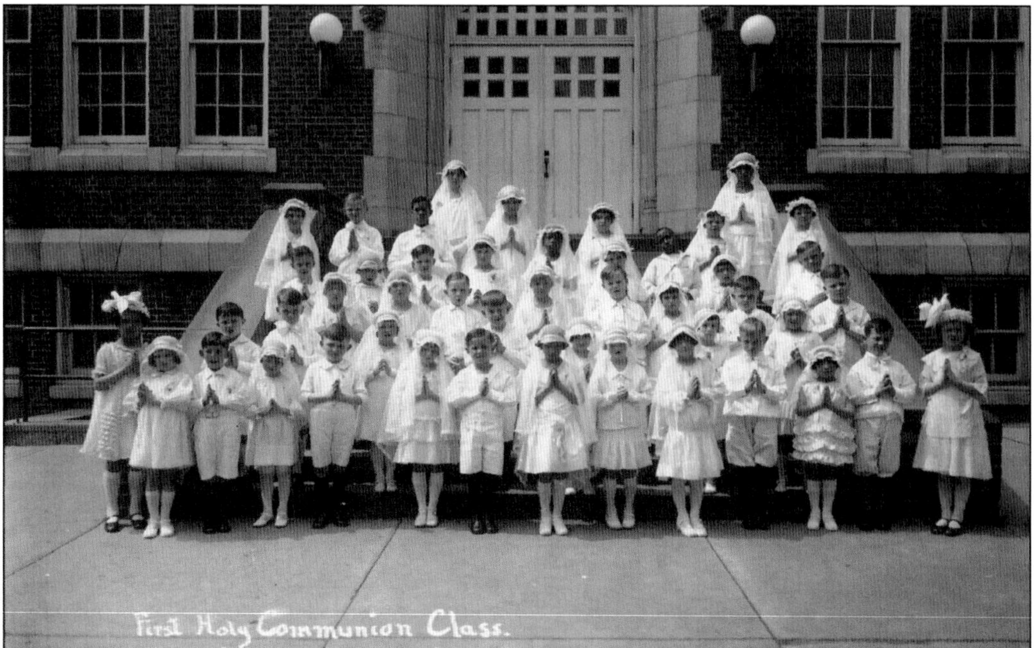

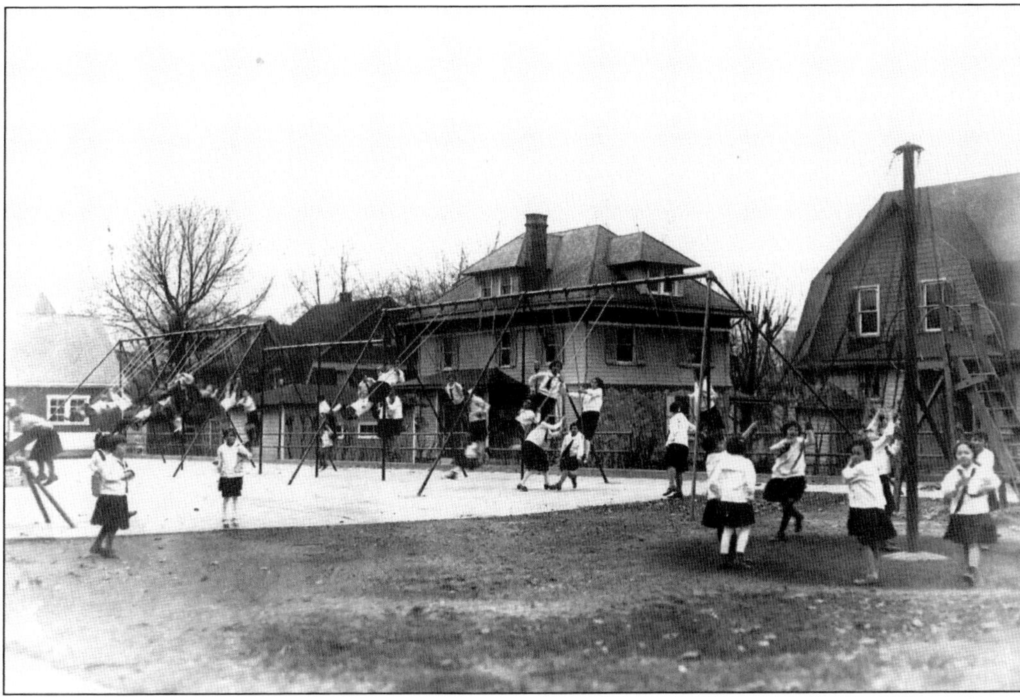

PLAYGROUND, 1926. It was common practice in 1926 to separate the girls from the boys during their recess. Pictured above is the girls' playground with its swing sets and sliding board. The girls are wearing their uniforms, a white blouse, dark skirt, and dark tie. The playground is behind the homes on Maple Avenue. The boys' playground below has the same equipment and a climbing pole. The boys' uniforms were similar to the girls' with a white shirt, dark knickers, and dark tie. (Courtesy of Holy Spirit Church.)

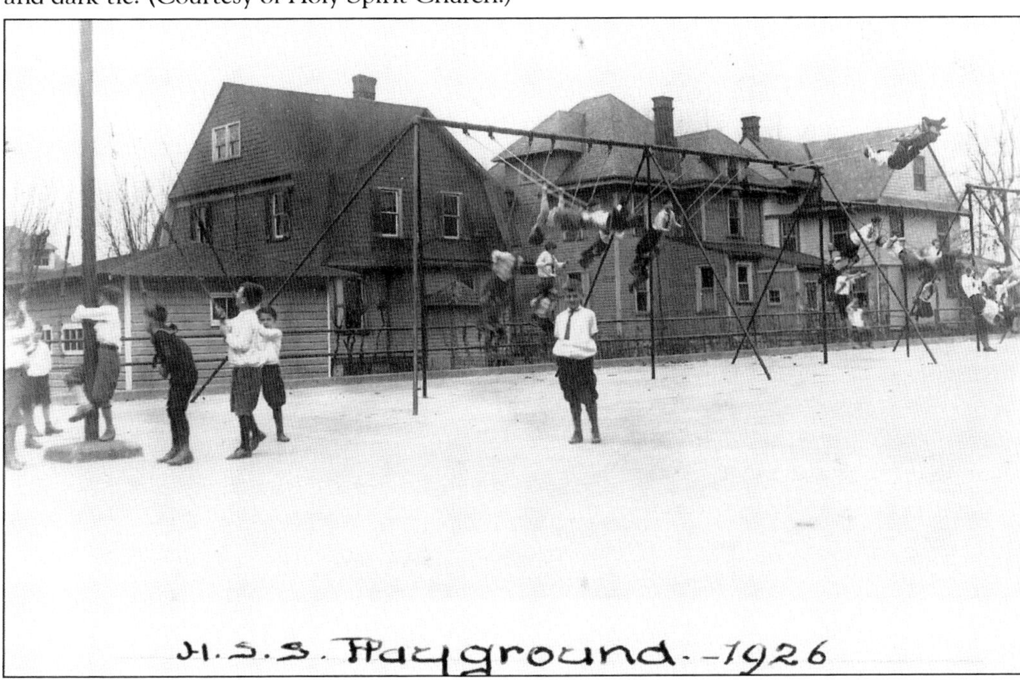

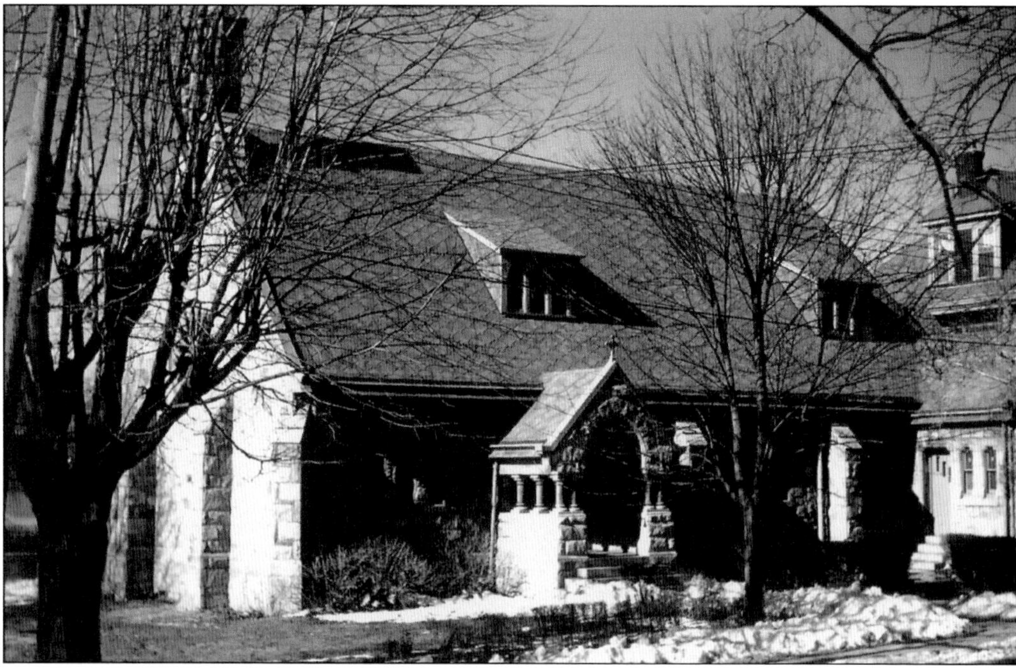

HOLY SPIRIT CHURCH, 1892. Fr. Thomas O'Neill of St. Clement's Church in Philadelphia built the first Holy Spirit Church as a mission church on the grounds where the present church now stands. The church accommodated 250 worshippers. It serviced the community for 68 years, until the new church was built in 1960.

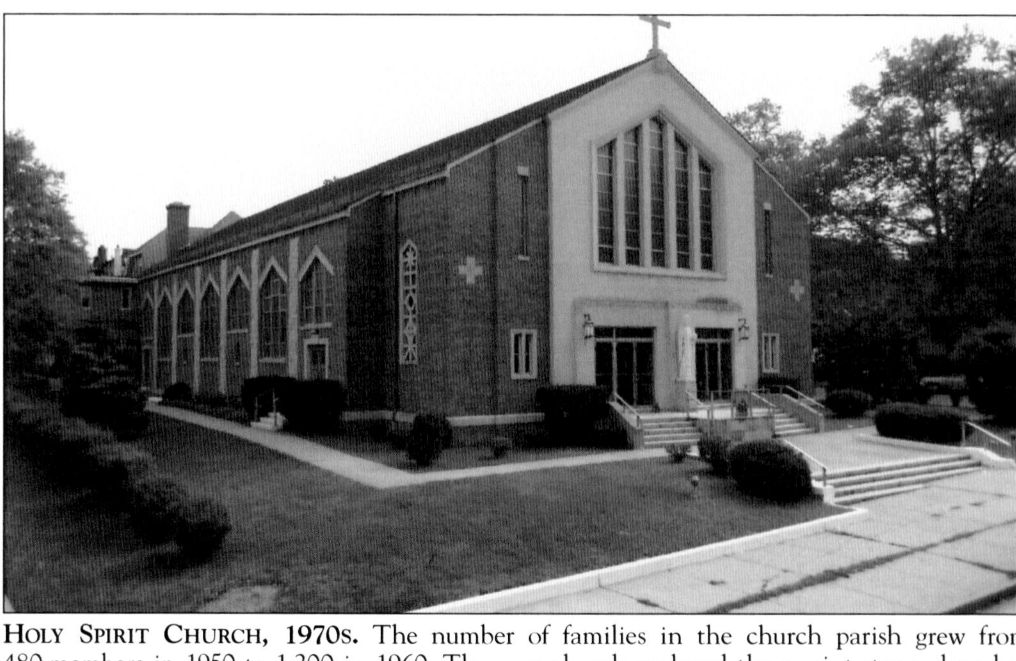

HOLY SPIRIT CHURCH, 1970S. The number of families in the church parish grew from 480 members in 1950 to 1,200 in 1960. The new church replaced the quaint stone chapel at the same site on Sharon Avenue and School Street. Archbishop (later Cardinal) John J. Krol officiated at the dedication ceremonies on March 17, 1960.

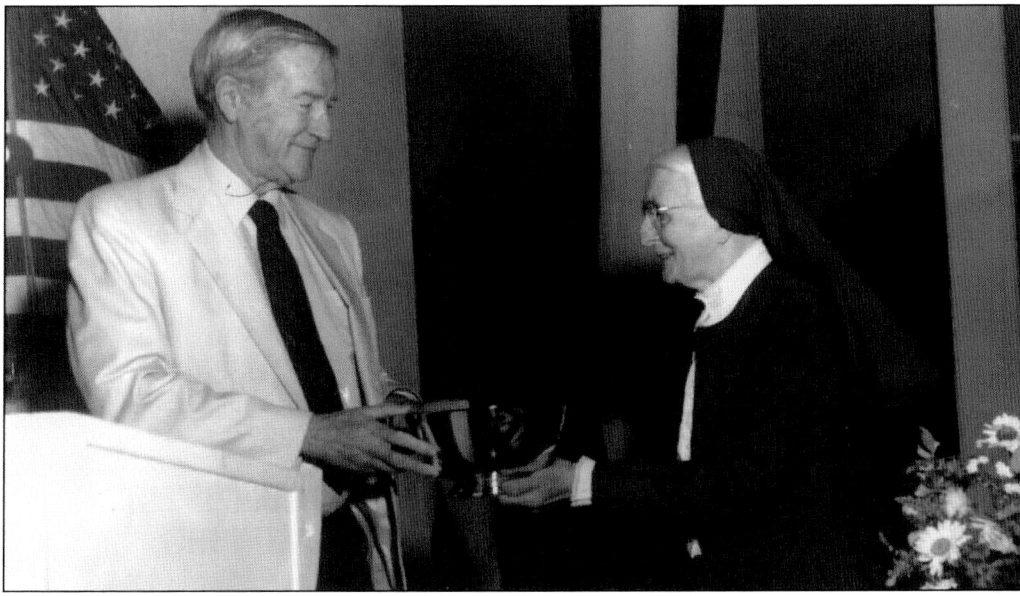

Sister Mary Liguori, SHCJ, 1980. Sr. Mary Liguori actively pursued the needy throughout the area: the homeless, the hungry, and anyone needing rental assistance, medication, or advocacy. Her membership and participation in a myriad of Delaware County and Philadelphia Archdiocesan organizations expanded her intense concern for improving the plight of those in need. Sister Liguori was one of only 10 persons awarded the prestigious *Philadelphia Evening Bulletin*'s Jefferson Award for her outstanding community service.

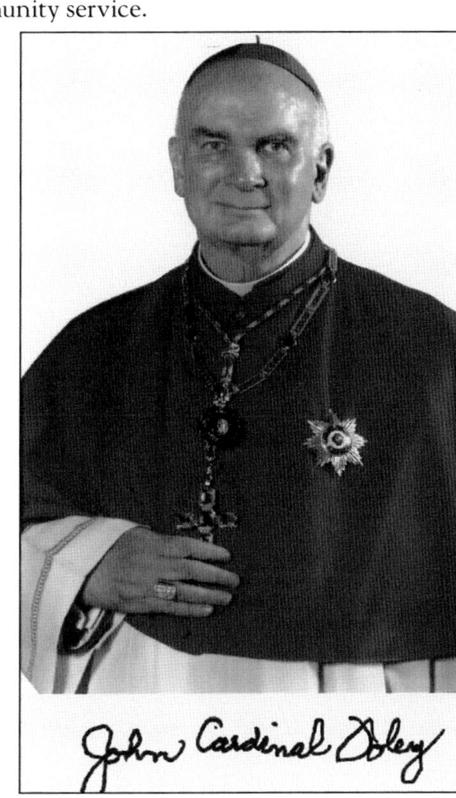

John Cardinal Foley, 2007. John Cardinal Foley attended Holy Spirit School. In 1970, Archbishop Foley was named editor of the *Philadelphia Catholic Standard and Times*. Rising through the ecclesiastical ranks of the Catholic Church, Archbishop Foley was appointed by Pope Benedict XVI to the eminent office of cardinal in 2007. He now serves as grand master of the Equestrian Order of the Holy Sepulchre of Jerusalem. (Courtesy of John Cardinal Foley.)

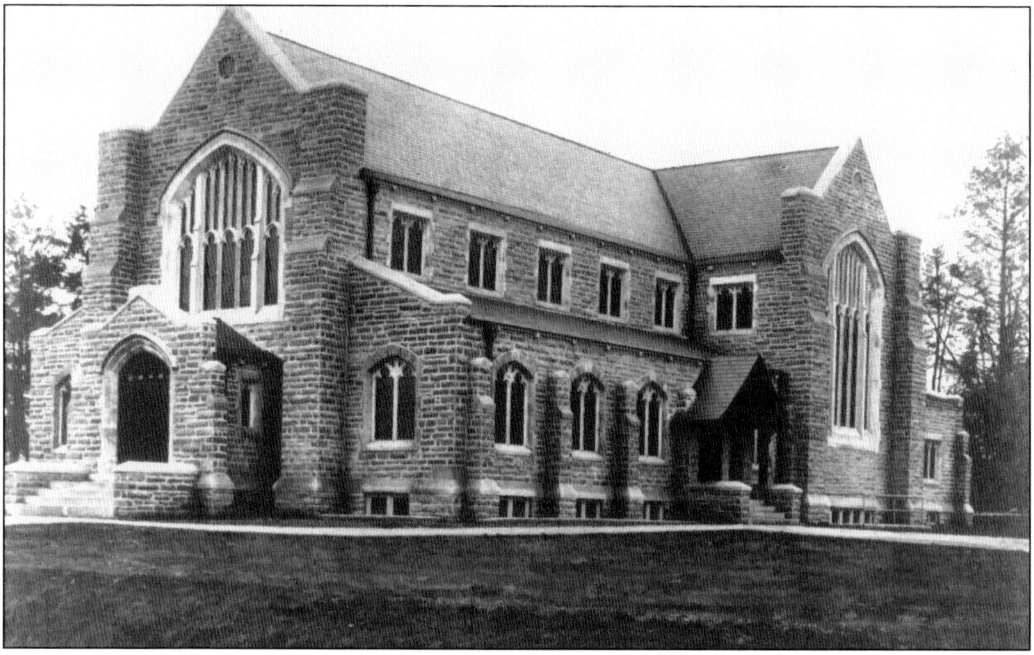

TULLY MEMORIAL PRESBYTERIAN CHURCH, 1912. The first meeting place of the planned Presbyterian Church was at the borough hall in 1908. Construction took place in 1912, and the church was named in honor of Rev. David Tully, who was the first moderator, friend, and helper to the newly formed group. In four years the congregation raised $60,000 to build this impressive edifice. The architect was Hazlehurst.

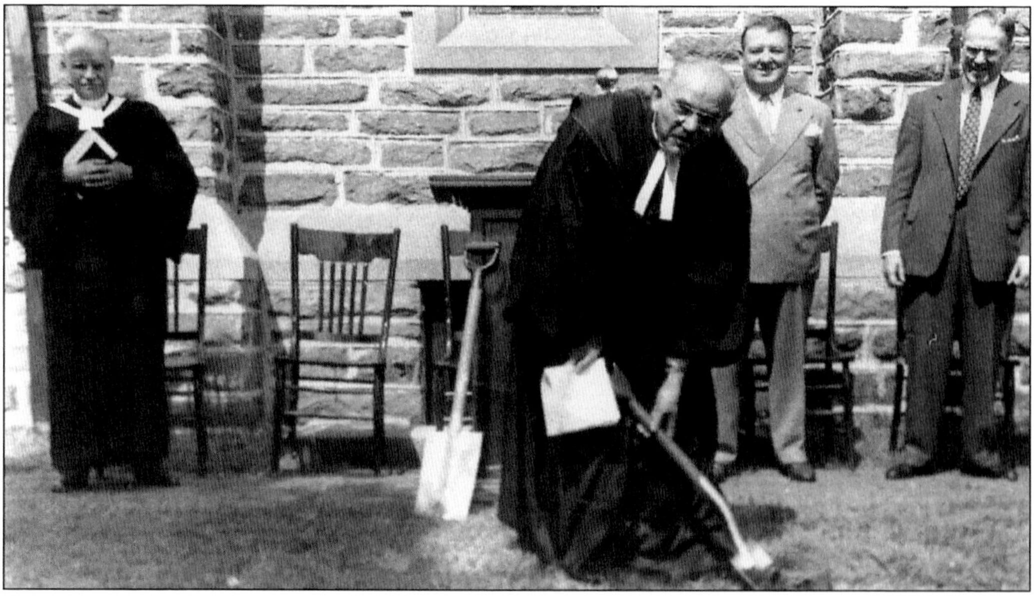

GROUNDBREAKING AT TULLY CHURCH, 1960. An addition to Tully Church was built and dedicated in 1960. It was named Knowlton Hall in honor of Rev. S. Brooks Knowlton, who retired in 1968, having served the church for 31 years. The picture shows Reverend Knowlton as he turns the first spadeful of earth for the addition. The shovel was the same one used in the groundbreaking of the original church in 1912.

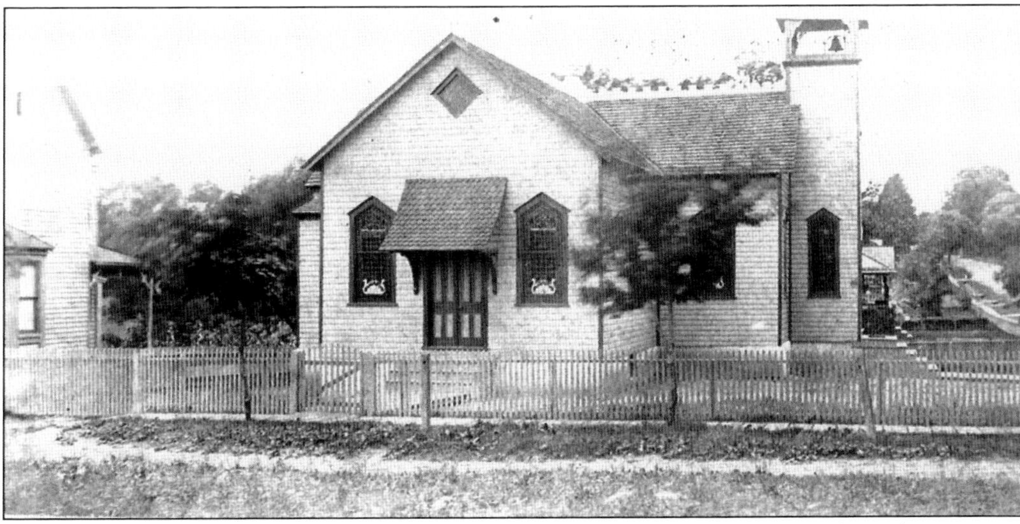

SHARON HILL METHODIST EPISCOPAL CHURCH, 1899. The congregation was formed in 1882 and held its first service in the Sharon Hill train station (the Philadelphia, Wilmington and Baltimore Railroad at that time). The first church building was constructed in 1883 at Spring Street and Sharon Avenue. The frame building with a bell tower was in use until the new church was built to accommodate the increased membership in 1899. This building was demolished in 1901.

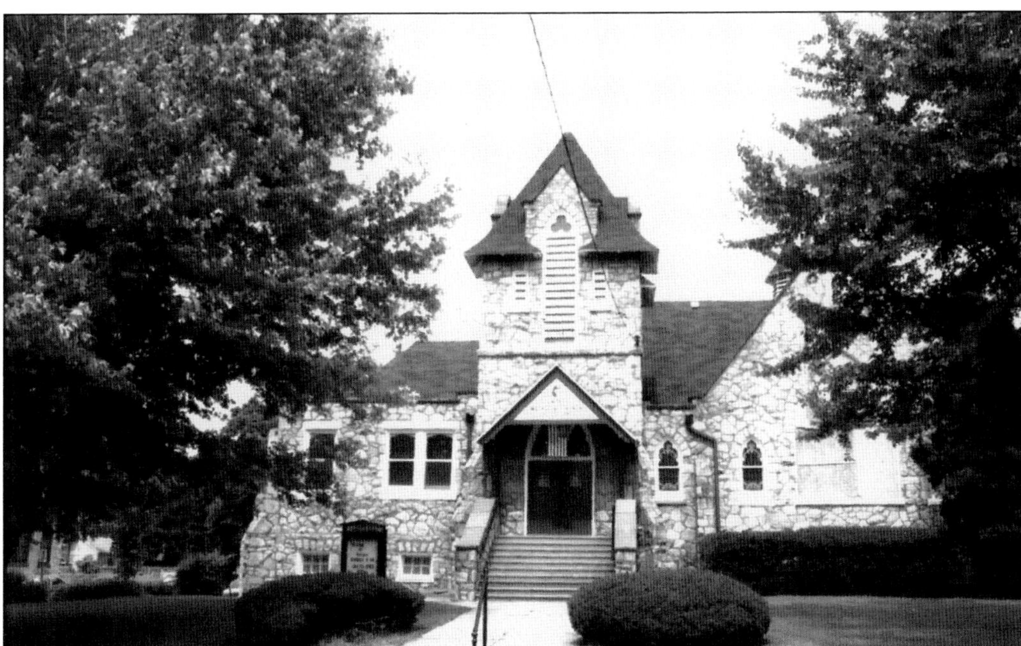

SHARON HILL UNITED METHODIST CHURCH, 1989. Increased membership led to the construction of this new Methodist church in 1899. Part of its expansion led to a new parsonage in 1912. In 1926, a Sunday school and recreational facility were built by the church on the grounds of the former public school. The structure was named the Roberts-Douglass Memorial Building. William Douglass was elected the chief burgess in the town's first council. He was instrumental in the building of the church.

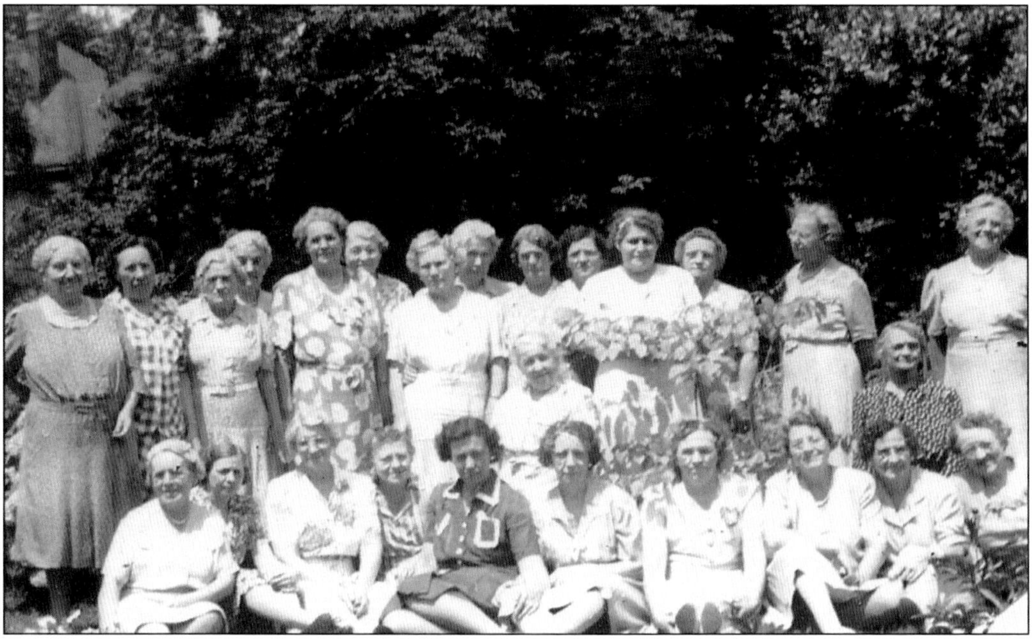

Miss Kendrig's Buds, 1940s. The women at this gathering of the Methodist Episcopal Church's first Sunday school class in the early 1900s represented the oldest members of the town and church at that time. Many of the women started in the Cradle Roll Class in 1915. They remembered well their pastor, Rev. George Paul Beck. (Courtesy of Marlene Larer.)

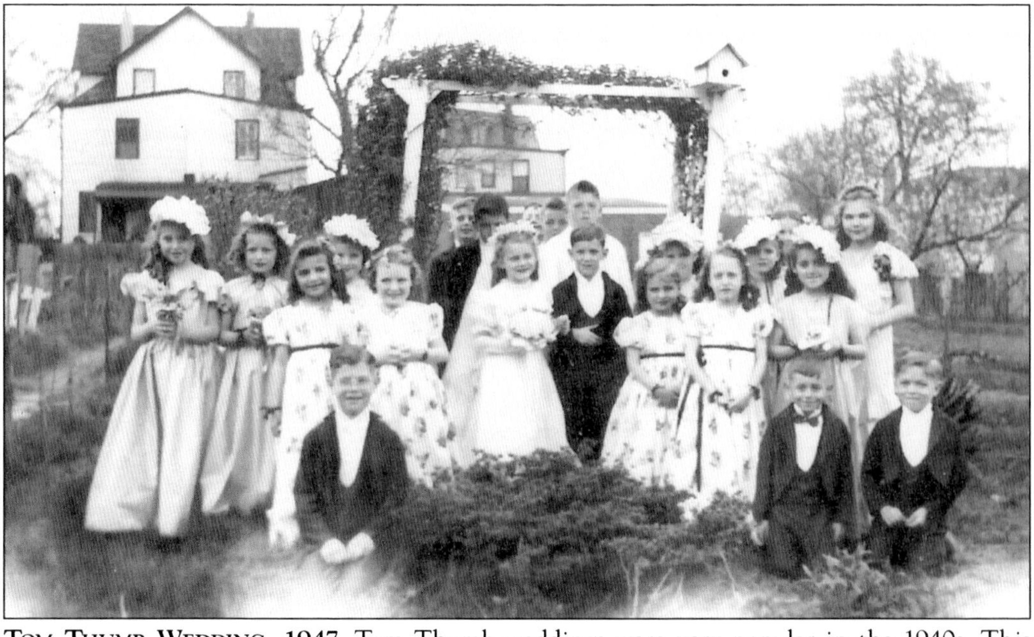

Tom Thumb Wedding, 1947. Tom Thumb weddings were very popular in the 1940s. This picture shows a group from the Sharon Hill Methodist Church dressed in their wedding finery and posing for the photographer in 1947. For some time this was an annual event for the Methodist Church and a favorite for both participants and guests. (Courtesy of Ken Watkins.)

Four

Commerce and Industry

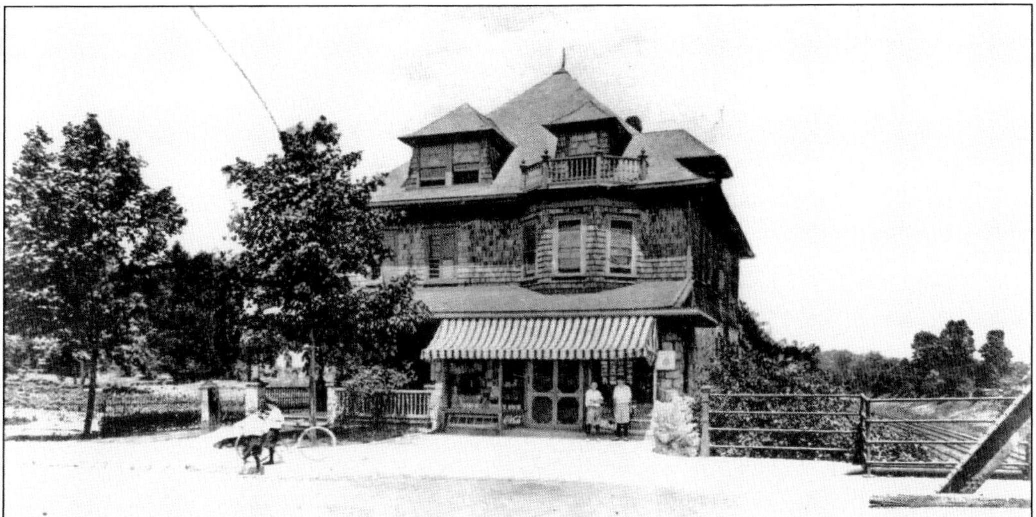

Sharon Hill Post Office, c. 1900. In 1899, the post office was moved from the Sharon Hill train station to Dr. David Dalton's Drug Store at 411 Sharon Avenue. Dr. Dalton acted as postmaster until 1908.

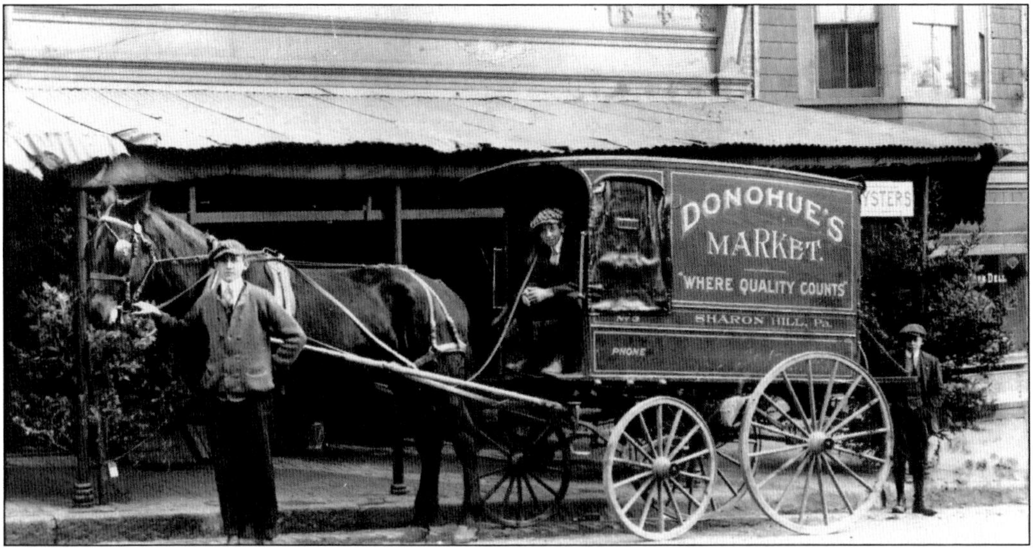

DONOHUE MARKET, C. 1906. The grocery wagon in this photograph is in front of Donohue's meat and grocery store on Sharon Avenue between Elmwood Avenue and the railroad tracks. Frank Donohue is holding the horse, and the driver is John Donohue. The horse is unhitched. If the fire ring was sounded, the horse would be ready to be hooked to the fire wagon. (Courtesy of Henrietta Donohue.)

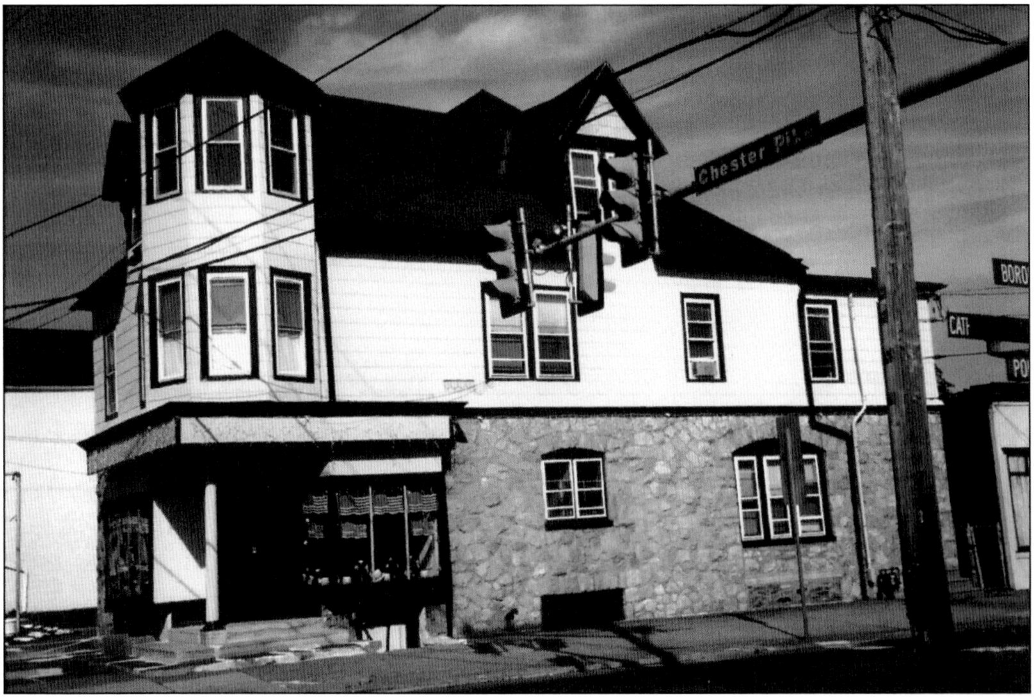

QUINN'S GROCERY STORE, 1970. Thomas Quinn was the owner of this store at Sharon Avenue and Chester Pike that was built in the late 1880s. It was one of the few grocery stores at the dawn of the 20th century. Families grew their own vegetables and raised chickens; meat and staples were brought from Philadelphia or other parts of Delaware County. Thomas Quinn was the health inspector for the borough in 1893.

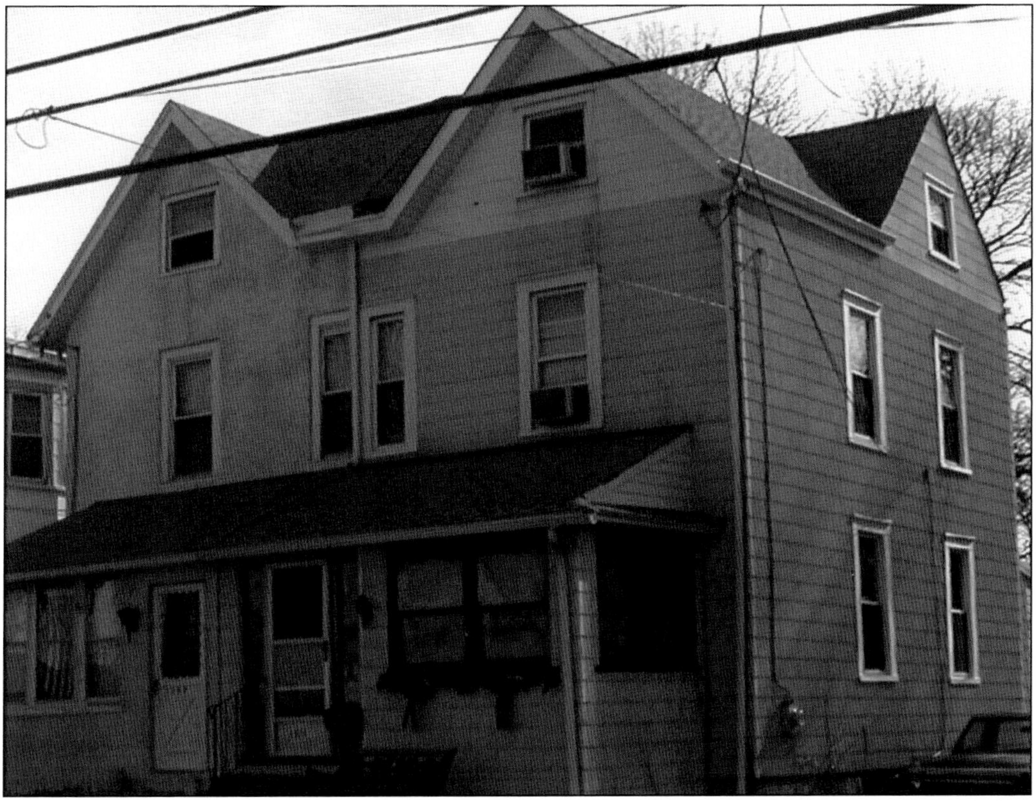

YANCK'S GLASS WORKS, C. 1965. Located on the south side of Elmwood Avenue below Felton Avenue once was a single building used by the glassworks. Rejects were discarded in the backyard, which extended to the Muckinapates Creek. The original factory was destroyed by fire. (Courtesy of Delaware County Planning Department.)

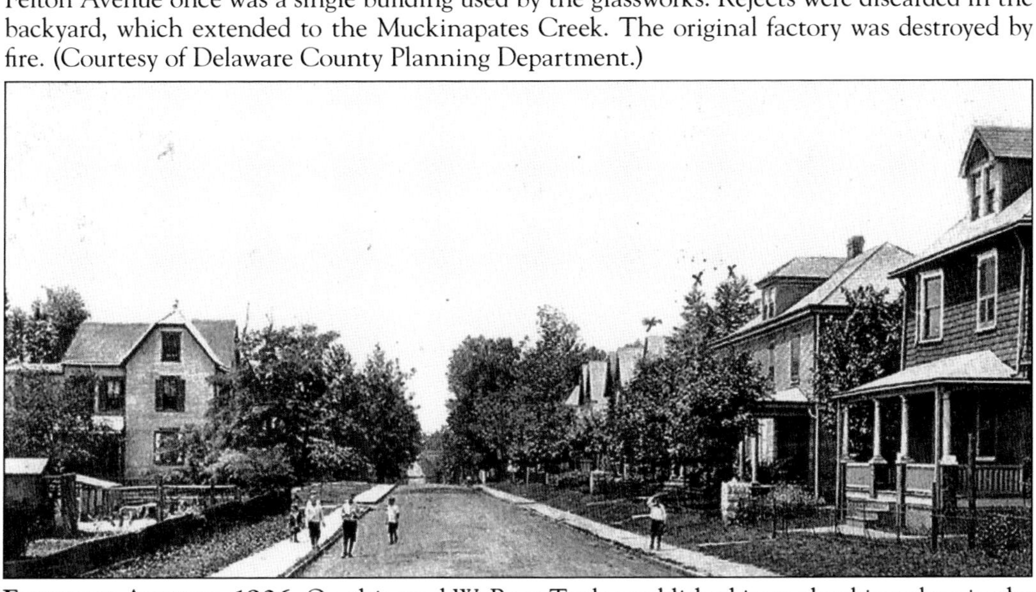

ELMWOOD AVENUE, 1906. On this road W. Rose Tools established its toolmaking plant in the 1880s. Yanck's Glass Works was also an early business, and its factory was located directly across Elmwood Avenue near Felton Avenue. Comfortable single and twin homes followed from Folcroft Avenue through Calcon Hook Road abutting what is now Henderson Industrial center.

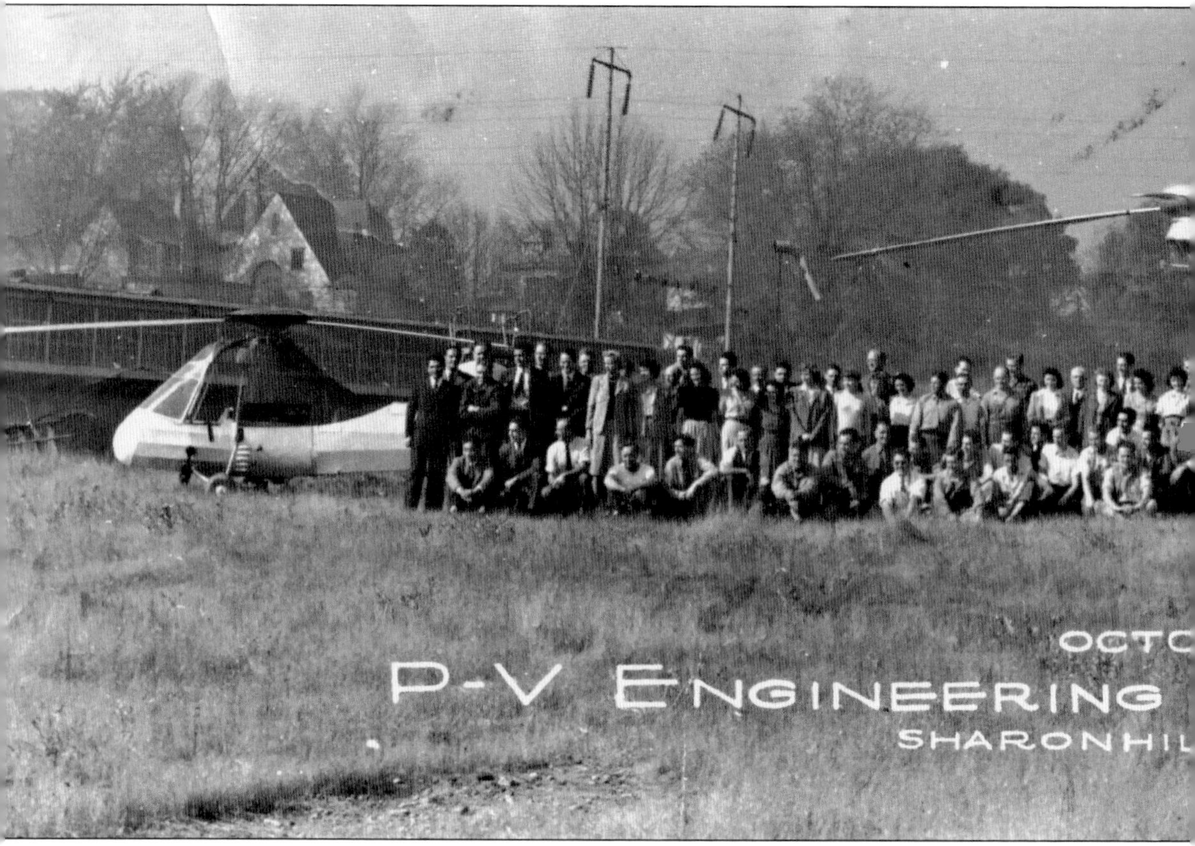

HELICOPTER INDUSTRY, 1945. For a period of time in the 1940s, Frank N. Piasecki, pioneer in the helicopter industry, based his company known at the time as P-V Engineering Forum Inc. in Sharon Hill. The company set up its plant and testing site in 1945 on the northeastern side of Elmwood Avenue below Calcon Hook Road. Residents of the homes in the background and the surrounding neighborhood were witnesses to Piasecki's initial testing flights over the

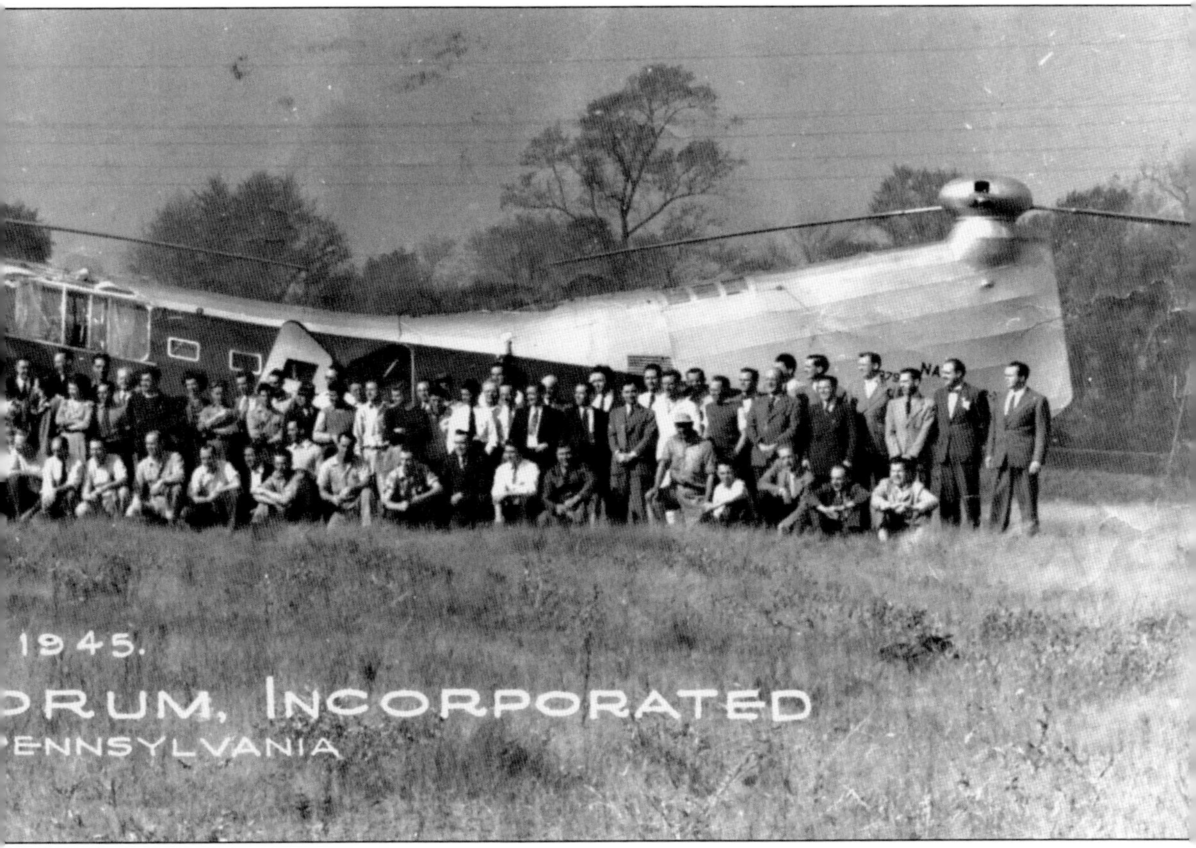

area. The whirling creatures flying overhead introduced a new and innovative kind of air flight, which later became important to both military and commercial personnel. Pictured is a gathering of the employees in front of an XHRP-I helicopter (right). Frank Piasecki is pictured second from the right in the second row. (Courtesy of the American Helicopter Museum and Education Center.)

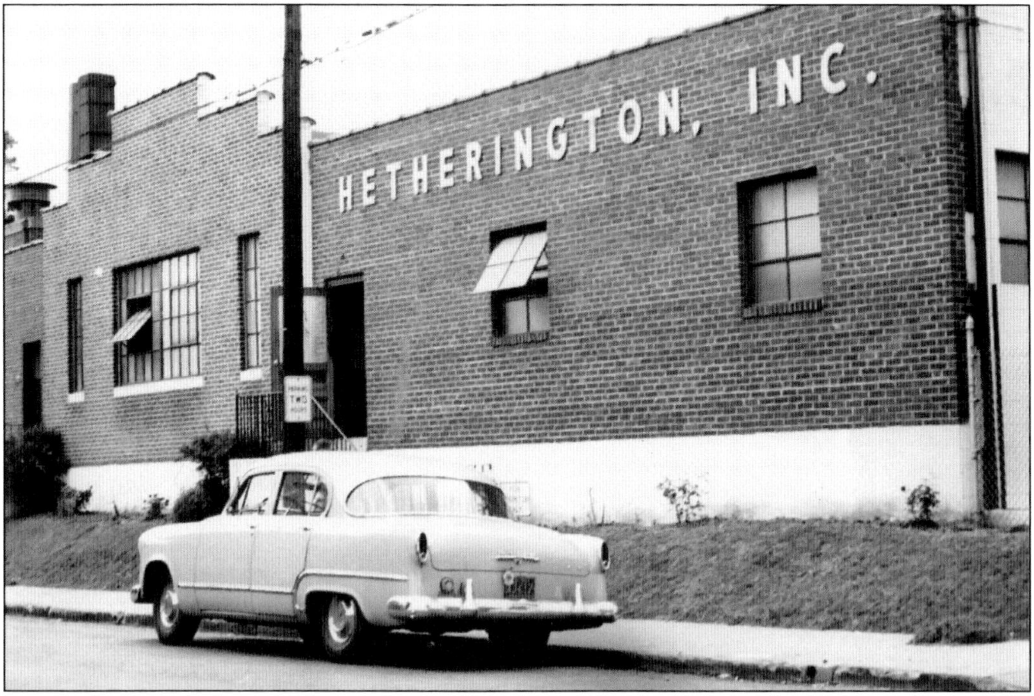

HETHERINGTON INC., 1950. Located on Elmwood Avenue, the mainstay of this company was manufacturing illuminated control switches for planes and helicopters. Starting out as a small machine shop in Sharon Hill, they are now a worldwide company. In 1961, Hetherington became the control switch division of Controls Company of America. (Courtesy of Joseph Walker Jr.)

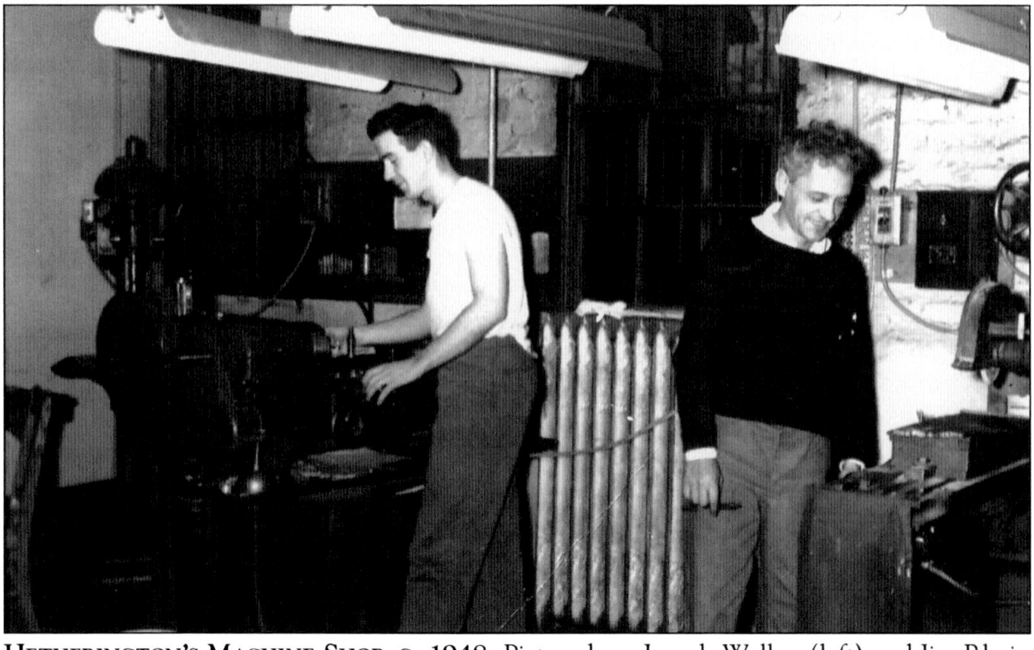

HETHERINGTON'S MACHINE SHOP, C. 1948. Pictured are Joseph Walker (left) and Jim Rhein (right), employees of Hetherington Inc., working on making parts for switches in the machine shop on Elmwood Avenue. (Courtesy of Joseph Walker Jr.)

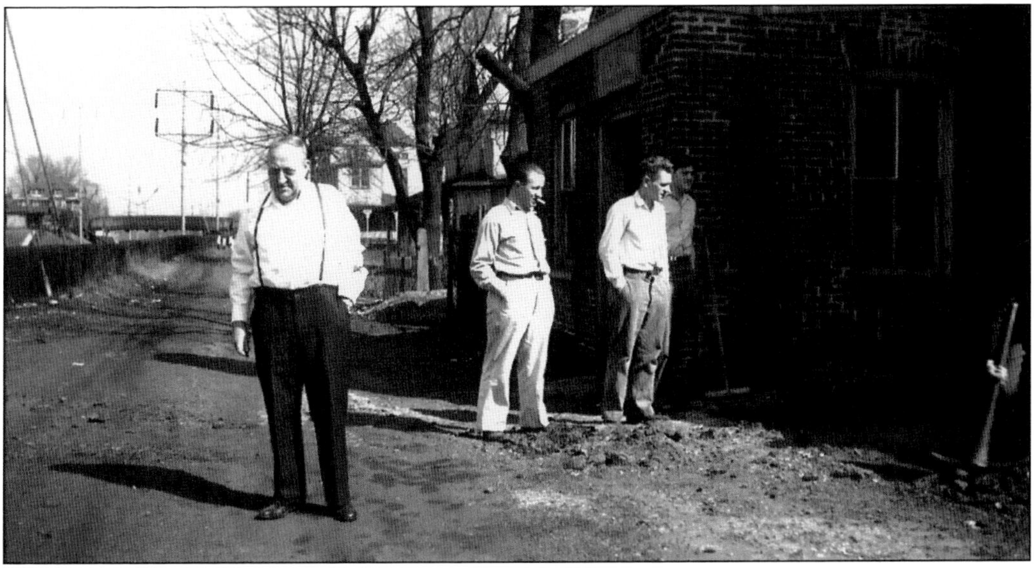

ROBERT HETHERINGTON, LATE 1940S. Pictured in the foreground is Robert Hetherington, founder of Hetherington Inc. In 1938, Robert Hetherington and Joe Schillman, in a garage on Garvin Boulevard, invented a device that helped guide fabric through the milling process. The Sharon Hill train station is in the background on the left. (Courtesy of Joseph Walker Jr.)

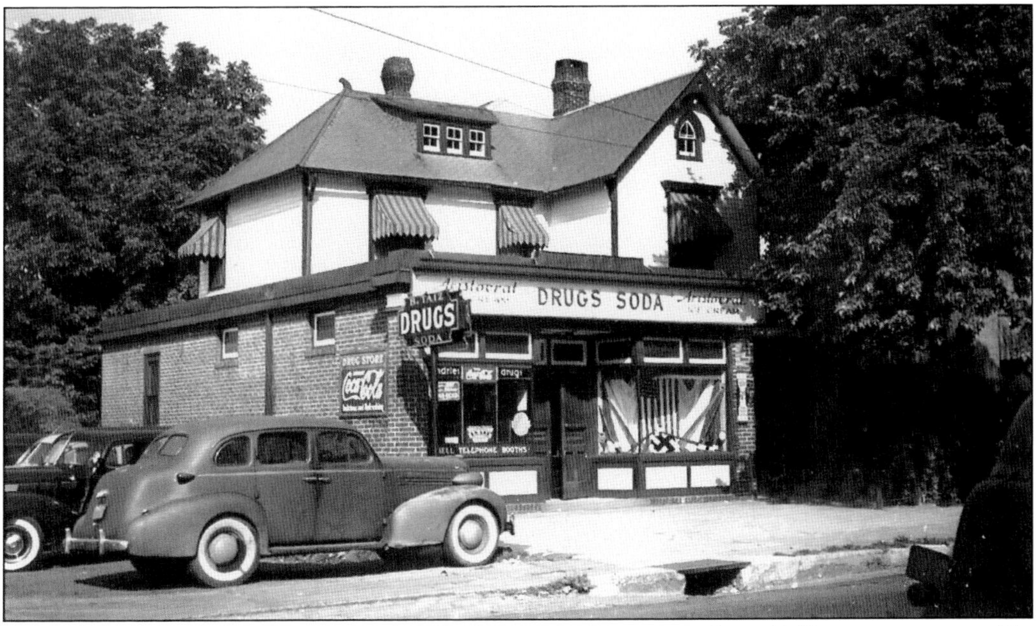

TAIZ'S DRUG STORE, 1945. Pictured is the drugstore as it appeared in a 1945 picture, operated by Bernard Taiz on Sharon Avenue next to the train station. The business was mainly a drugstore; however, the store also had a soda fountain and became known for its "take-away sundae," a scoop of ice cream served in a flat-bottomed pleated paper cup, topped with chocolate syrup and a cherry on top. The treat was eaten with a wooden spoon and was popular with all ages.

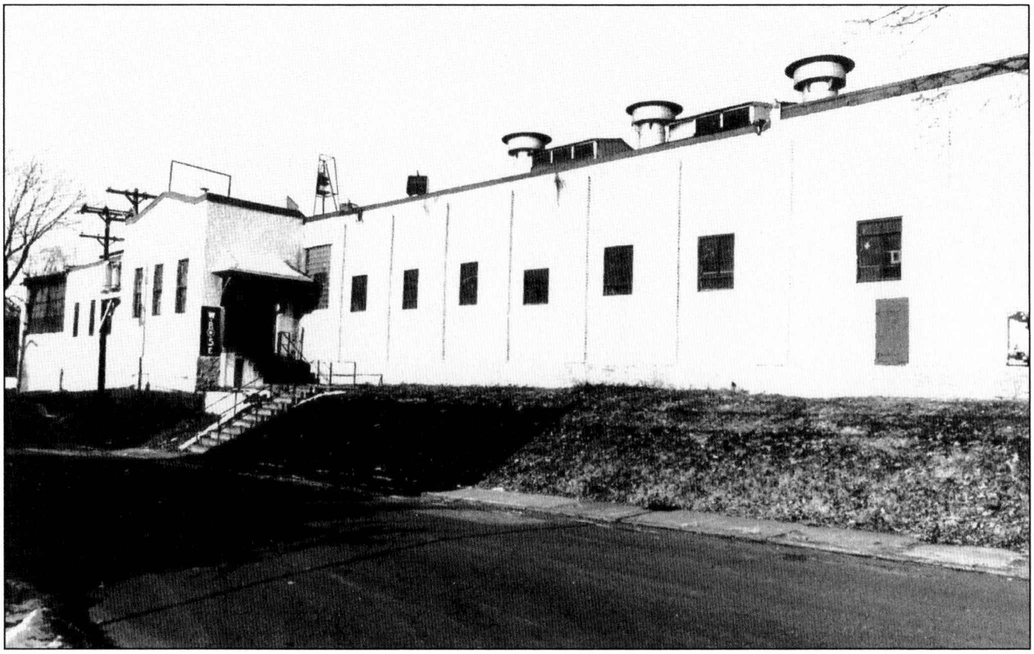

ROSE TOOL COMPANY, 1997. The oldest operating business in Sharon Hill, Rose Tool was started in Philadelphia in 1789. During the War of 1812 and the Civil War, it made swords and bayonets for the U.S. Army. The company moved to Sharon Hill in the 1880s. Octavius Goodwin purchased the building pictured at an auction in 1894. The Goodwins added more buildings until 1967. The company is noted for making high-quality tools. In 1995, having been in business for 197 years, the State of Pennsylvania commended W. Rose Inc. It was noted as one of only 12 manufacturing businesses that were in continuous operation since before the year 1800.

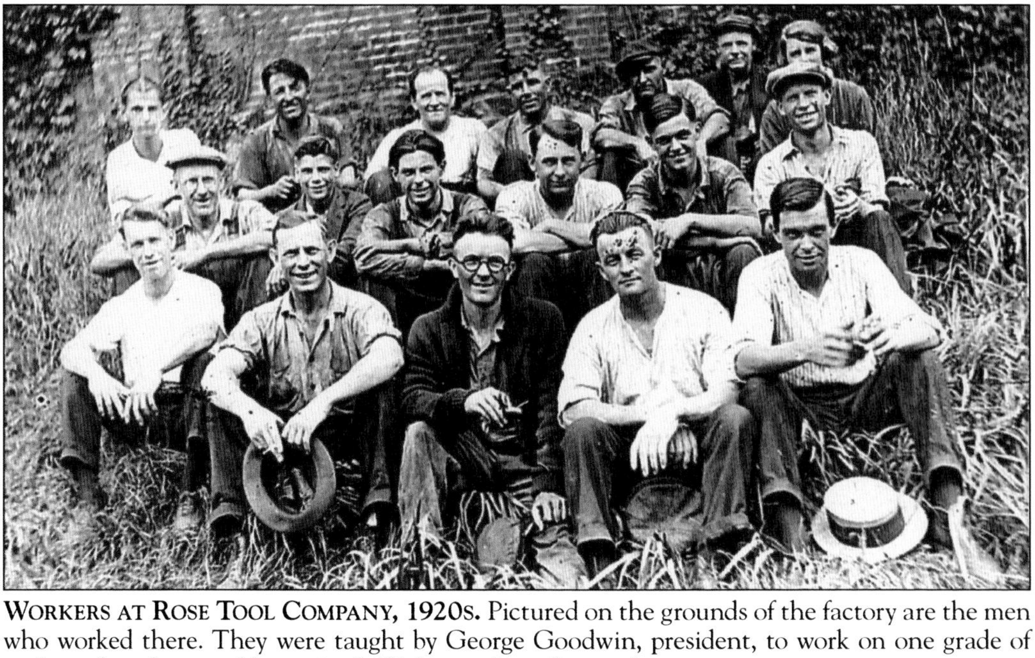

WORKERS AT ROSE TOOL COMPANY, 1920S. Pictured on the grounds of the factory are the men who worked there. They were taught by George Goodwin, president, to work on one grade of tools so that they would remain skillful in making fine tools.

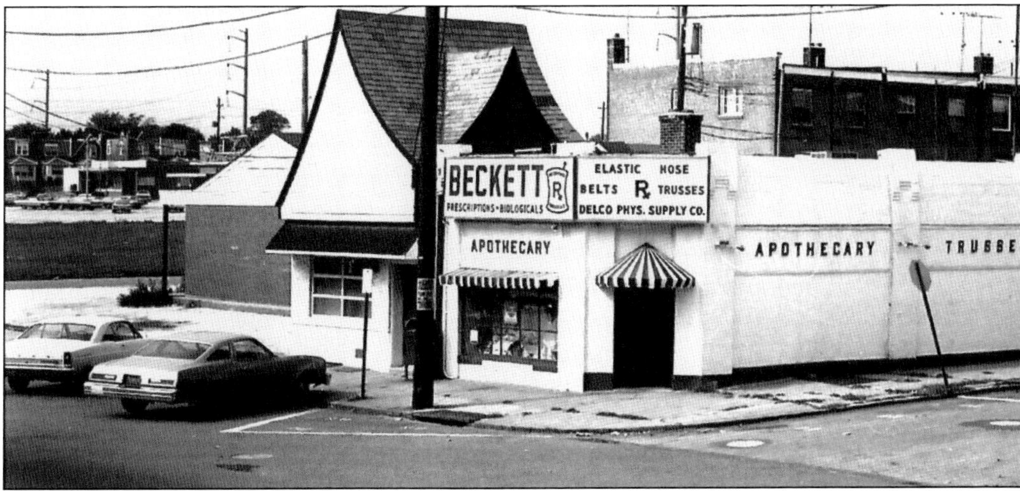

BECKETT APOTHECARY, 1975. Originally on the corner of Barker Avenue and Chester Pike (as shown), Beckett's, now known as Beckett's Home Care Products Inc., came into being in the 1940s. In 1975, the business moved to its present site on Burnside Avenue (the former site of the Open Pantry). Beckett's offers a wide range of health care products.

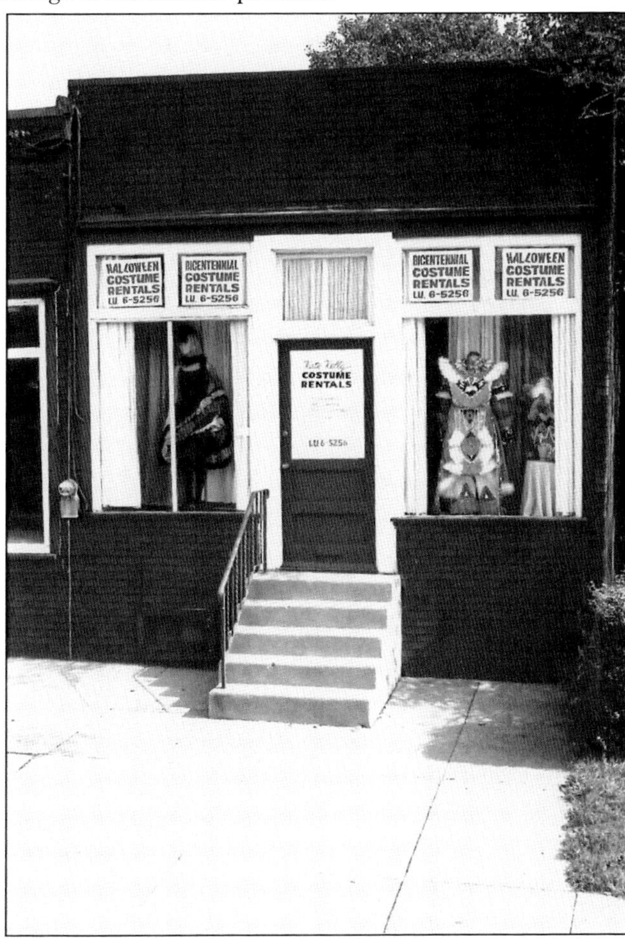

KATE KELLY'S ANTIQUE CLOTHING, C. 1960. The shop located on Sharon Avenue just below Chester Pike was managed by local historian Kate Kelly. The shop featured authentic antique clothing and accessories and supplied the outfits for Kelly's fashion shows, which were used as fund-raisers for Delaware Valley church, school, and charity events. The clothing received national attention when Kelly appeared on television programs *What's My Line* and *To Tell the Truth.*

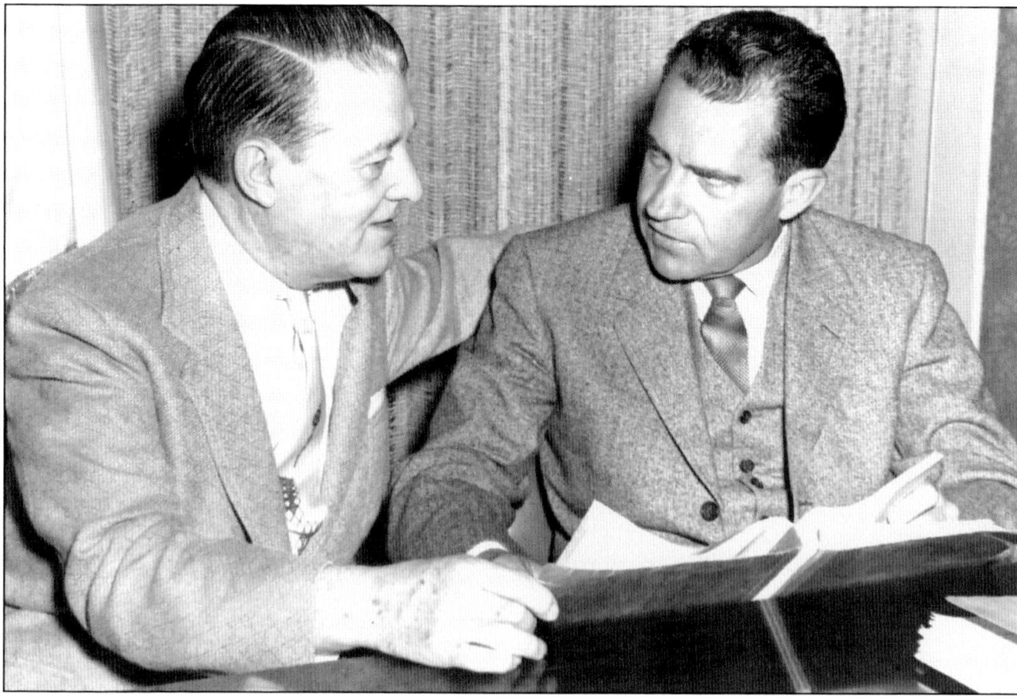

WILLIAM H. MILLIKEN JR., 1969. Shown here with Pres. Richard Nixon, William H. Milliken Jr. attended the old public school at Sharon and Maple Avenues. Later he attended Drexel Institute of Technology. Before his election to the Pennsylvania House of Representatives in 1943, Milliken was a local council member and chief burgess of Sharon Hill for 10 years. He also was clerk of the court in Delaware County from 1950 to 1958. In 1969, Milliken was elected to congress and served for three terms on the House Appropriations Committee. Milliken died in 1969.

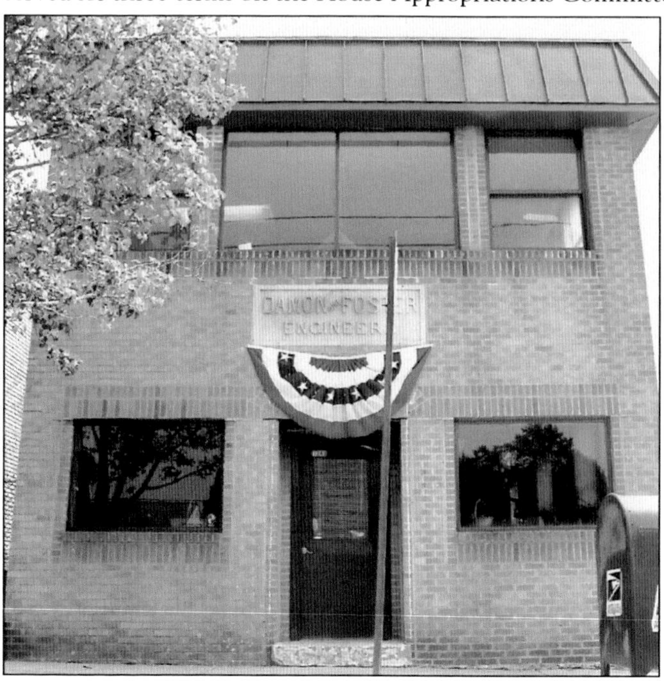

DAMON ENGINEERING, 1927. Located at Chester Pike and High Street, and serving the borough for over 100 years, the Damon Engineering Company has been located in its present office since 1927. It has been in continuous business since 1894, when the business was founded by A. F. Damon Jr. in Darby. At present the company is being managed by David P. Damon, who represents the fourth generation of the Damon family.

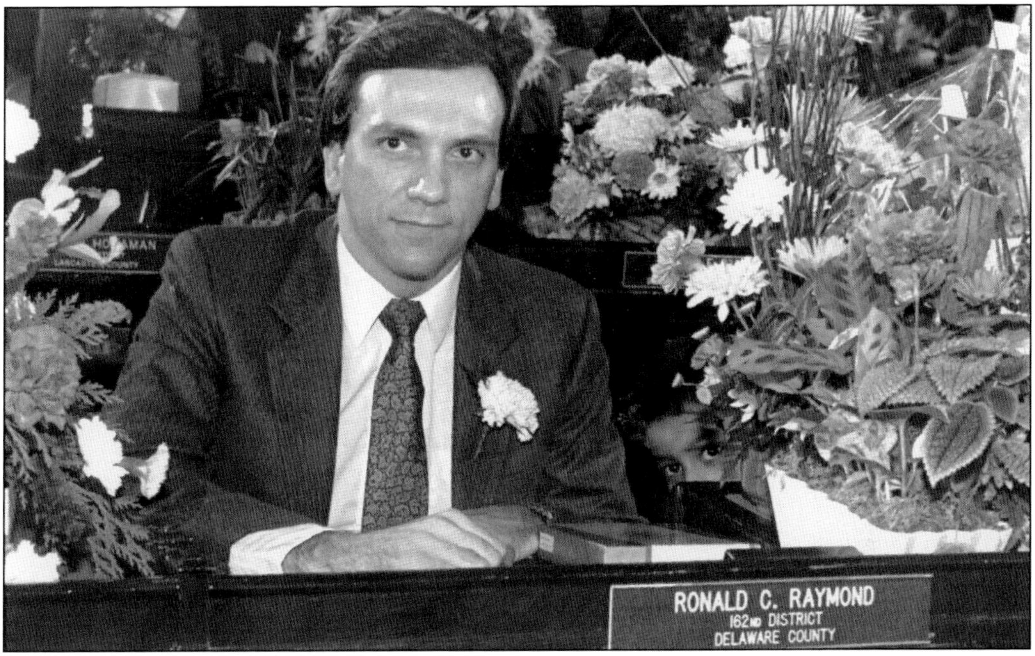

RONALD C. RAYMOND, C. 1990. Ronald Raymond served on the borough council and as mayor of Sharon Hill. He was elected to the state legislature in 1985, where he served with distinction until he retired in 2008.

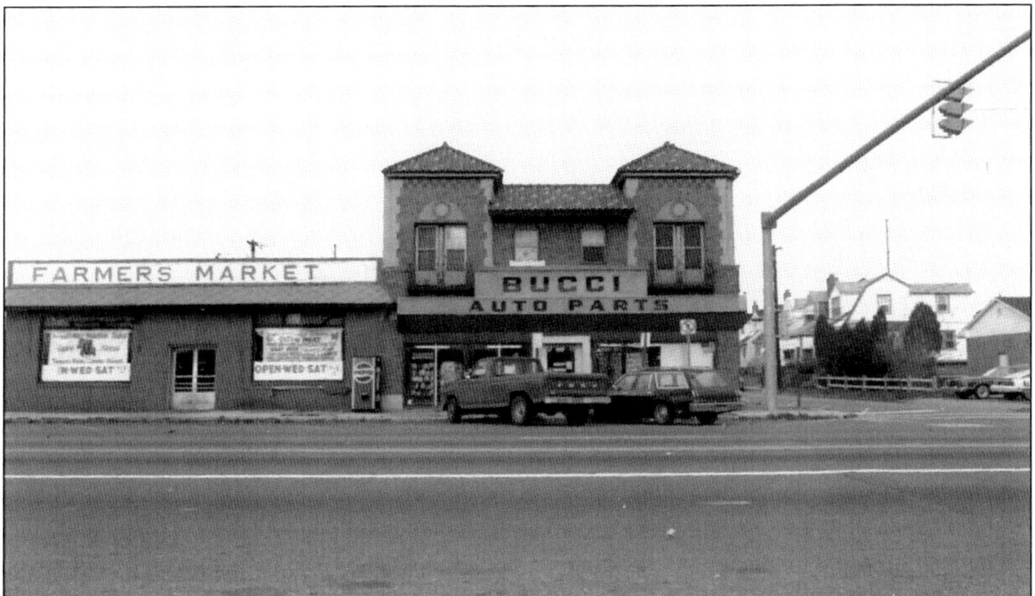

LANCASTER COUNTY FARMERS MARKET, 1997. Decorative wrought-iron balconies and a Spanish tile roof embellished the building that housed the Collingdale millworks. In 1934, it became the Lancaster County Farmers Market. The market was a very busy place where up-country farmers, butchers, and meat processors in quaint garb brought their wares twice a week (Wednesdays and Saturdays). At one time the market occupied the entire building and included a restaurant in the basement. The building was demolished in 1999.

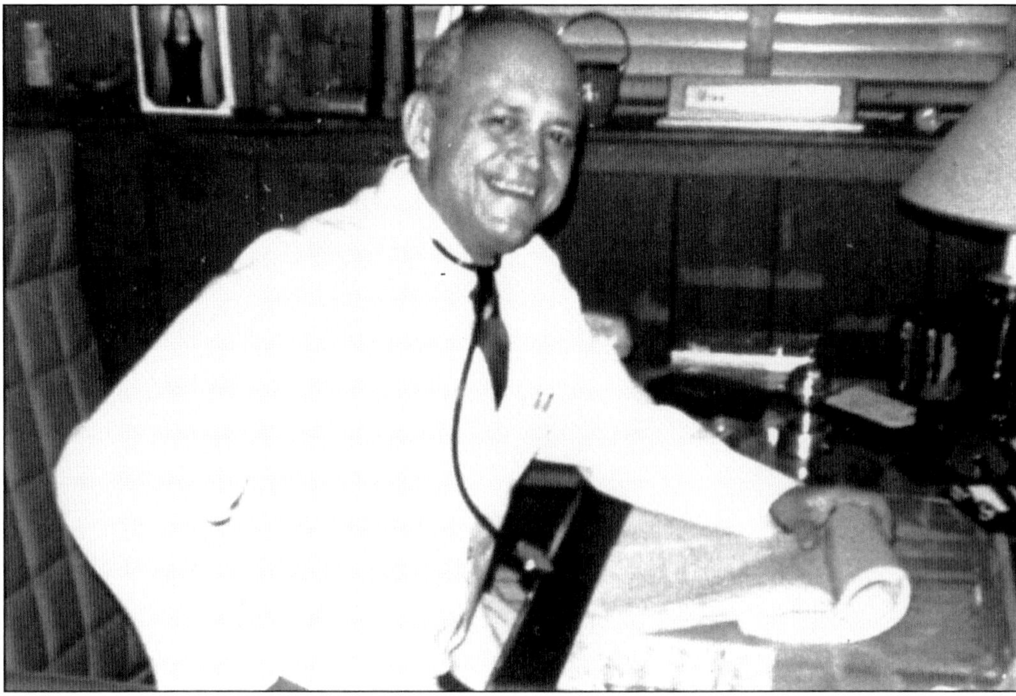

FRED T. WICKIS, M.D., 1973. Dr. Fred T. Wickis graduated from Sharon Hill High School in 1939 and served in the military during World War II. He was a graduate of Rutgers and Princeton Universities. After receiving his medical degree from Temple University, he established his practice at Barker Avenue and Chester Pike. Dr. Wickis was a well-respected, well-liked, and very important part of the community.

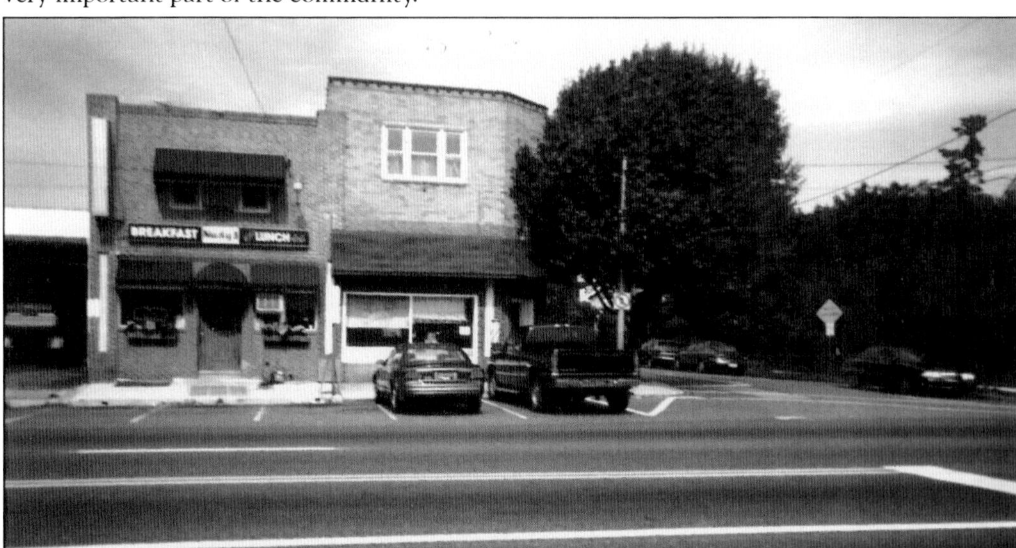

THE OWL, 1999. Formally known in its day as Rita and Harry's Luncheonette, the Owl obtained its name as the frequent favorite stop of students from Sharon Hill High School, whose school mascot was the owl. When the business was sold in 1984, it became known as Nudy's and more recently known as Jimmy's, an eating establishment for over 60 years at Chester Pike near Ridley Avenue.

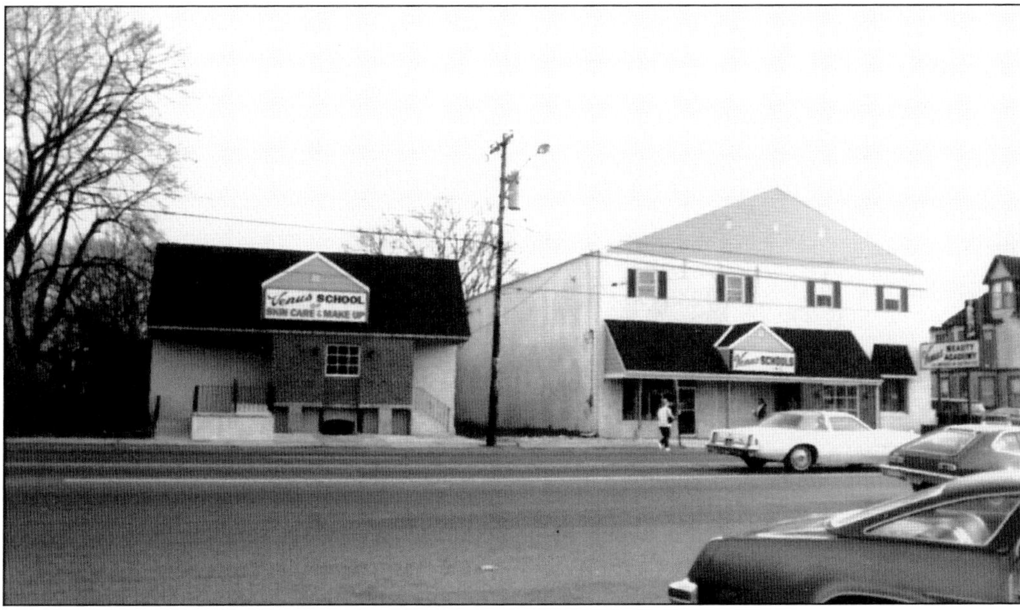

VENUS BEAUTY SCHOOL, 1964. The beauty school was located on Chester Pike on the site of the former post office building. The property was purchased in 1964. The business expanded in 1982 and took over the old Bell Telephone Company building, which was later razed, and with the purchase of adjoining properties made way for an office building and parking lot.

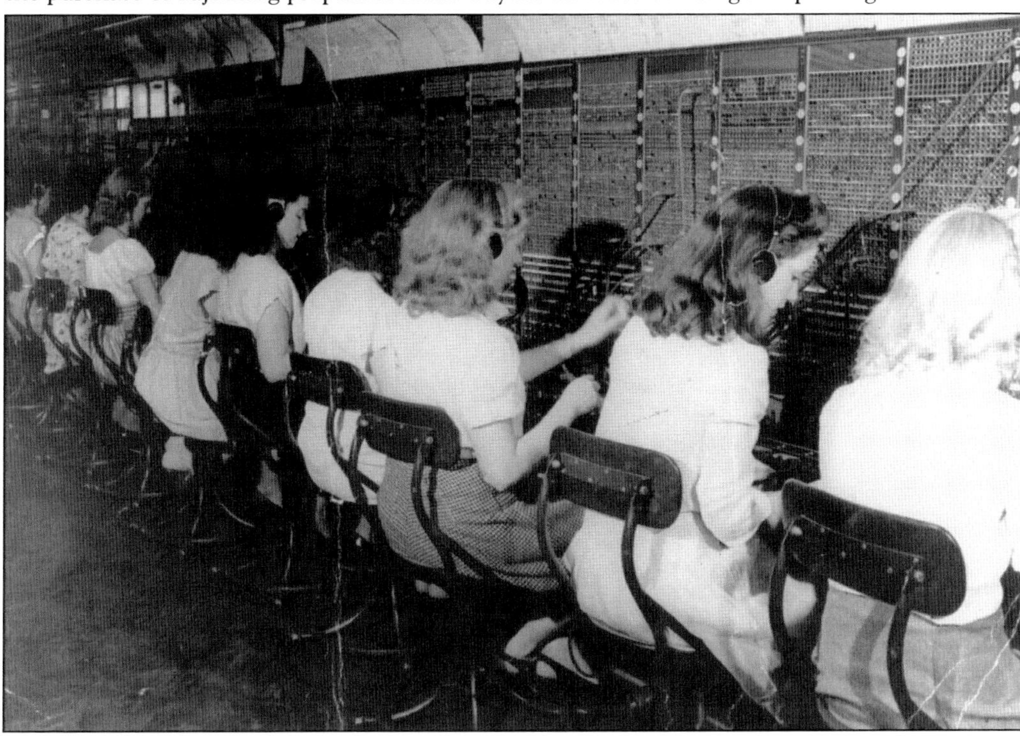

BELL TELEPHONE OPERATORS, C. 1945. On land presently occupied by the Venus Beauty School at 1029 Chester Pike, Bell Telephone built its first office in the borough in 1906. Pictured are a group of switchboard operators and the busy boards they handled. (Courtesy of Mary B. Baker.)

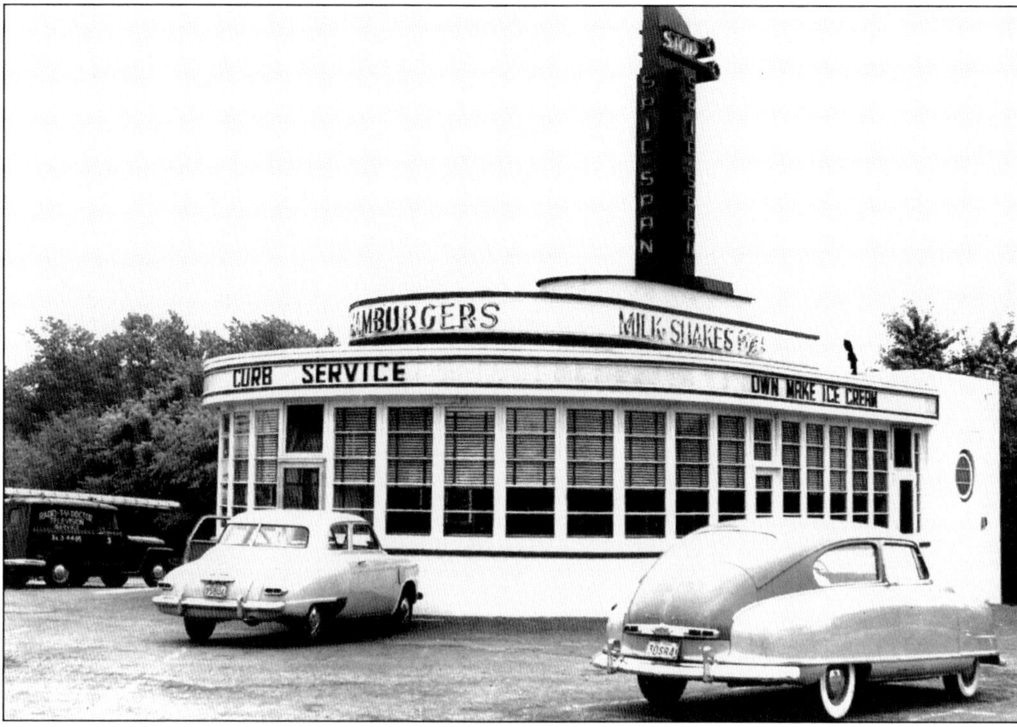

SPIC AND SPAN RESTAURANT, C. 1950. A favorite for young and old alike, the Spic and Span was the first drive-in eatery in town. The restaurant held a prominent spot in the borough on Chester Pike near Felton Avenue. But alas the Spic and Span like the two automobiles in the picture (Nash Ambassador on the right and the Studebaker on the left) disappeared from the scene. The building was demolished and the ground purchased by the Southland Corporation, who built the 7-Eleven store in 1966, which is still in operation today. (Courtesy of Dolores Orner.)

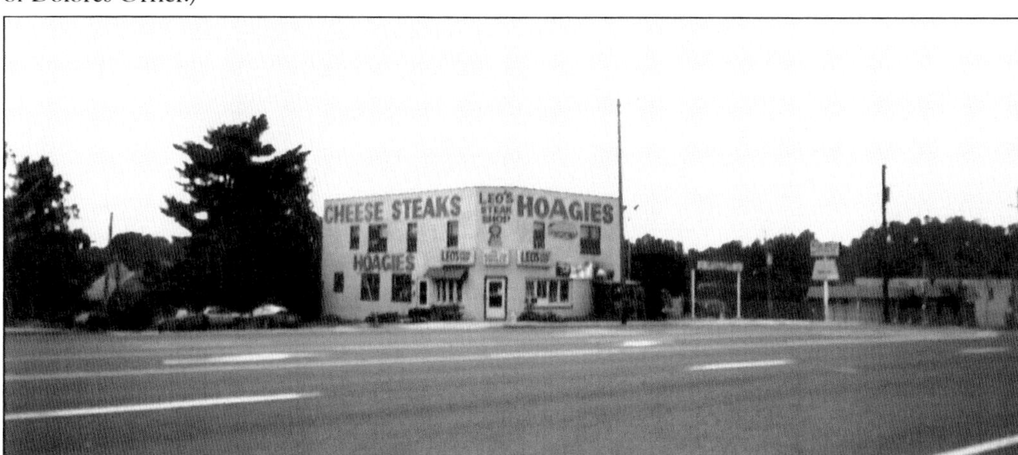

MARTIN'S FLORISTS/LEO'S STEAKS, 1988. Formerly the building of Martin's Florist, the Mullens purchased the property on the corner of Chester Pike and Burton Lane in 1987. With Leo's Steaks, the Mullen family had already established itself in the food department with its wonderful cheesesteaks and hoagies. The Mullens had several other restaurants, including one on Sharon Avenue, another at the trolley station, and several out-of-town locations.

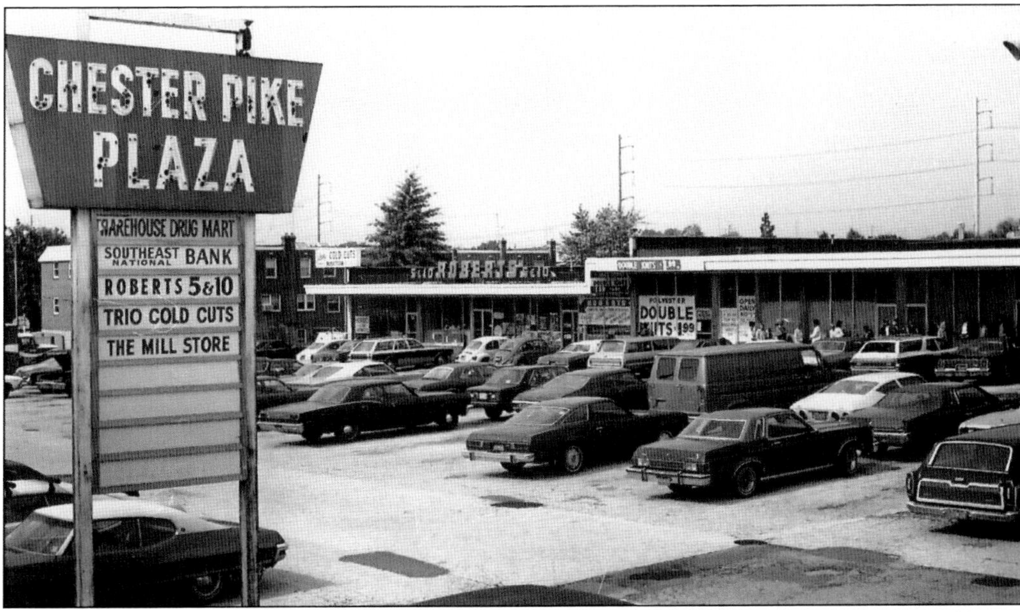

Chester Pike Plaza, c. 1960. Land for the property that contains five and one half acres of ground and is now known as Sharon Hill Plaza was purchased by Food Fair Stores in 1953. Former home of one of the town's last mansions, the Carson estate, and part of the Mallon estate, the property was located on Chester Pike just west of the trolley station. Although the Food Fair was the first occupant, other stores quickly followed; among them were the Delaware County National Bank, Robert's 5 and 10, Bob Walter Men's Shop (he was a local), and Goodman's.

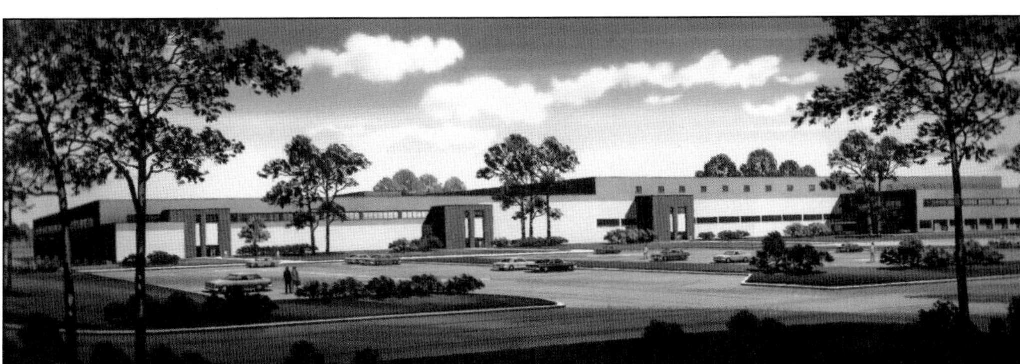

Henderson Group's Folcroft Industrial Park East, 1980. This light industrial park is located on Calcon Hook Road and stretches from Elmwood Avenue to Bonsall Avenue. It encompasses 100 acres of land once occupied by Curtis Publishing Company until 1969 and then by S. S. Kresge Company in 1973.

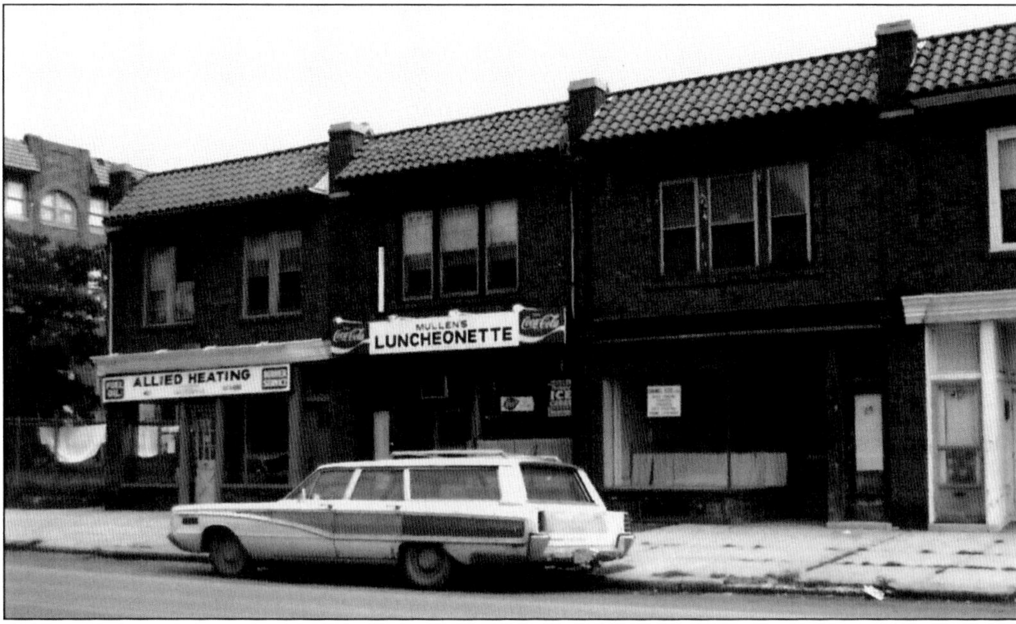

COMMERCIAL STRIP, 1970S. This group of stores was constructed in 1925 as a commercial area. Numbered 411 through 417 Sharon Avenue, the stores were located near the railroad station. In 1942, No. 411 housed the post office. These brick buildings with their Spanish-tiled roofs were demolished to make way for a housing development, the Sharon Hill Commons.

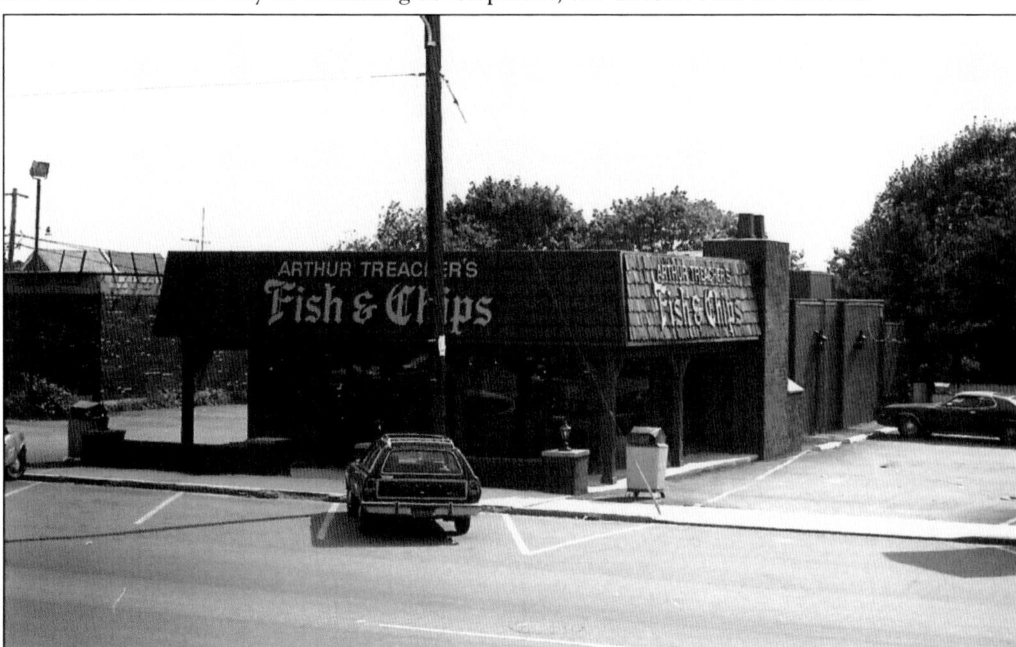

ARTHUR TREACHER'S FISH AND CHIPS, C. 1960. A stylish building housed this fish and chip house named for the consummate English butler of movies and television, Arthur Treacher. A chain store operation, the business was built just west of Brainerd Boulevard. (Courtesy of Dolores Orner.)

Five

POLICE AND FIRE DEPARTMENTS

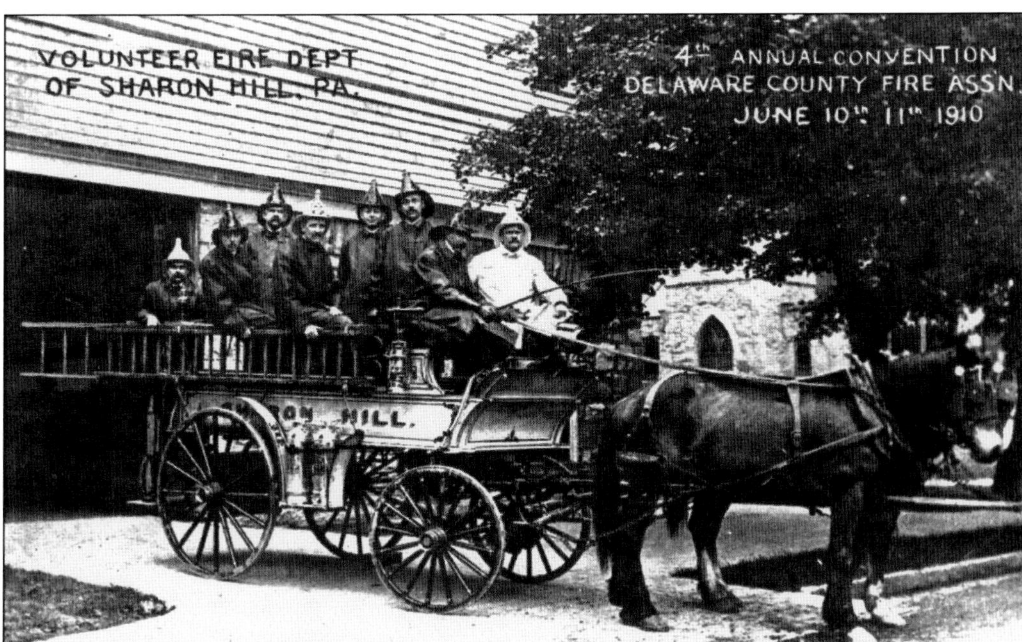

HORSE-DRAWN FIRE COMPANY WAGON, 1910. Within a few years the company had graduated from a hand-drawn two-wheeled reel of hose with a couple of buckets and axes to a horse-drawn wagon, when Chief Garvin, Tuppeny, Atchinson, Duncan, Blank, McCadden, and Wagner posed for this photograph at the fourth annual convention of the Delaware County Fire Association on June 10 and 11, 1910.

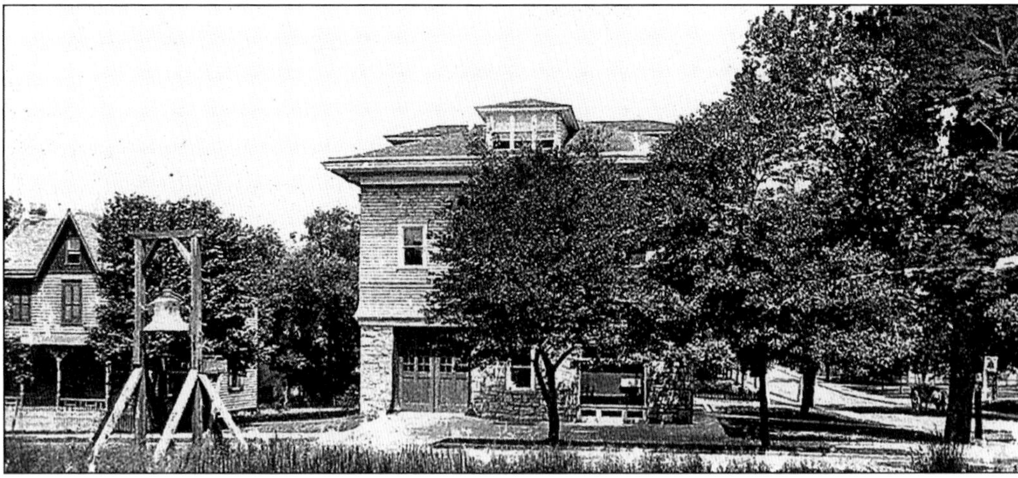

FIREHOUSE AND TOWN HALL, 1912. In 1912, the Sharon Hill Fire Company was headquartered in the building owned by Sharon Land Association on Sharon Avenue and Spring Street. The building erected in 1906 was known as the Sharon Hill Borough Hall. Sharon Hill Borough Council held its first meeting there. The ground floor was used for a meeting room and fire engine room. The bell in the foreground was used as an alarm. The engraving on the bell reads, "McNeely and Kimberly, Founders Troy NY 1872."

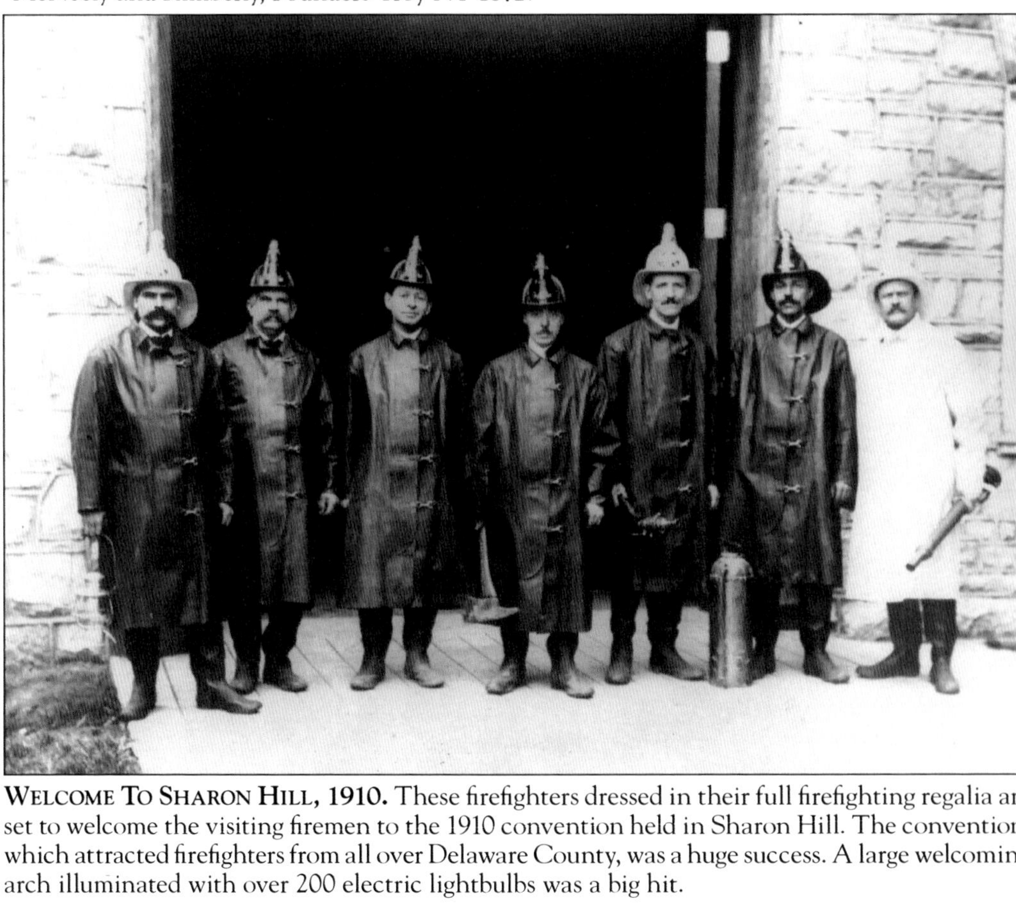

WELCOME TO SHARON HILL, 1910. These firefighters dressed in their full firefighting regalia are set to welcome the visiting firemen to the 1910 convention held in Sharon Hill. The convention, which attracted firefighters from all over Delaware County, was a huge success. A large welcoming arch illuminated with over 200 electric lightbulbs was a big hit.

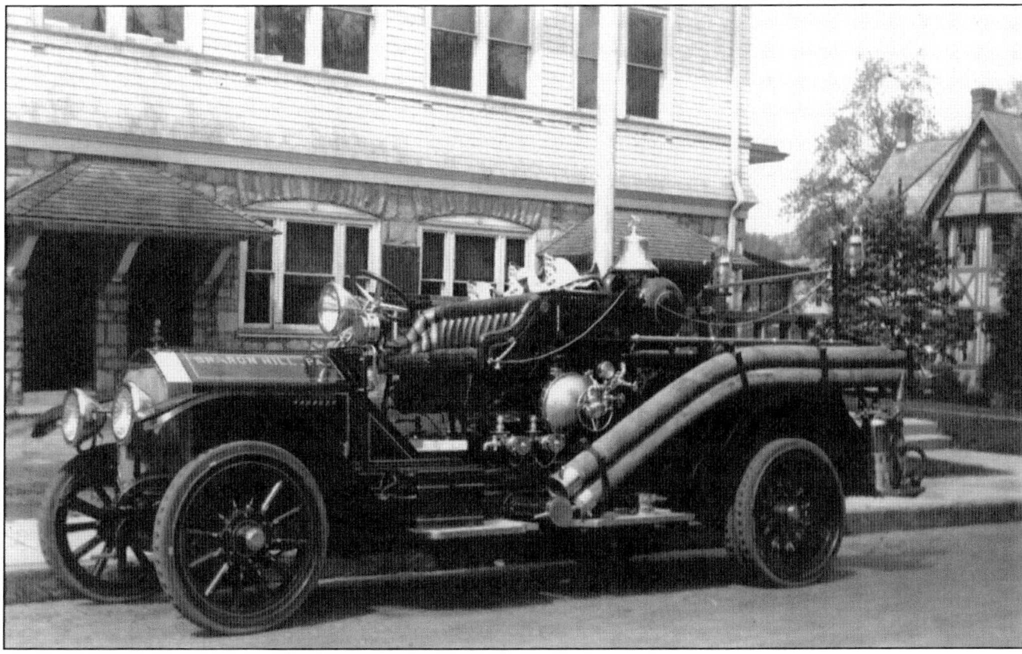

NO. 120 FIRST PUMPER, 1917. This 1917 American La France 750-gallon pumper became the first mechanized pumper in service in the Sharon Hill Fire Company's arsenal. It was in service for 24 years.

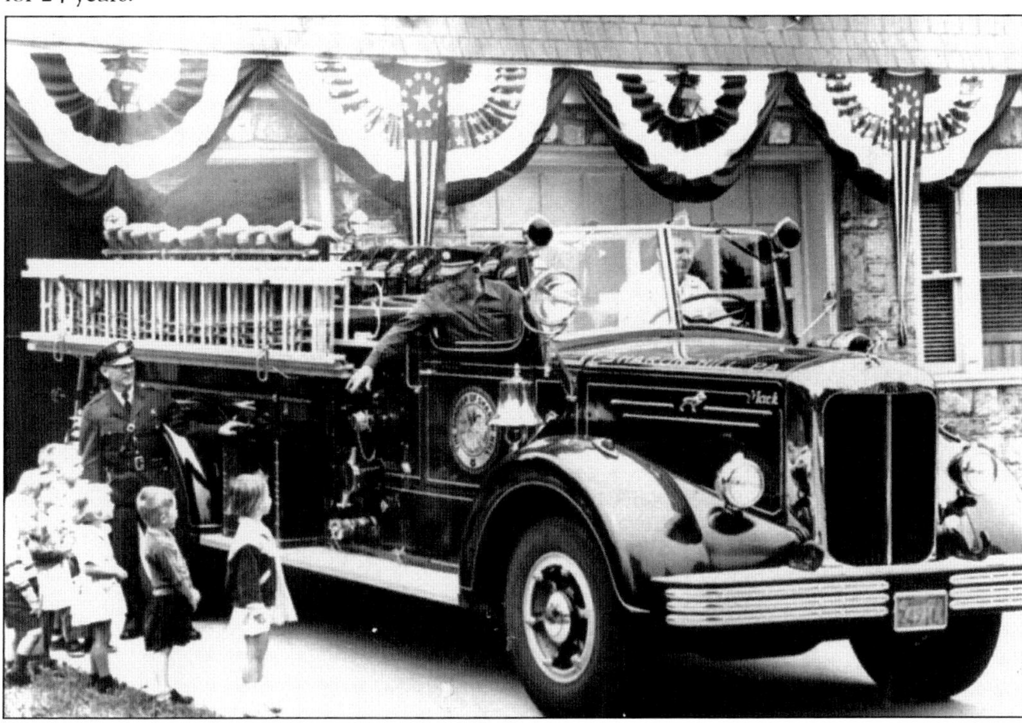

NEW FIRE ENGINE, 1951. Fire Chief Frank Truax and his driver Charles Hauger show off their new fire truck, a 1951 Mack 750-gallon pumper. The duly impressed onlookers are police officer Elwood Casey and a group of local schoolchildren.

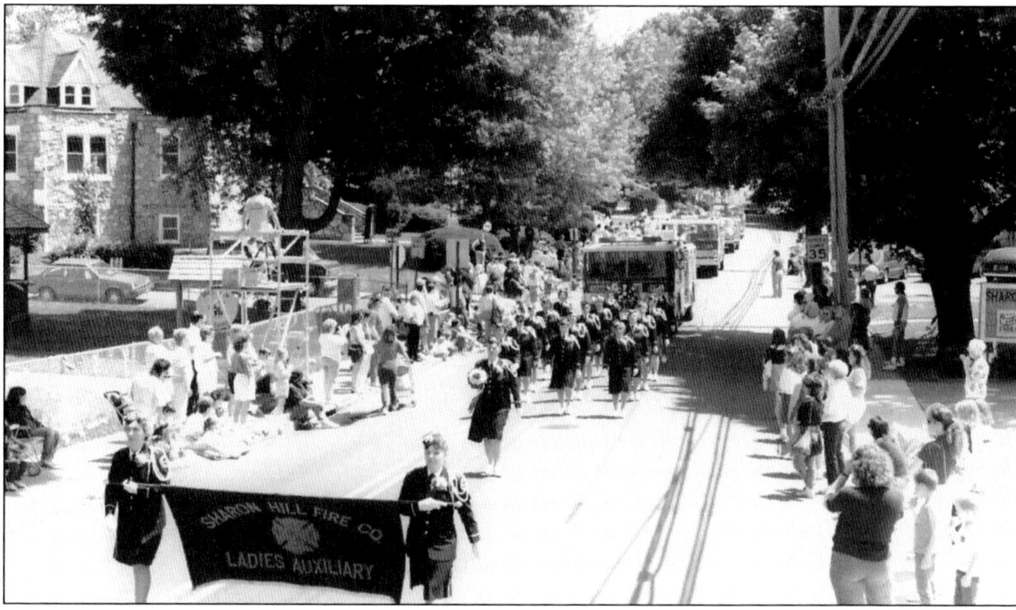

SHARON HILL FIRE COMPANY LADIES AUXILIARY, 1990. The ladies auxiliary shown in the photograph is marching in the centennial parade on Sharon Avenue. The auxiliary was organized in 1908 with 178 members. Their goal is to aid firemen. Throughout the year they hold fund-raisers to help the firemen with their finances, purchase equipment, and provide refreshments when needed.

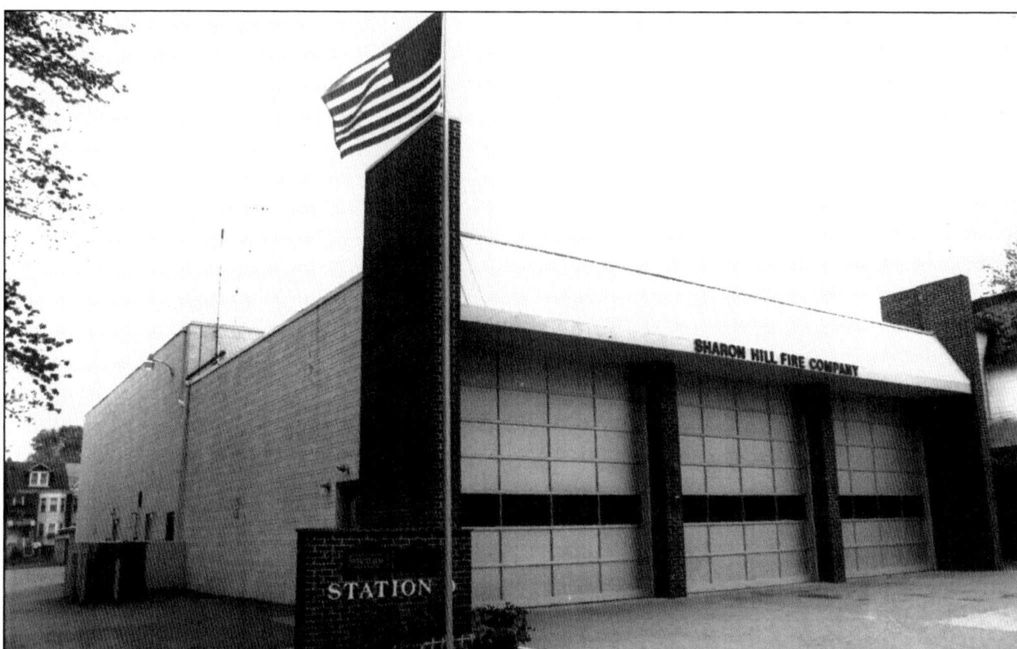

SHARON HILL FIRE COMPANY, 1987. In 1979, a new building on Sharon Avenue was dedicated followed by a small parade. A new fire engine was purchased in 1988, but the fire company decided to wait until the centennial in 1990 before the ceremonial rite called "housing" was held for the latest vehicle, a Pierce pumper. (Courtesy of the Delaware County Times.)

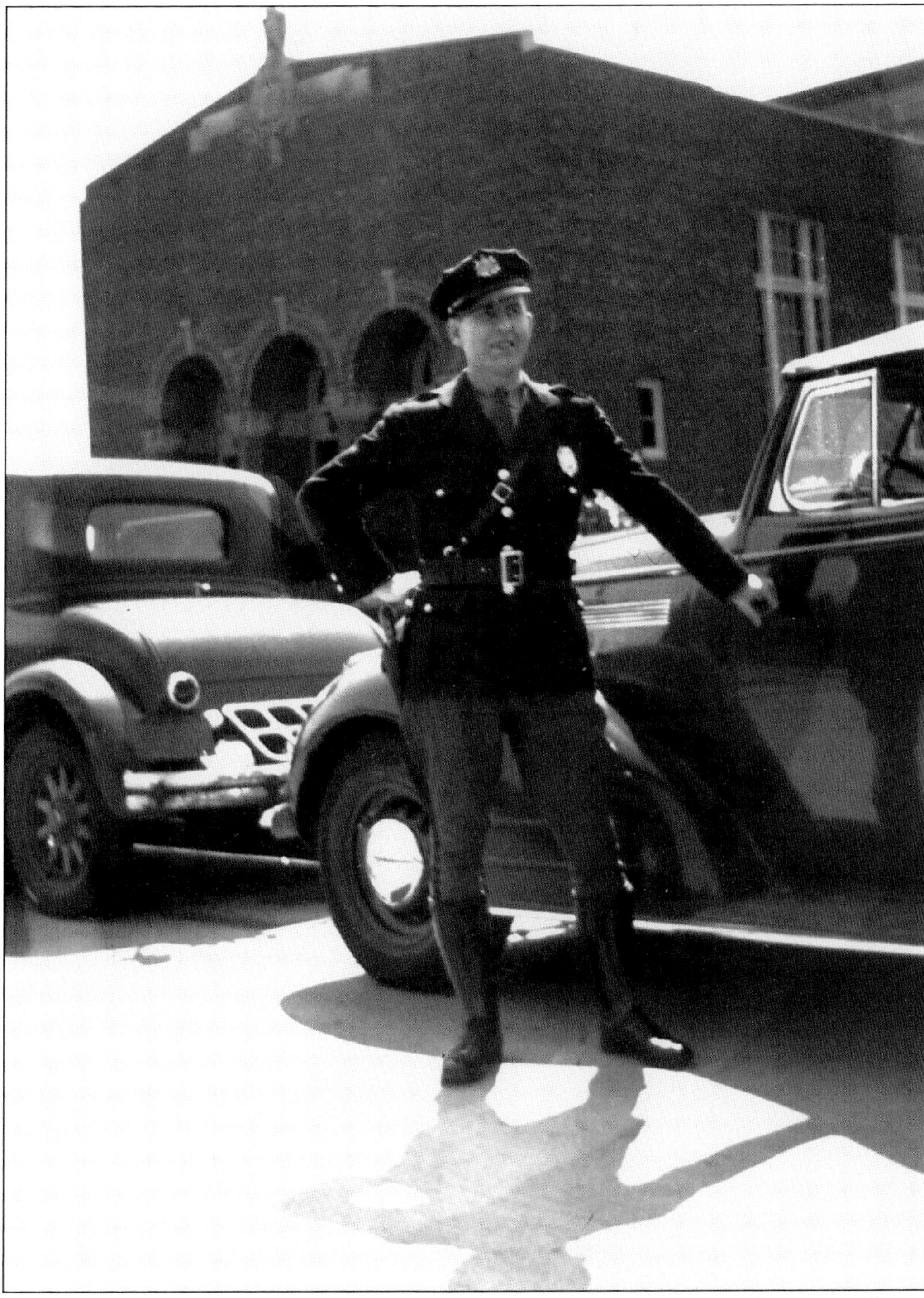

POLICE OFFICER, 1930S. William Malloy, a newly hired police officer, stands next to a line of cars in front of the Sharon Hill High School. His wages in 1930 were $130 a month. He was named chief of police in 1960.

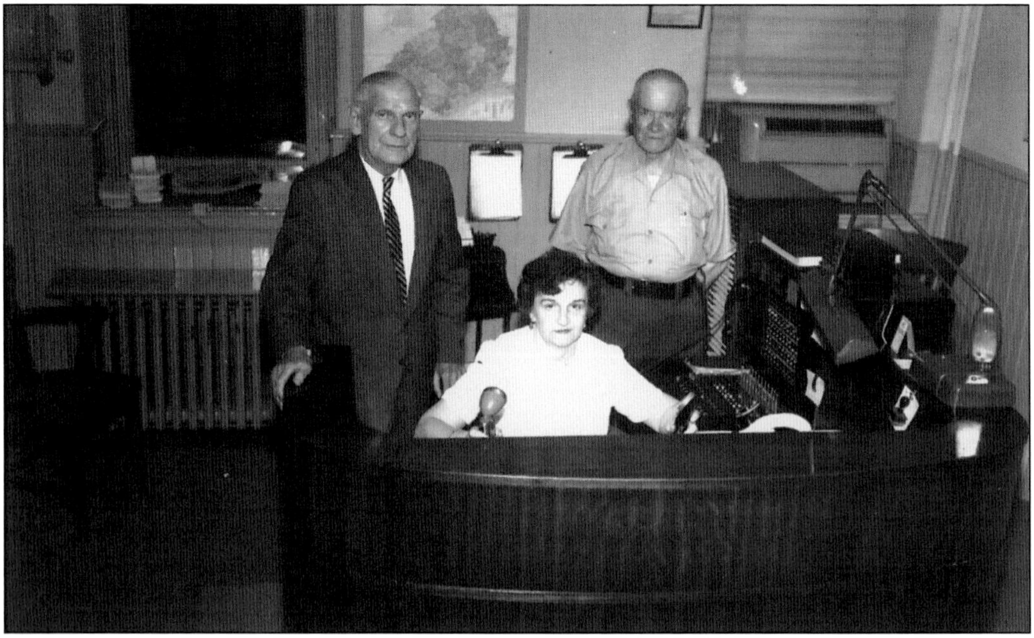

POLICE RADIO ROOM, 1950S. In 1934, a police radio room was put into operation. It provided 24-hour service for police and fire calls to nine communities. Pictured here are operator Martha Kennedy with Al McNair (left) and police chief Frank Truax. The radio room was located in the borough hall.

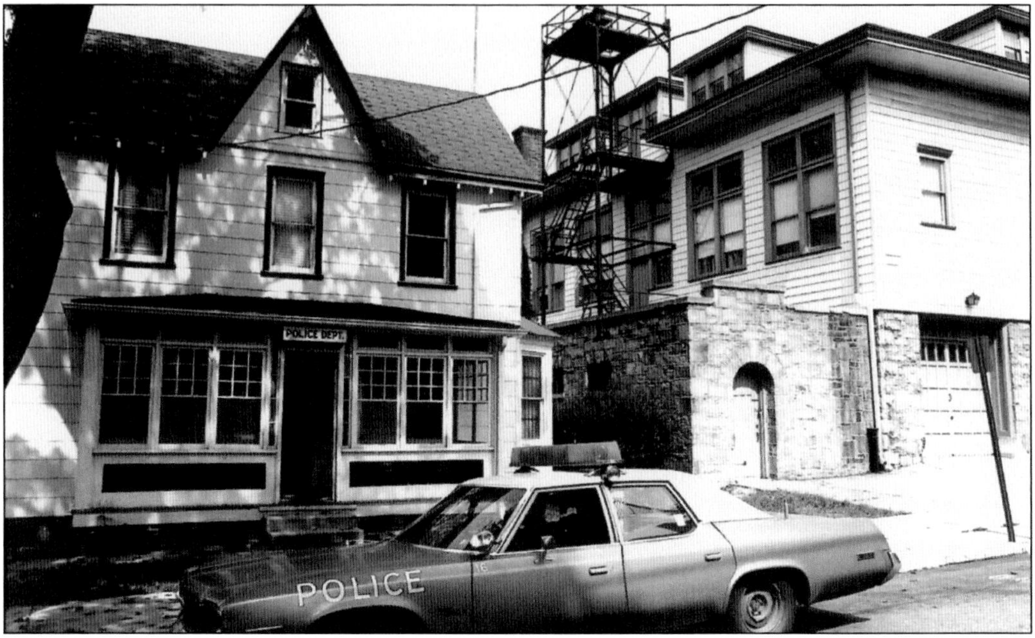

POLICE HEADQUARTERS, C. 1974. This property at 1110 Spring Street was built in the early 1900s. It was known as the McConnell house in the 1920s and later as Nicholson's. It was acquired by the borough in 1974 to be used as a police headquarters, since space was at a premium in the borough hall. The tower shown on the right contained the bell that was sounded for fire and police emergencies.

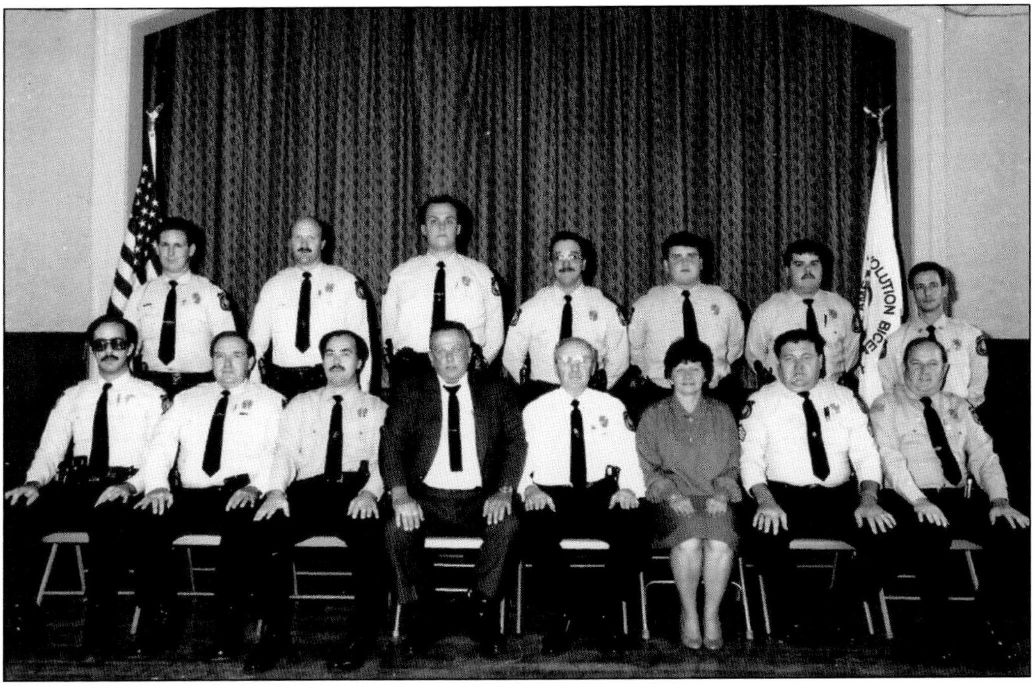

SHARON HILL POLICE FORCE, 1989. The force in 1989 consisted of nine full-time officers, seven part-time officers, Chief William Hanna, and Sergeants James Montieth and Ray Cain. Pictured from left to right are (first row) W. Orr, D. Klauder, J. Kelly, Sgt. Ray Cain, Chief William Hanna, L. Strumsky (secretary), Sgt. James Monteith, and J. Mills; (second row) J. Hoffner, H. Tinsley, D. McDonald, W. Smith, S. Kennedy, G. Faulkner, and S. Mummo.

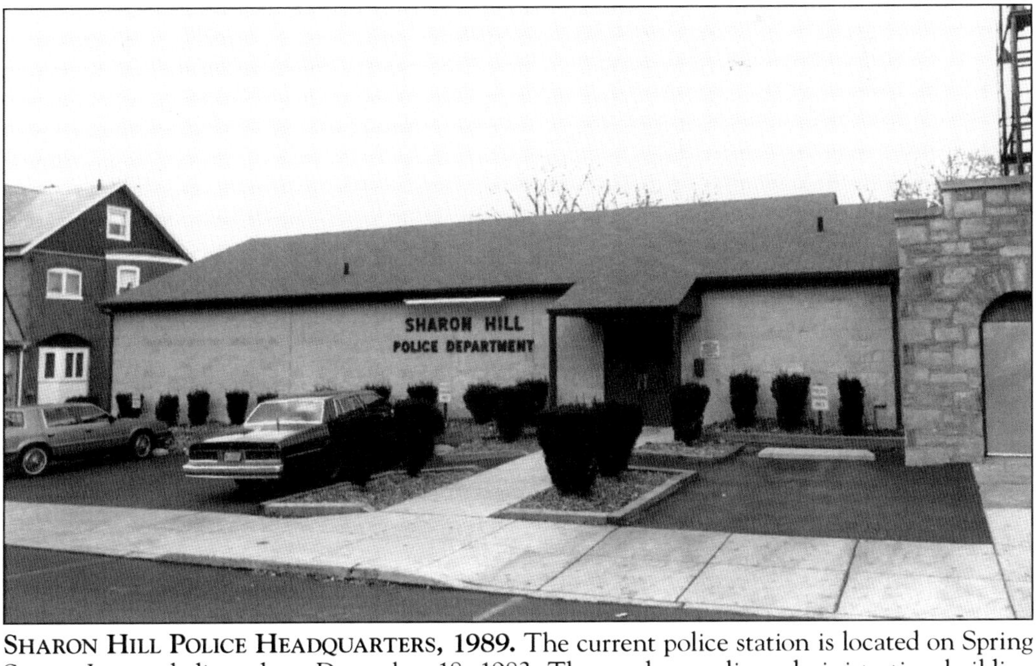

SHARON HILL POLICE HEADQUARTERS, 1989. The current police station is located on Spring Street. It was dedicated on December 18, 1983. The modern police administration building provided more space for the growing department.

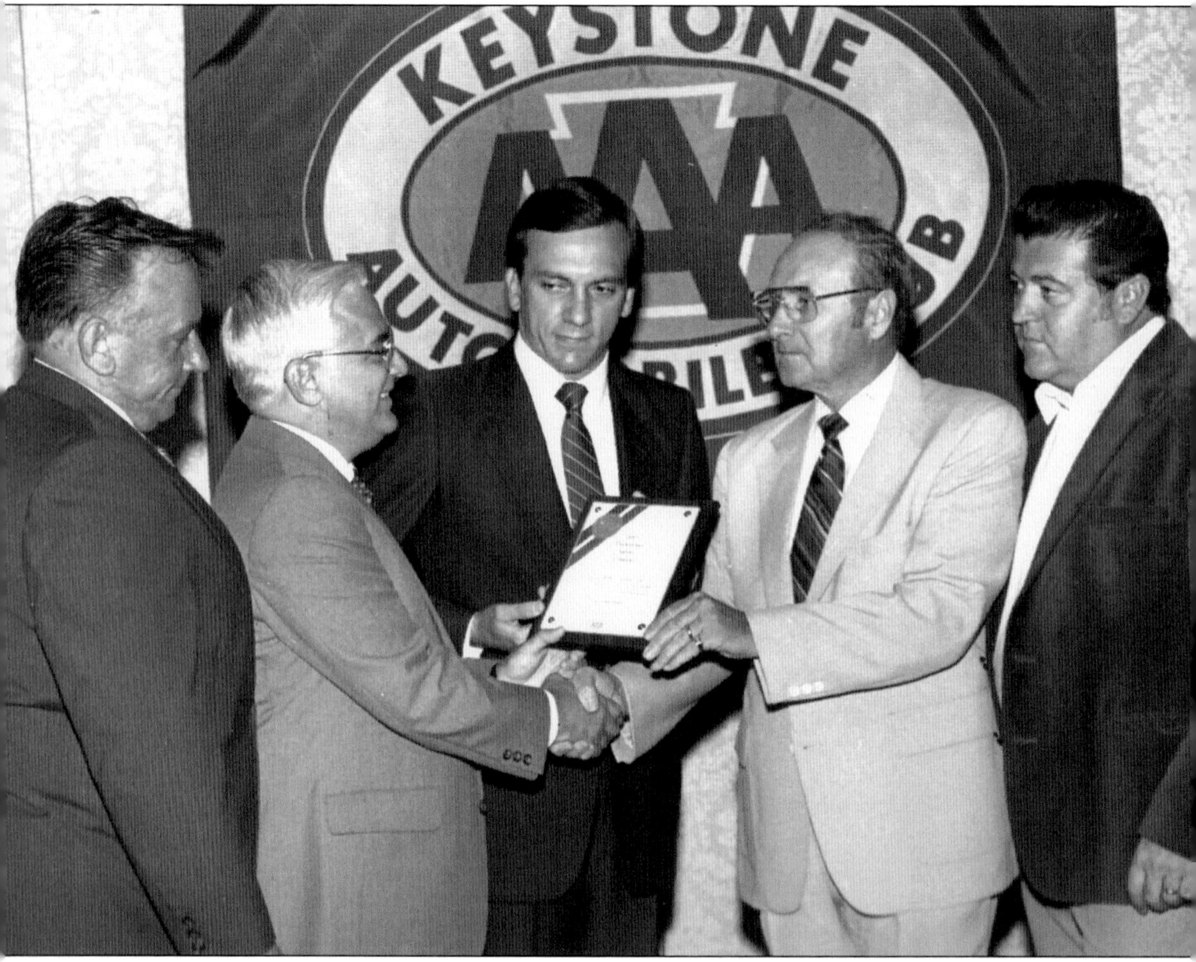

KEYSTONE AUTOMOBILE CLUB AWARD, C. 1980S. Police Chief William Hanna (second from right) and Rep. Ron Raymond (center) accept an award from the representative of the AAA Keystone Automobile Club for the borough's outstanding traffic safety record. Also appearing in the picture are Sgt. Ray Cain (left) and Sgt. James Monteith (right).

Six

CITIZEN GROUPS AND COMMUNITY ACTIVITIES

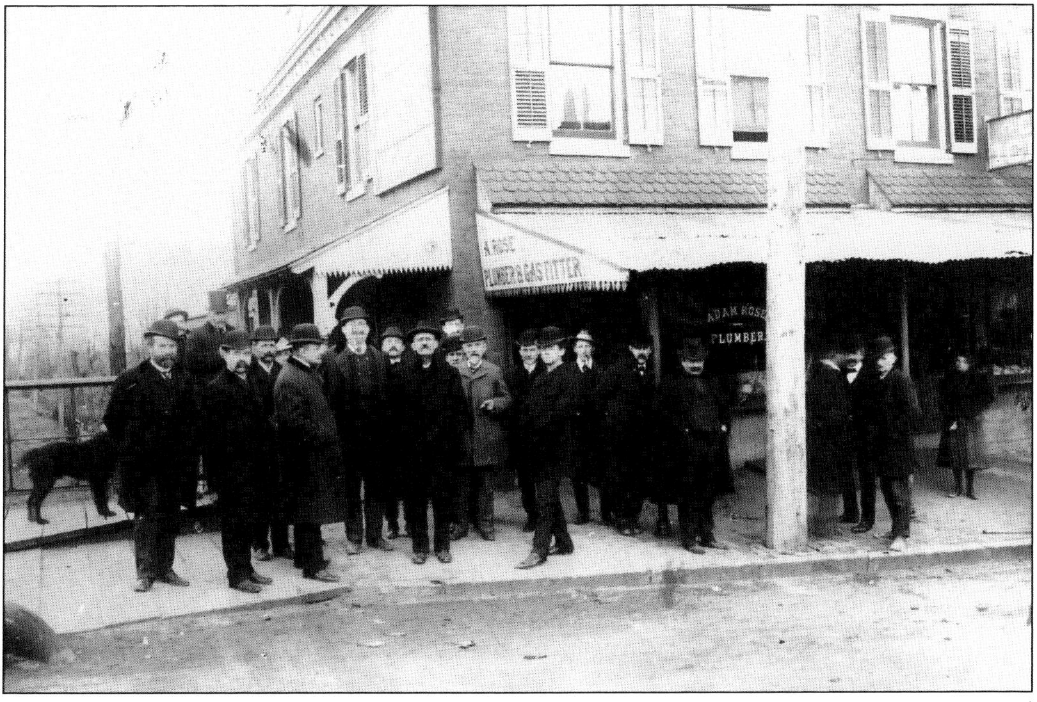

ELECTION DAY, 1896. Voters gathering at the Adam Rose store located on Sharon Avenue and the railroad on August 31, 1896, voted down the proposition to increase the indebtedness of the borough to $11,000 for the purpose of constructing sewers.

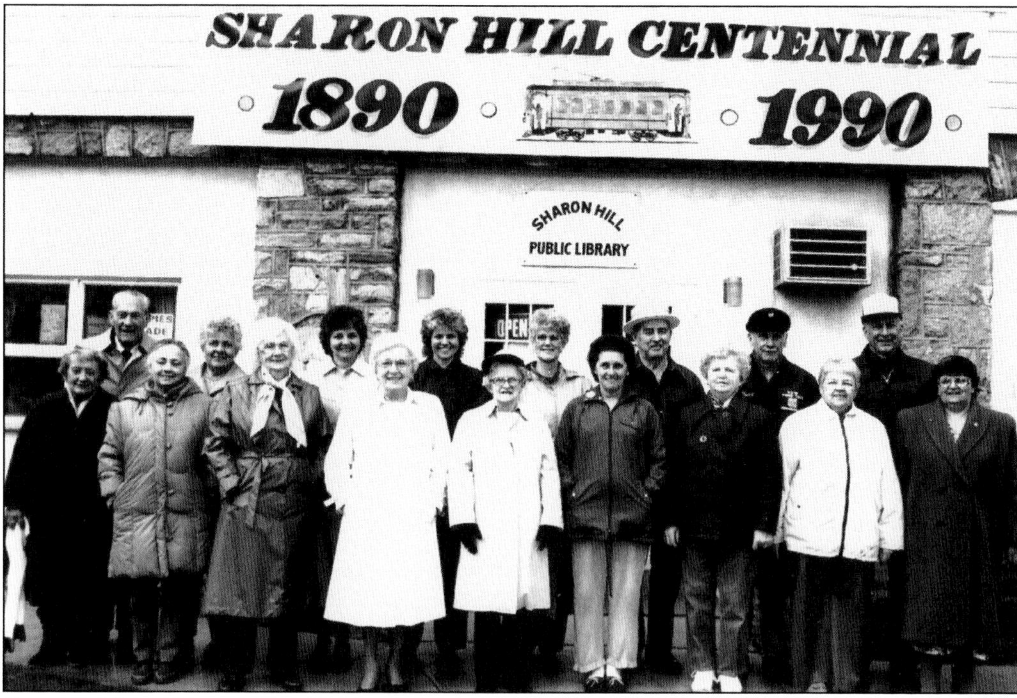

SHARON HILL CENTENNIAL COMMITTEE, 1990. Members planned many events to celebrate the borough's 100 years of incorporation: a reenactment of the first council meeting, a historic tour and display of memorabilia, and a community parade and picnic. Pictured from left to right are (bottom row) Dorothy Grover, Synmi Stroh, Kate Kelly, Val Long, Cass Mc Shea, Dolores Orner, Jean Shiber, Helen Hewish, and Peg McCann; (top row) Ralph Brower, Annabelle Valent, Peg Foster, Kathleen Dowd, Sandy Malloy, Bob Ritter, Ed Davis, and Charlie Miller.

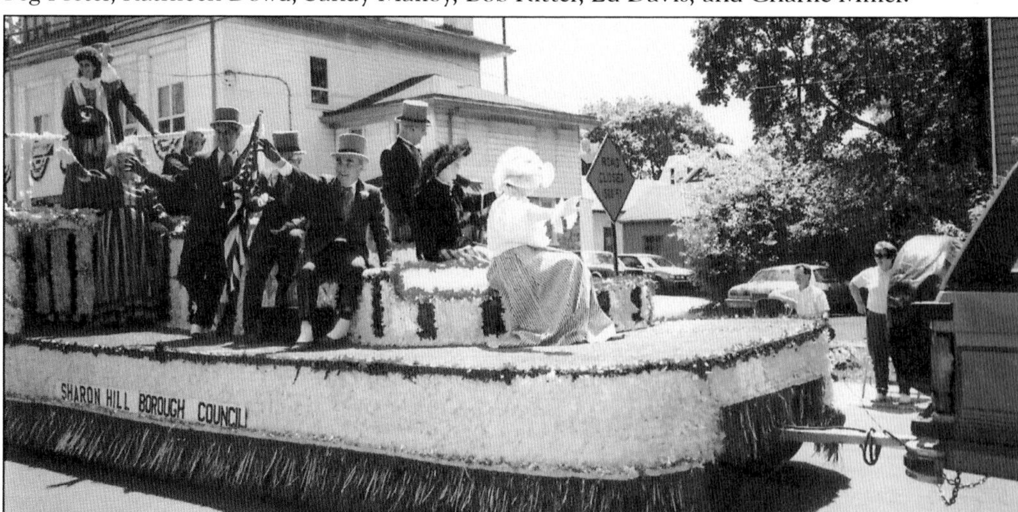

BOROUGH COUNCIL, 1990. Members of the borough council, from left to right, Mayor Carmen Cavacini, Agnes O'Toole, Mary Schraepfer, solicitor Richard Tinucci, Bernard Foster, Francis McCourt, Joseph Kelly, president Ralph Brower, Sandra Malloy, and borough manager Mildred Enderle wave to residents during the centennial parade. Council members also participated in a reenactment of the first council meeting as part of the year's events.

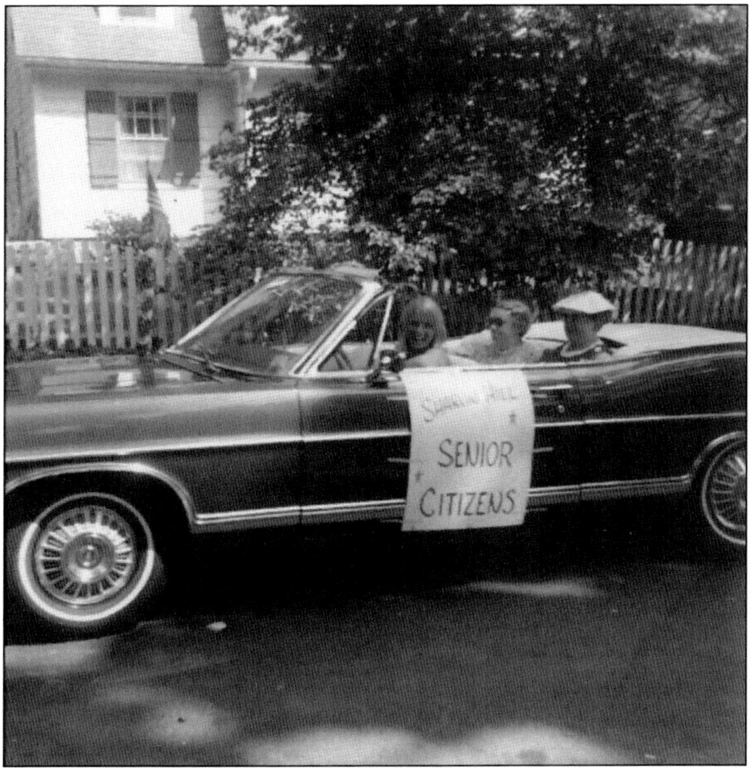

SHARON HILL FOURTH OF JULY PARADE, 1967. During the Fourth of July parade in 1967 Kathy Moulder drove the convertible carrying Mrs. Otto Leinhauser (center) and Mrs. Francis Schneider. They represented all the senior citizens who were honored that day. The automobile is passing the home at 734 Woodland Terrace.

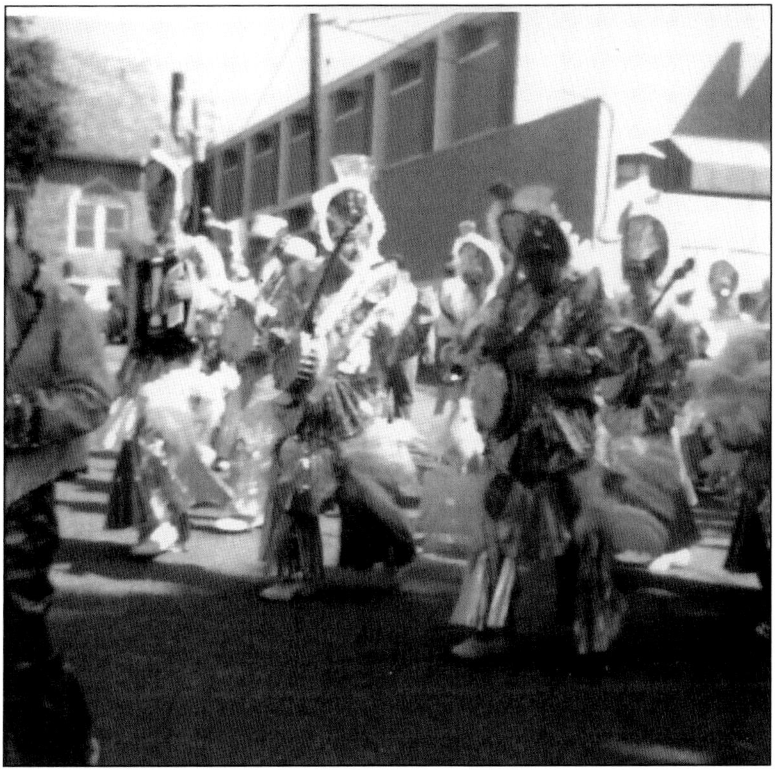

UPTOWN STRING BAND, FOURTH OF JULY PARADE, 1981. Each year Sharon Hill Borough invites a local string band to play in the Fourth of July parade. String bands are very popular in the Philadelphia area. They perform on New Year's Day in the Mummers Parade. Mummers wear fancily decorated costumes usually with feathers. String bands play stringed and reed instruments only.

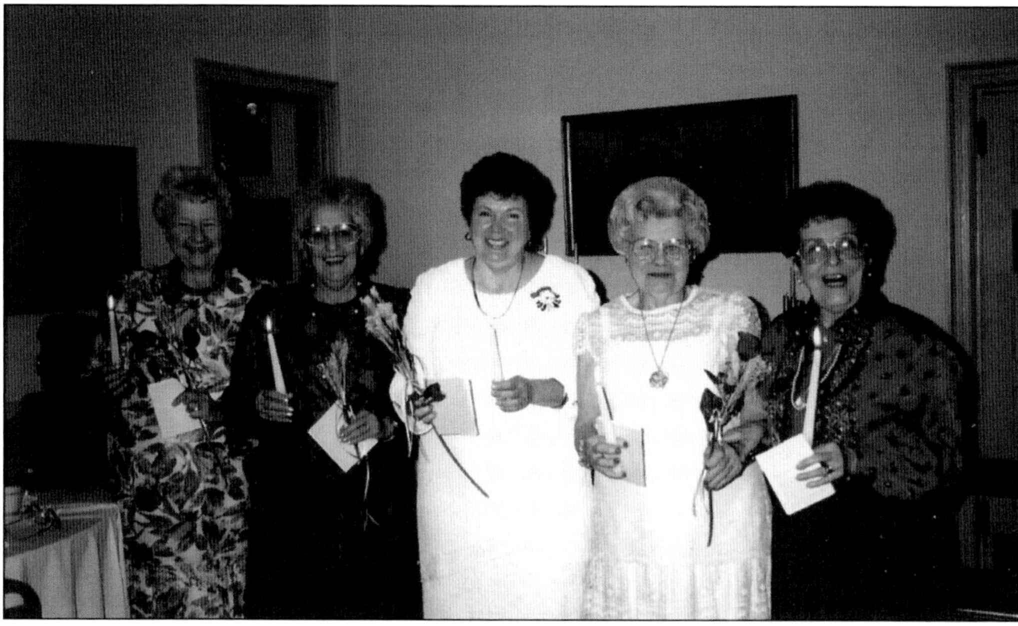

General Federation of Women's Clubs, Women's Club of Sharon Hill, 1994. Organized in 1924, the club has provided many services to the community. During the wars, the Depression, and in good times the women used their skills and resources to help the people, groups, and organizations in need. Pictured at the initiation of new members at a Christmas dinner from left to right are Doris Simpson, Esther Morrison, Barbara Middleton, Mary Grady, and Norma Gaul, president. (Courtesy of Norma Gaul.)

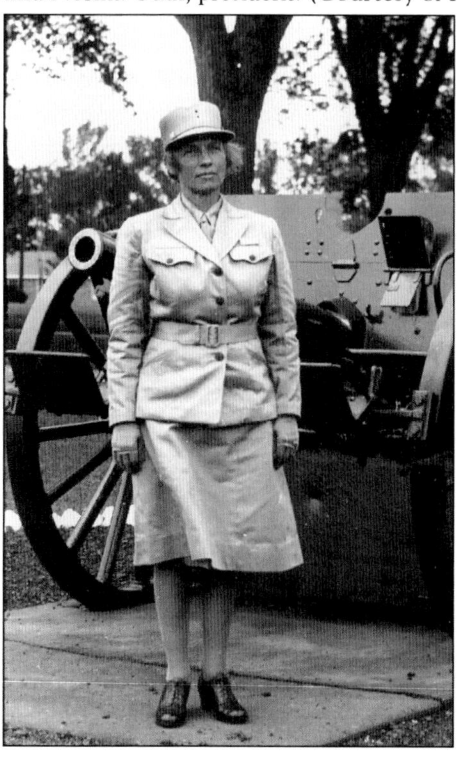

Lt. Ruth W. Brainerd, 1940s. Brainerd Boulevard was named for Ruth Brainerd, who resided on School Street. Brainerd attended college at Vassar and later joined the WACs. She attained the rank of major in the U.S. Army and worked in communications at the Pentagon in Washington, D.C. Later she worked at the Bell Telephone Company and was the first woman engineer, which was a very significant accomplishment for a woman of her day. Brainerd was instrumental in the changeover to the dial system.

WORLD WAR I MEMORIAL, 1936. This memorial honors the servicemen from Sharon Hill who served in World War I. Originally the plaque was attached to the wall at the borough hall. In 1936, the ladies auxiliary of the Sharon Hill Fire Company donated the seven-foot stone shaft for the bronze plaque. It is now in front of the borough hall.

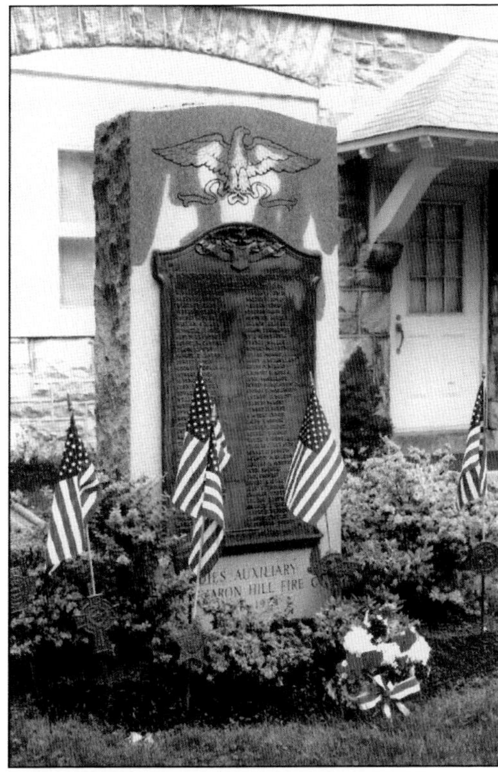

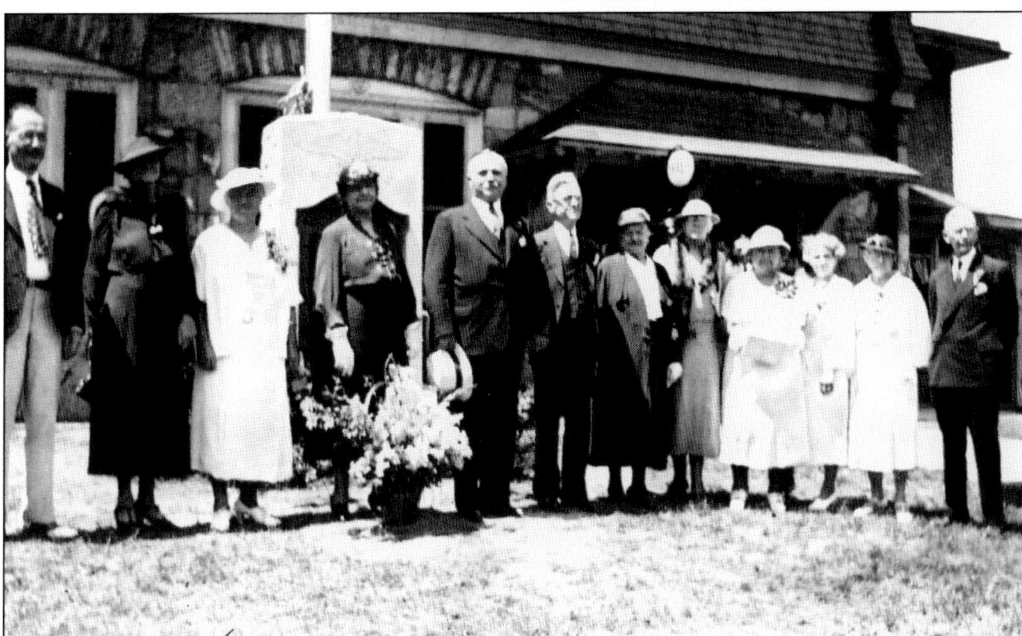

THE UNVEILING OF THE WORLD WAR I MEMORIAL, 1936. The dedication of the war memorial remembering the "war to end all wars" was held in 1936. The memorial, which stands in front of the borough hall, was donated to the community by the ladies auxiliary of the Sharon Hill Fire Company.

FIRST DAY COVER, MAY 1938. This first day cover celebrated the first national air mail week from May 15 through May 21, 1938. First day cover collectors had their choice of different denominations of bicolored stamps from 6¢ to 16¢ and two sizes of air-stamped envelopes. Ralph B. Althouse was the postmaster.

GOLDEN ANNIVERSARY CACHET, 1940. Sharon Hill held a weeklong celebration for the 50th anniversary of its incorporation as a borough. This cachet dated September 9, 1940, commemorates that special occasion.

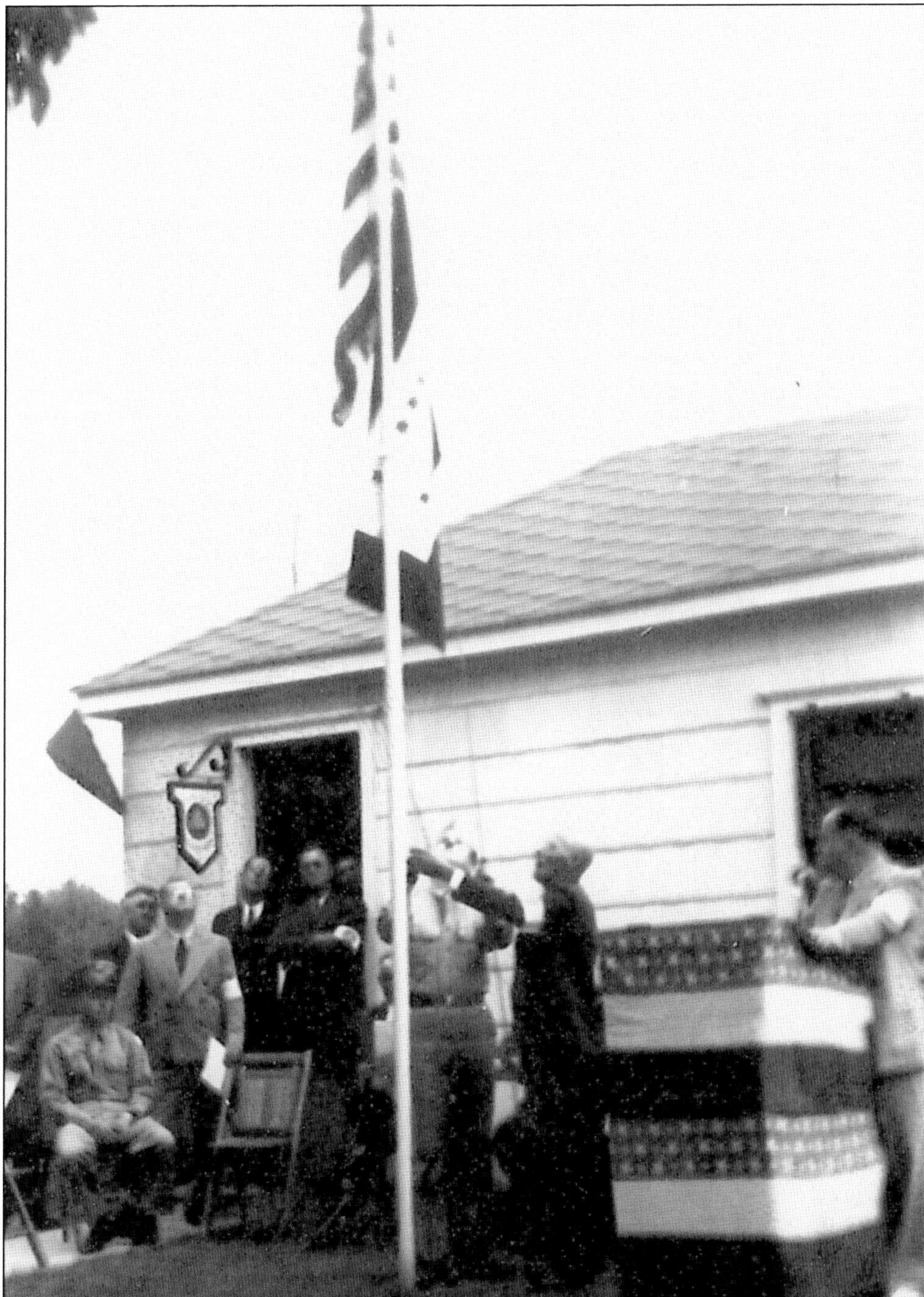

CIVIL DEFENSE HEADQUARTERS, 1943. Located at 1342 Elmwood Avenue, the Civil Defense headquarters was dedicated on May 30, 1943. Known as civil defense area No. 5, the World War II air raid wardens kept their equipment and flashlights in this building along with other civil defense paraphernalia for use in blackouts and air raid drills. (Courtesy of Mary Donaghy Breeze.)

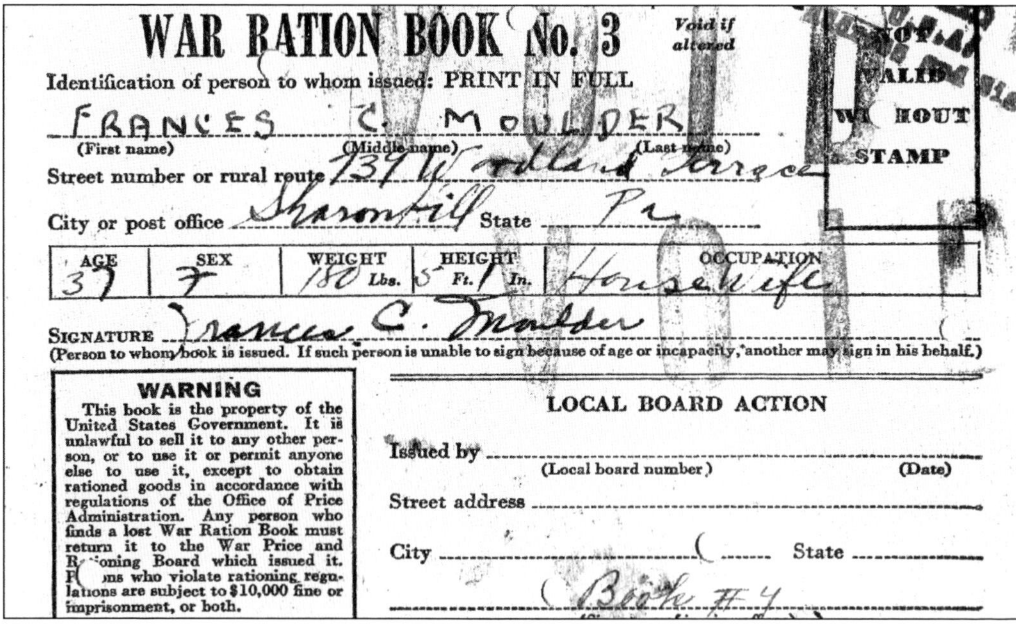

WAR RATION BOOK No. 3 — Void if altered

Identification of person to whom issued: PRINT IN FULL

FRANCES C. MOULDER

(First name) (Middle name) (Last name)

Street number or rural route 139 Woodland Terrace

City or post office Sharon Hill State Pa

AGE	SEX	WEIGHT	HEIGHT	OCCUPATION
37	F	180 Lbs.	5 Ft. 1 In.	Housewife

SIGNATURE Frances C. Moulder

(Person to whom book is issued. If such person is unable to sign because of age or incapacity, another may sign in his behalf.)

NOT VALID WITHOUT STAMP

WARNING

This book is the property of the United States Government. It is unlawful to sell it to any other person, or to use it or permit anyone else to use it, except to obtain rationed goods in accordance with regulations of the Office of Price Administration. Any person who finds a lost War Ration Book must return it to the War Price and Rationing Board which issued it. Persons who violate rationing regulations are subject to $10,000 fine or imprisonment, or both.

LOCAL BOARD ACTION

Issued by (Local board number) (Date)

Street address

City State

(Book #4)

WAR RATION BOOK, 1944. Ration books were distributed during World War II. They were used for meat, sugar, clothing, shoes, gasoline, and liquor. The book was not transferable, and misuse was punishable by imprisonment, fines, or both.

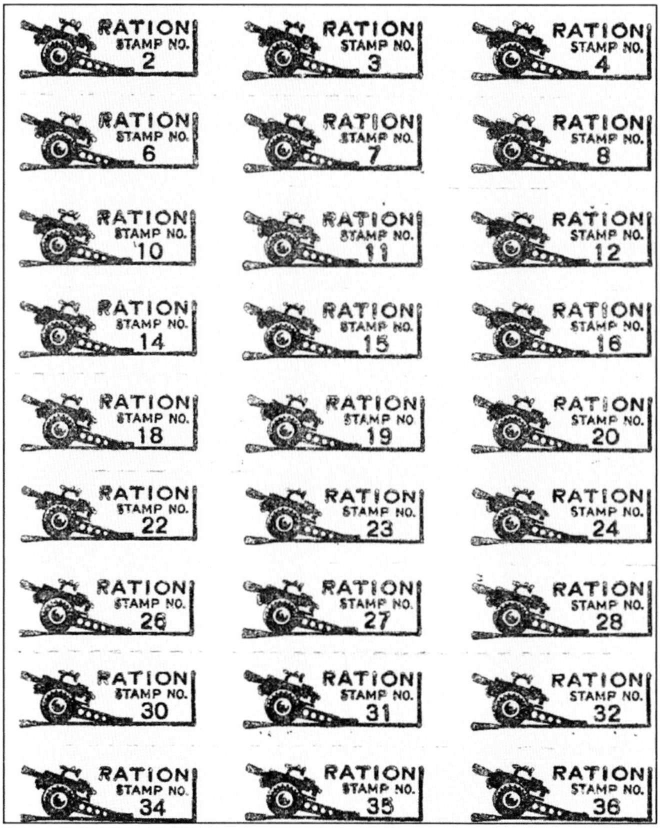

WAR RATION STAMPS, 1944. Pictured are World War II ration stamps individually numbered. They were used to purchase the rationed items listed above.

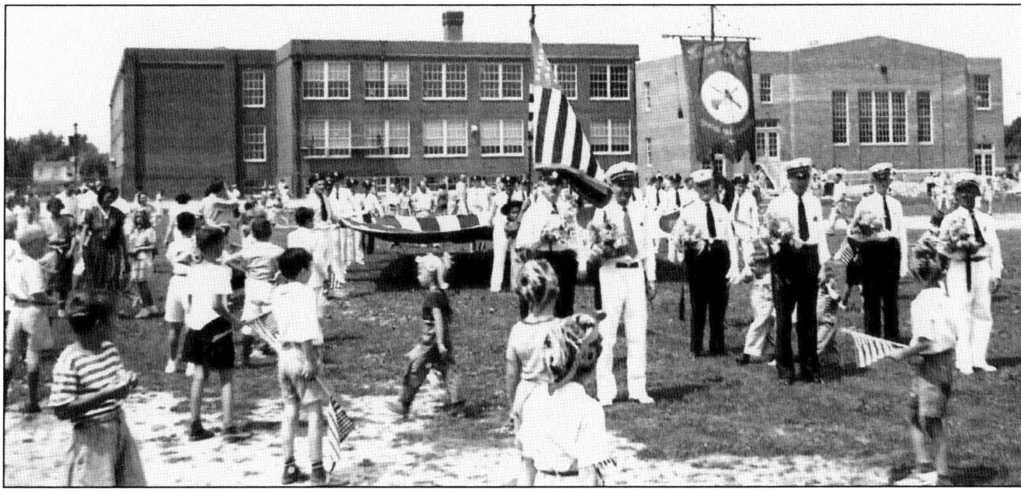

FOURTH OF JULY, 1940S. The Fourth of July has always been special for Sharon Hill: hats and flags for youngsters, a patriotic parade, a baby parade, games, and fun for all ages. In the early years, there were vaudeville shows, talent shows, and sometimes fireworks. Free hot dogs and soda and maybe ice cream in the past were the norm. This picture shows a typical assembly of marchers and spectators on the high school field.

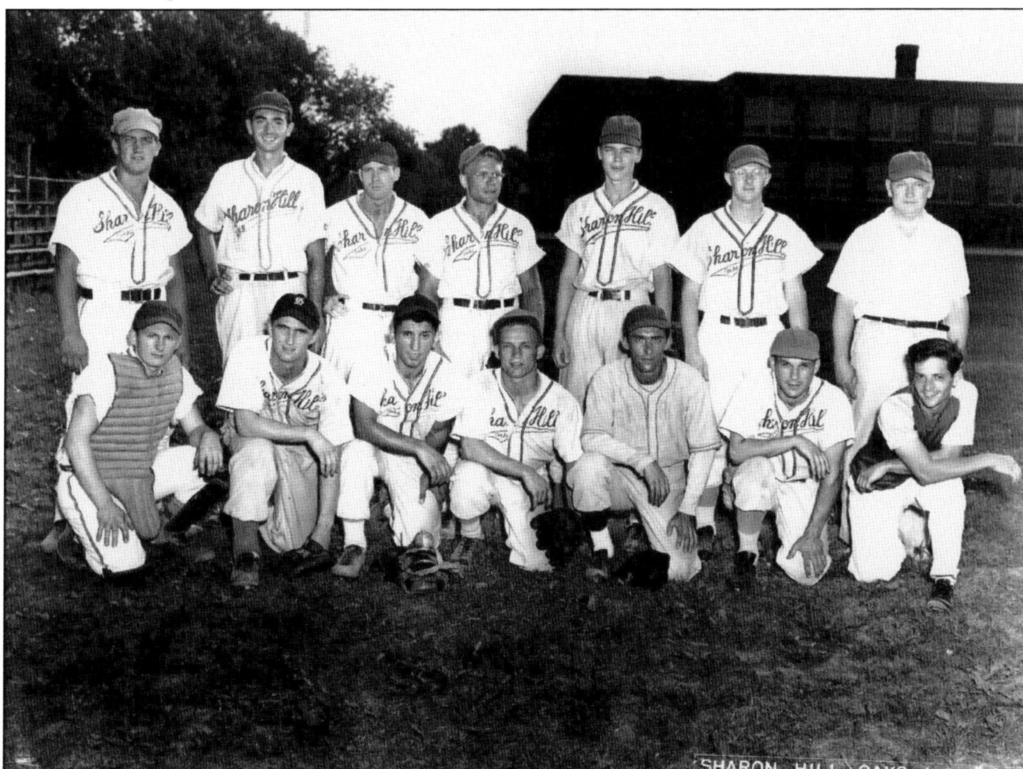

SHARON HILL OAKS ATHLETIC CLUB, 1949. The Sharon Hill Oaks was a very successful baseball team that played in the Interboro League. The very competitive league featured teams from Collingdale, Folcroft, and Norwood. The proximity of the teams made for large enthusiastic crowds.

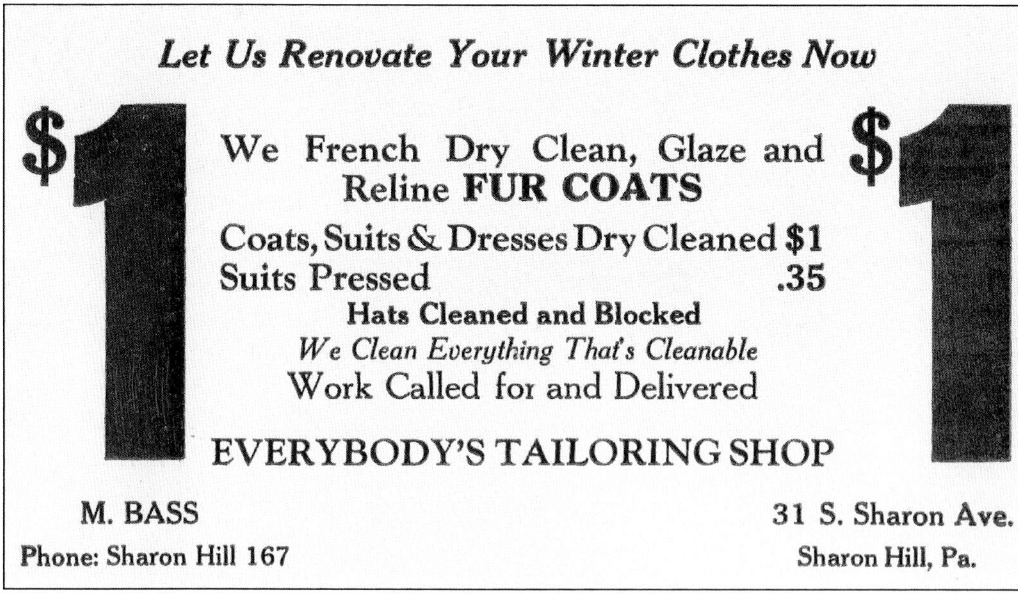

ADVERTISING BLOTTER, 1930S. There is no reason not to look one's best at these prices. Do not bother to call the number, nobody answers.

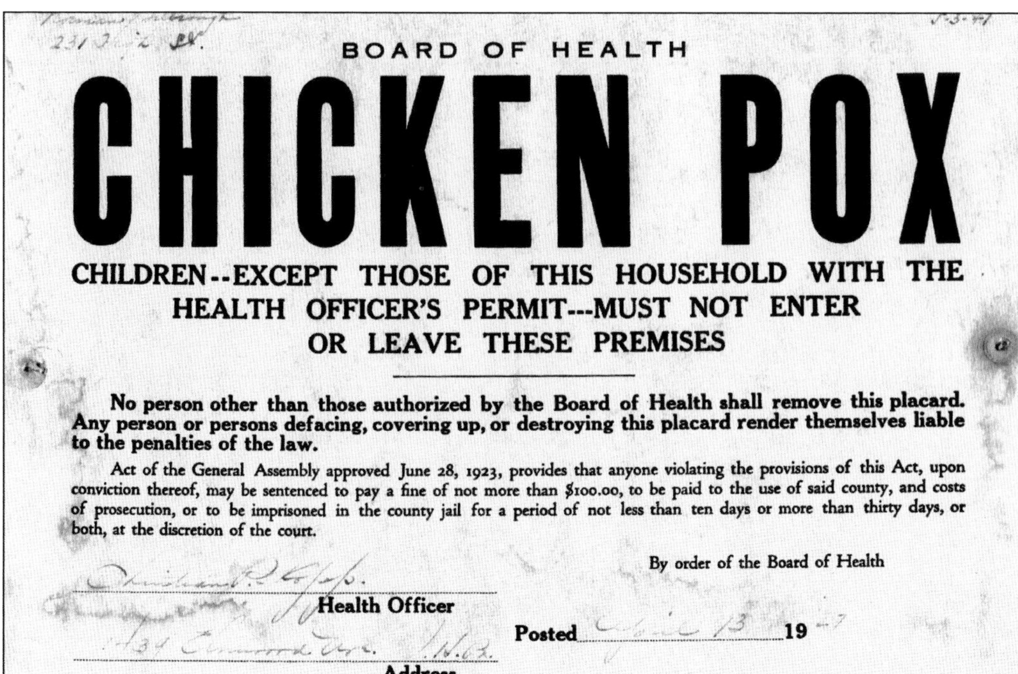

BOARD OF HEALTH QUARANTINE, 1947. This sign was a familiar sight in the late 1940s. The health officer was Christian Kopp, and this sign was placed at 231 High Street on April 13, 1947.

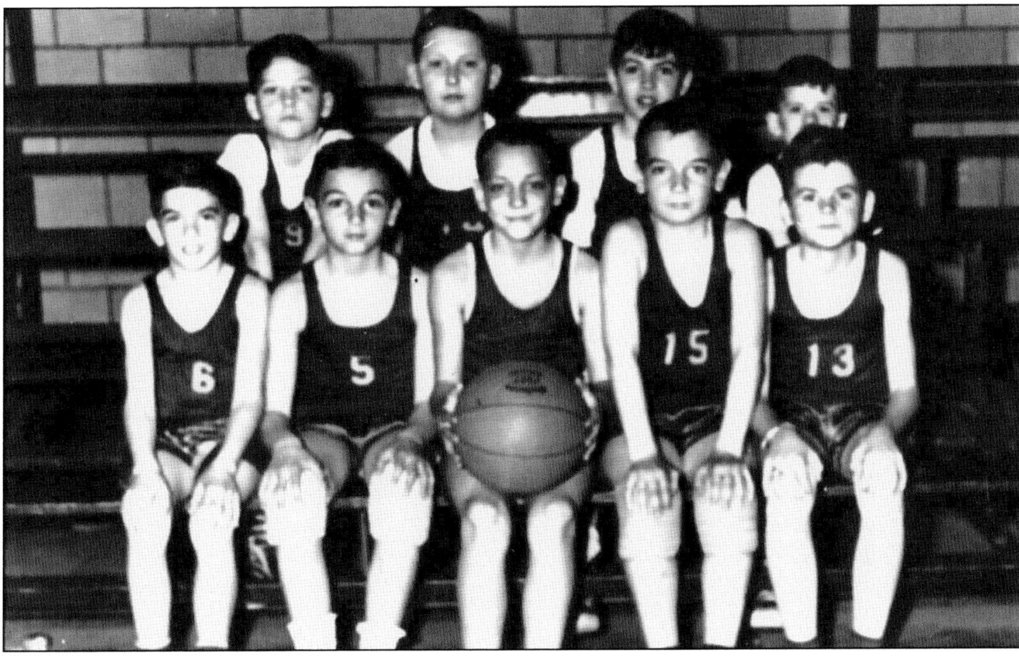

THE SHARON HILL ATHLETIC ASSOCIATION, 1959. The Sharon Hill Athletic Association was officially chartered in 1960. However, its roots go back to the 1950s. The purpose of the association was to stimulate, foster, develop, and provide the members with an opportunity to enjoy the highest type of clean and wholesome indoor and outdoor sports. A basketball league was founded in 1954.

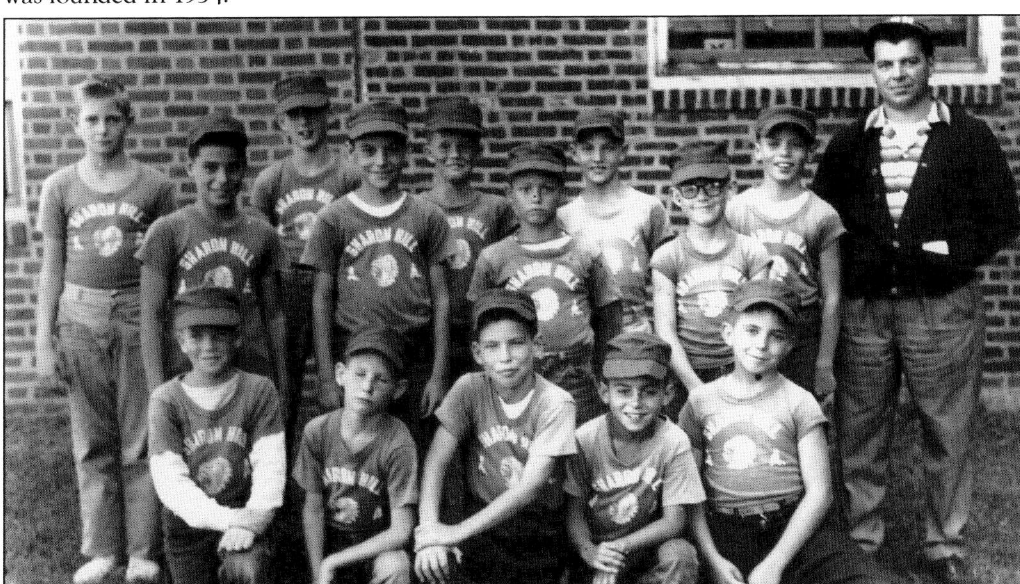

SHARON HILL ATHLETIC ASSOCIATION BASEBALL, 1959. In 1954, 30 people met at the borough hall to form the Sharon Hill Athletic Association. A basketball league was sponsored as the first activity. Fund-raising activities, such as bake sales and carnivals, financed the first baseball team in 1955, complete with uniforms. Later the highly successful program was funded yearly by the borough.

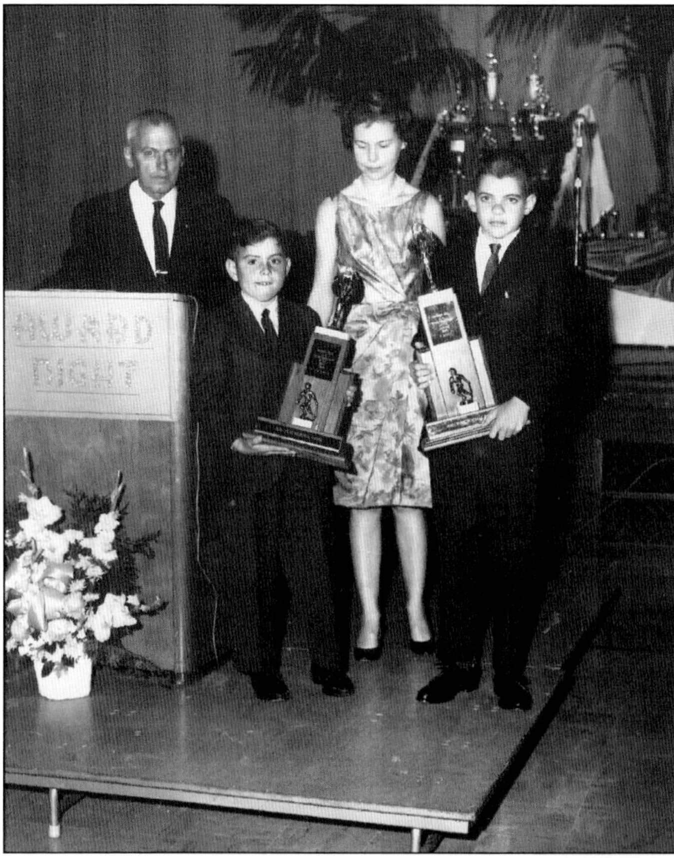

ATHLETIC ASSOCIATION AWARDS, 1960S. Bob Wiederwax and Marie Rowe presented the John Rowe Memorial Award for Sportsmanship to Rodger Fitzgerald and P. Boyle. Bob Wiederwax was president of the athletic association in 1967 and was instrumental in bringing the Phillies Home Run Derby to Sharon Hill. The Little League field on Elmwood Avenue is named after him. (Courtesy of Kathleen Fitzgerald Sharkey.)

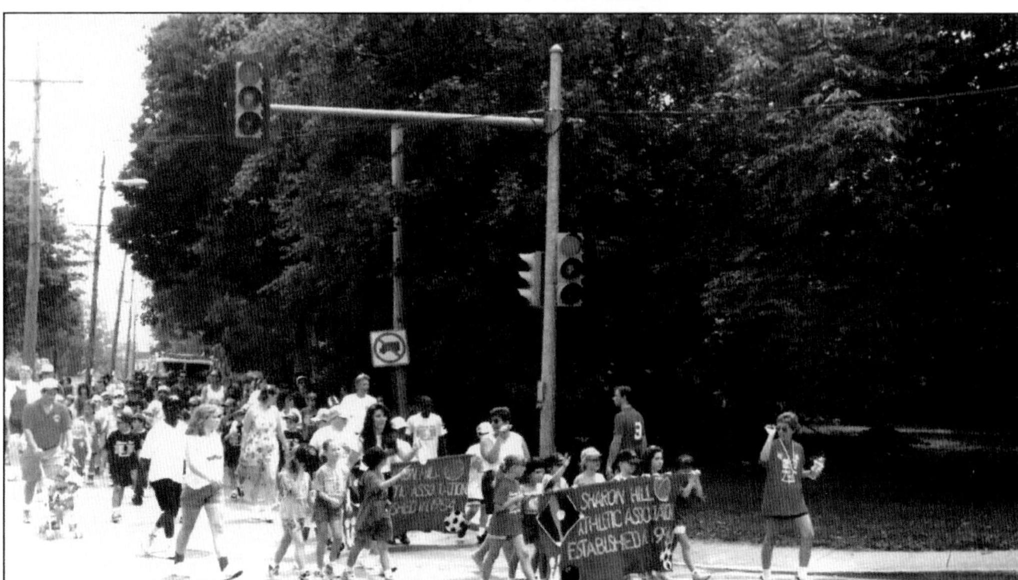

FOURTH OF JULY PARADE, 1998. The Sharon Hill Athletic Association banner, held by some of the younger participants in the Fourth of July parade, turns the corner from Poplar Street onto Calcon Hook Road. The parade is one of the most popular annual events in Sharon Hill.

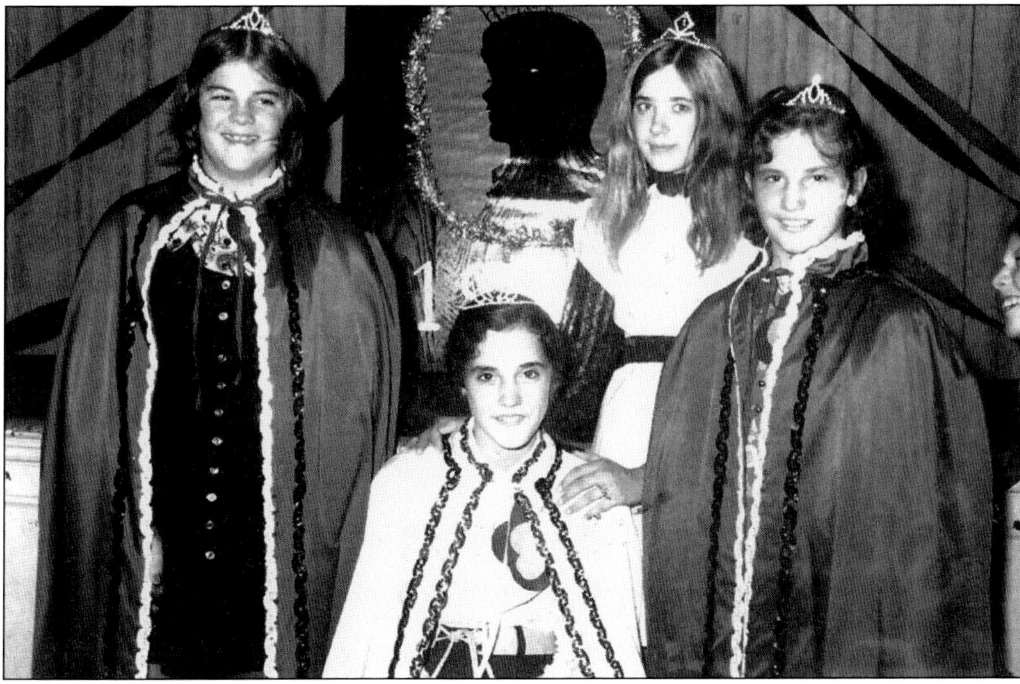

SHARON HILL RAMBLER QUEEN, C. 1970. One lucky girl was chosen each year to reign over the football bowl game at the high school field in November. This year's Sharon Hill Ramblers queen is shown with her court.

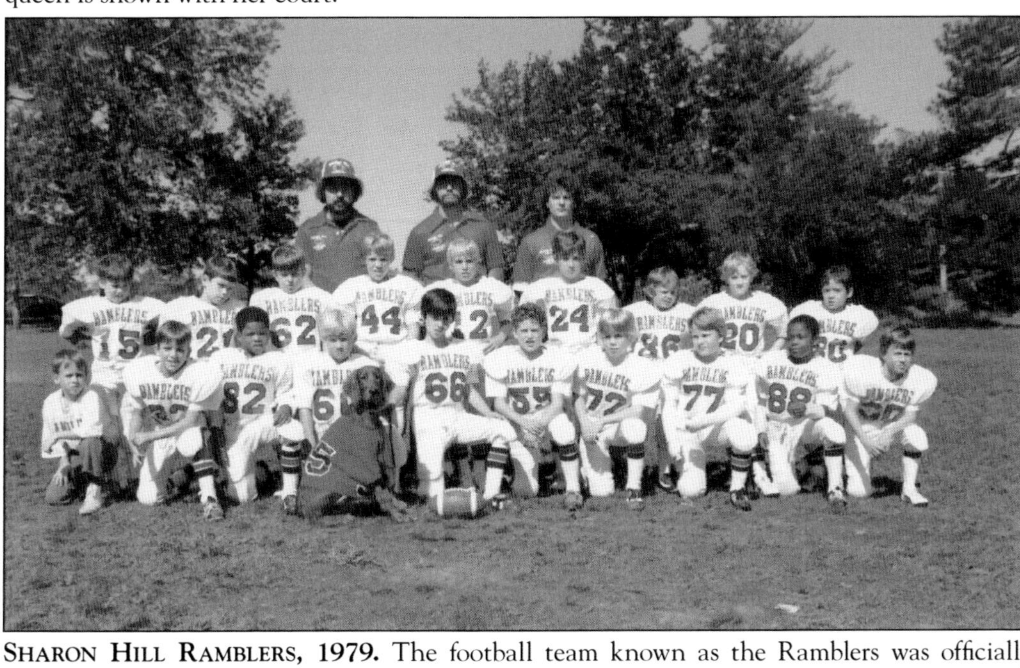

SHARON HILL RAMBLERS, 1979. The football team known as the Ramblers was officially chartered in 1972. The charter called it a "program of service to youth to sponsor organized, supervised, weight-controlled football." However, long before the charter, Jerry Coyne, who had organized the group, served as its president until his move from the borough. (Courtesy of Michael Franz.)

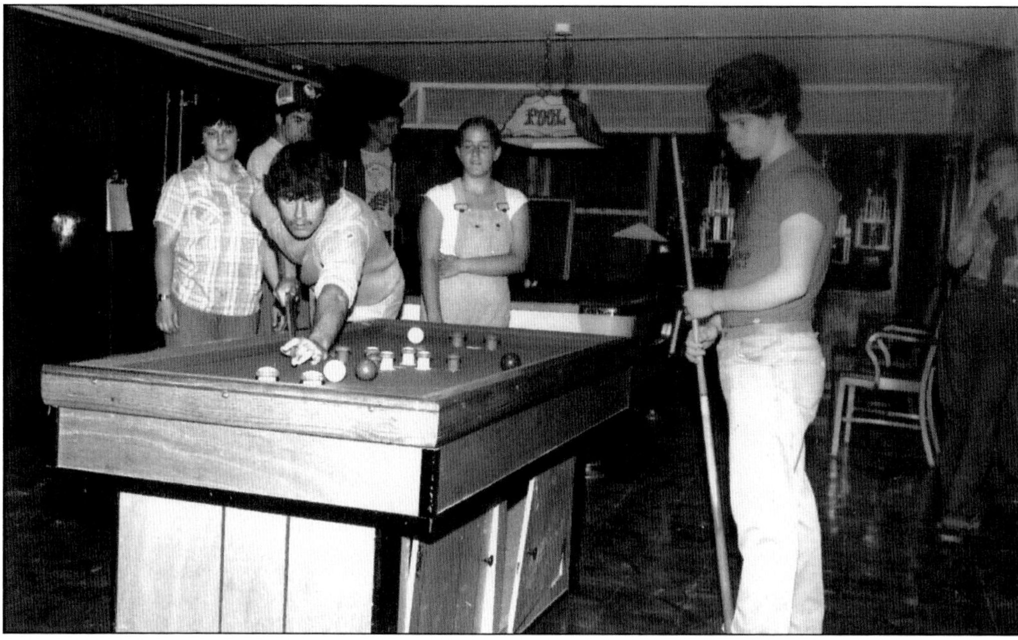

THE SHARK, C. 1979. The Sharon Hill Athletic and Recreation Klub (SHARK) was the brainchild of Al Dyson, Bernie Foster, and Paul Azarian, officers of the athletic association. Its purpose was to provide indoor activities for the youth of the borough. Supervised by the parents of the members, various activities, such as pinball, table tennis, air hockey, and pool, were available. The "klub" met in the basement of the borough hall on weekday evenings. Each Saturday the space was turned over to the physically challenged children of the borough.

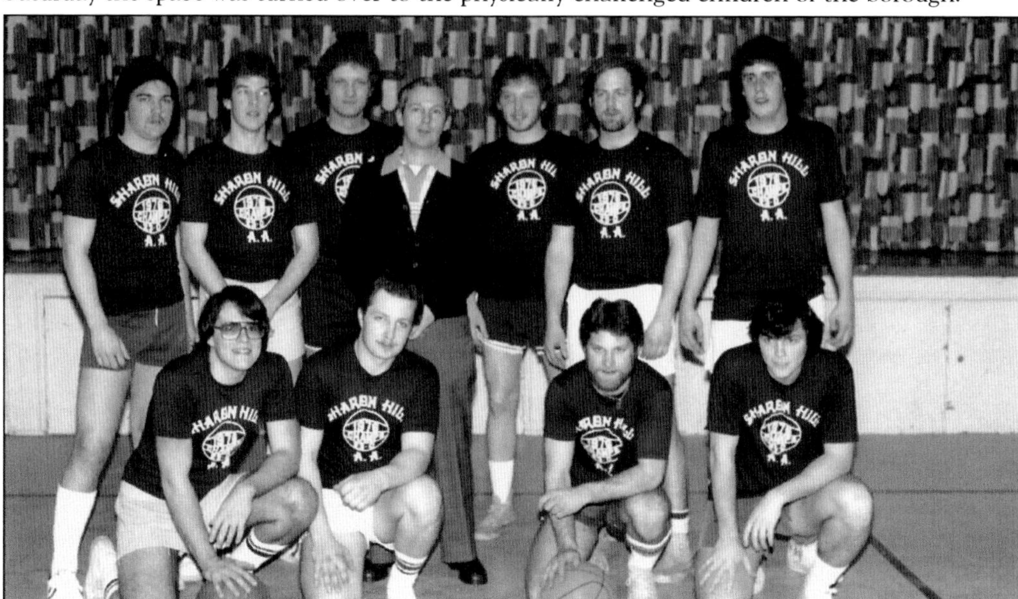

SHARON HILL ATHLETIC ASSOCIATION UNDEFEATED EDCO BASKETBALL CHAMPIONS, 1976. Pictured from left to right are (first row) John Marchetti, Rich Mateau, Mike Homyak, and Rick Pattinson; (second row) Tom Coleman, Kevin Scanlan, Joe Foster, coach Mike Franz, Dennis Collington, Matt Frick, and Joe McKee. (Courtesy of Michael Franz.)

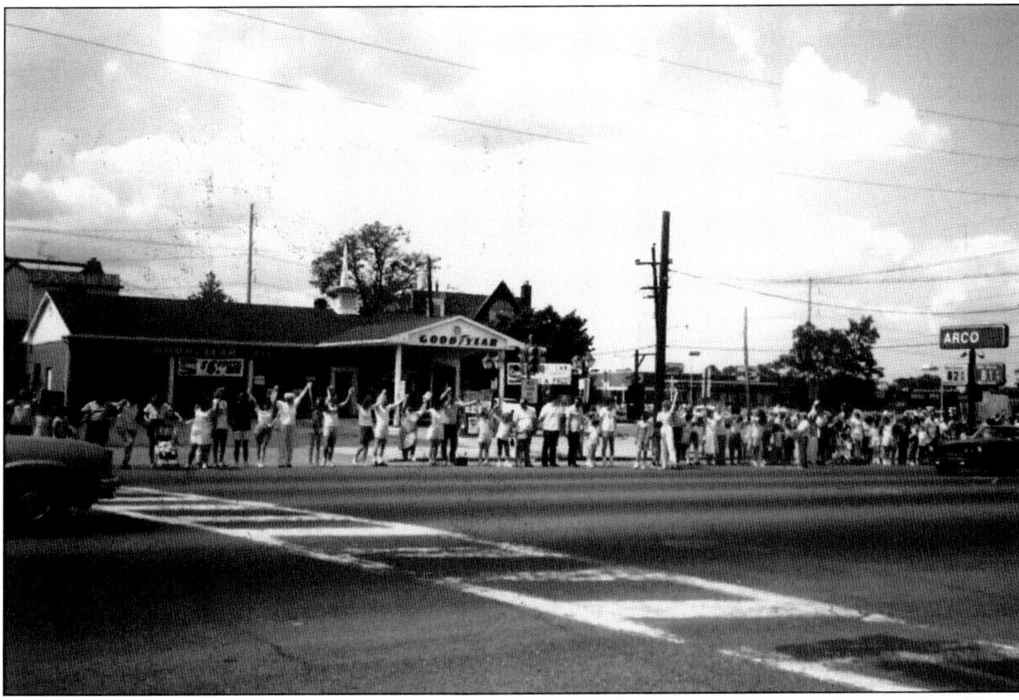

HANDS ACROSS AMERICA, 1986. Hands across America was a benefit event and publicity campaign staged on Sunday, May 26, 1986, in which approximately seven million people held hands in a human chain for 15 minutes along a path across the continental United States. Participants paid to reserve their place in line; the proceeds went to local charities to fight hunger and homelessness.

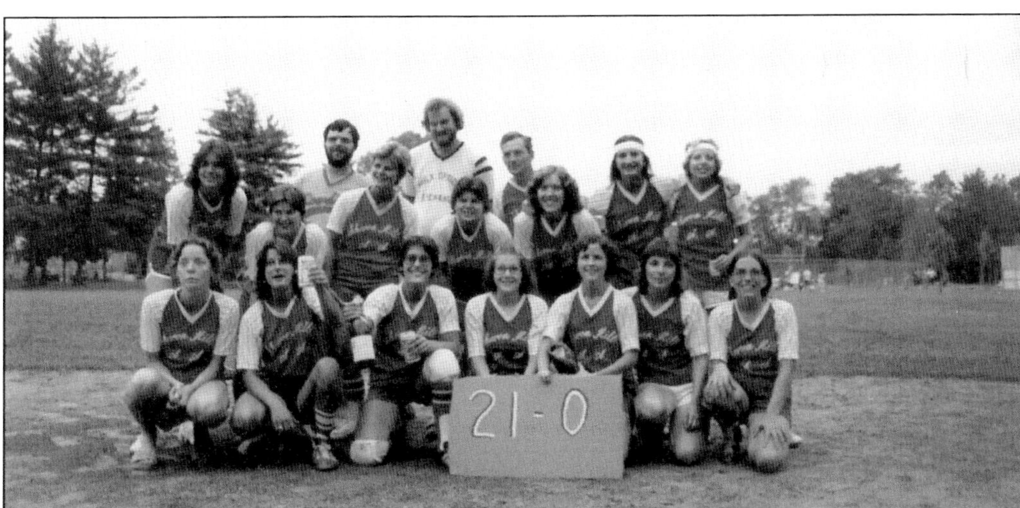

SHARON HILL ATHLETIC ASSOCIATION WOMEN'S SOFTBALL, 1978. The women's fast-pitch softball team was founded in 1977. The women participated in the local, state, regional, and national levels. This 1978 team with its coach Mike Franz had the only undefeated season in league history (21-0). (Courtesy of Michael Franz.)

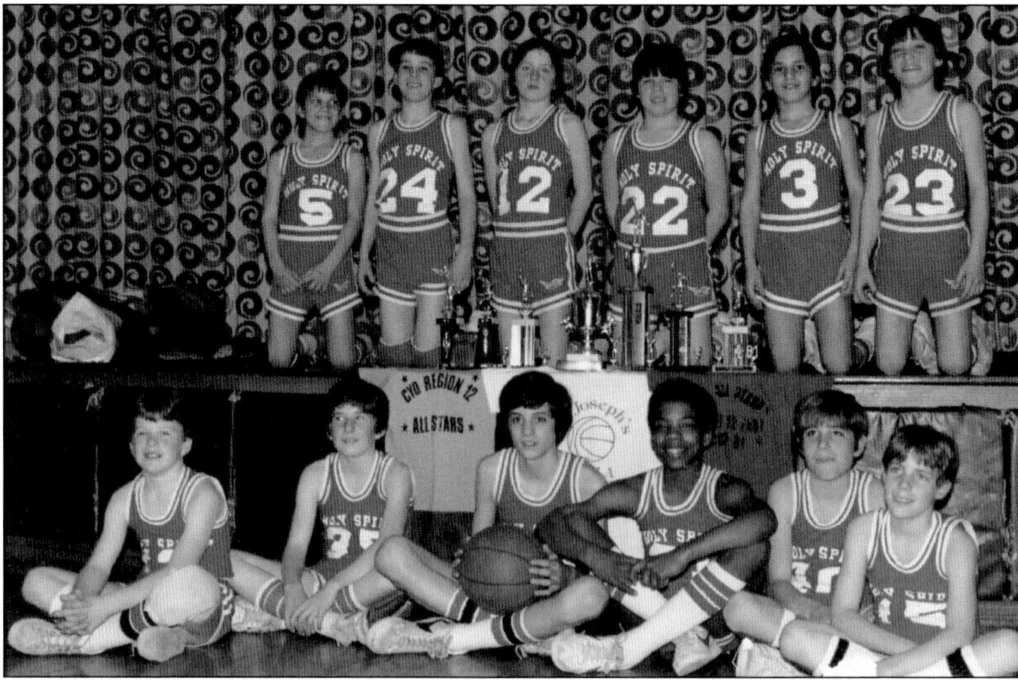

HOLY SPIRIT CATHOLIC YOUTH ORGANIZATION REGION 12 CHAMPIONS, 1980–1981. Pictured are the fifth- and sixth-grade region 12 champions, from left to right, (first row) Pat Lynch, Marty Cormican, Tom Leinhauser, Larry Clark, Ted Mulroy, and Neil Hamilton; (second row) Bill Franz, Mike Lynch, Andy Shiber, Robert Scanlon, Andy Franz, and Ned Rossi. (Courtesy of Michael Franz.)

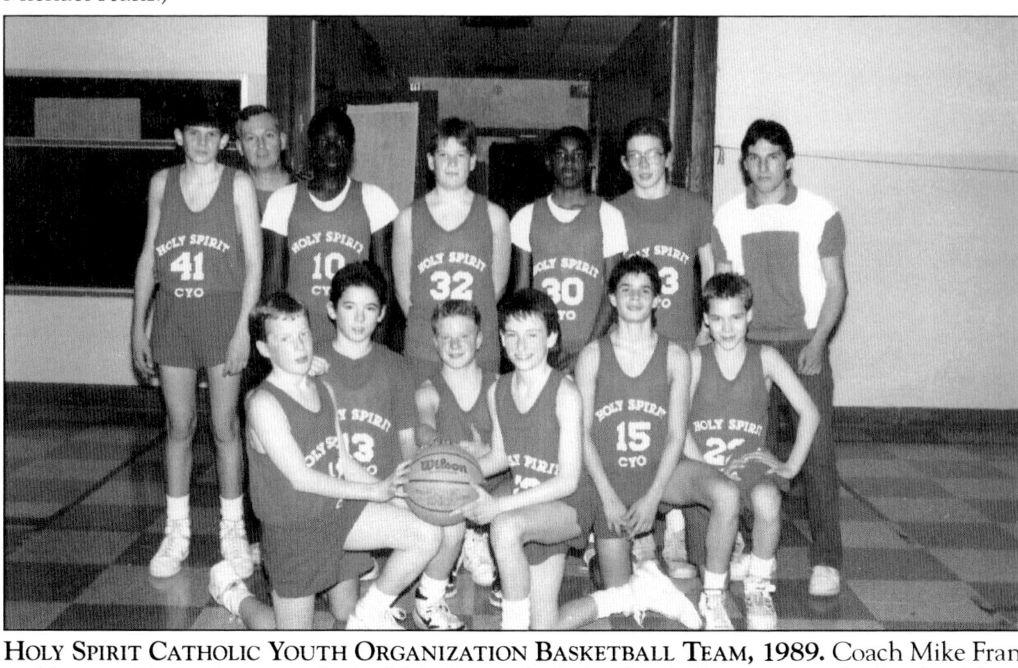

HOLY SPIRIT CATHOLIC YOUTH ORGANIZATION BASKETBALL TEAM, 1989. Coach Mike Franz and his son Michael pose with the Holy Spirit Catholic Youth Organization high school boys' basketball team, which went undefeated in 1989. (Courtesy of Michael Franz.)

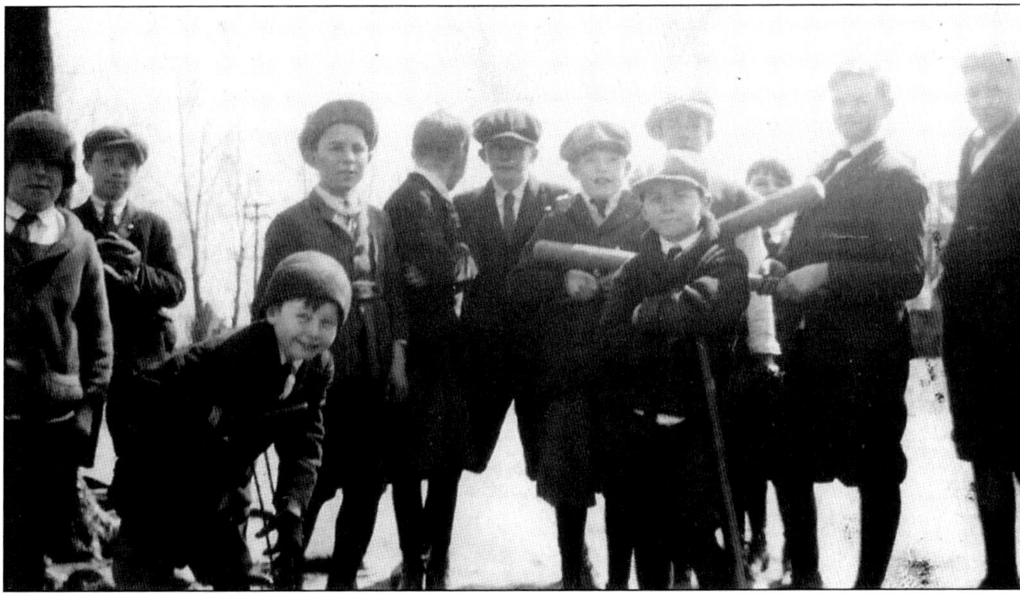

READY FOR SOME BASEBALL, 1924. This group of Holy Spirit boys gathers at the ball field to choose sides for a pickup game. Needless to say, this was before Little League. (Courtesy of Holy Spirit Church.)

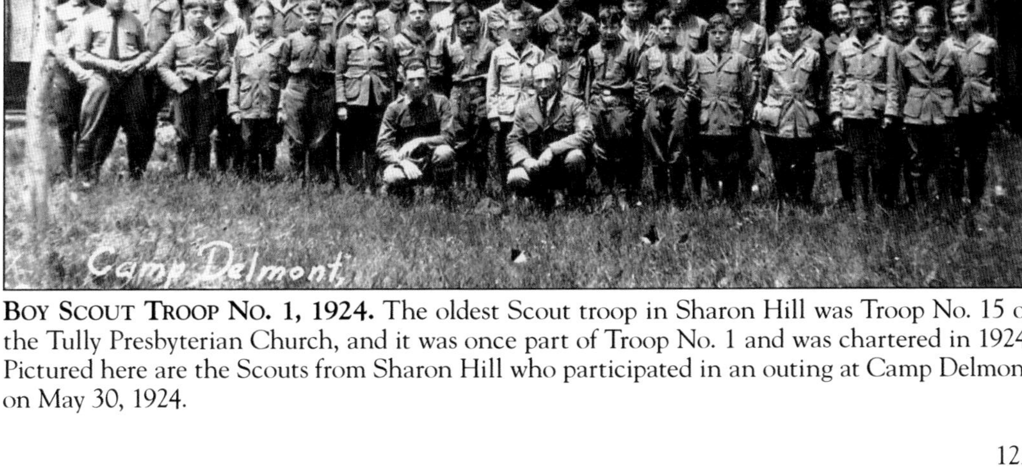

BOY SCOUT TROOP NO. 1, 1924. The oldest Scout troop in Sharon Hill was Troop No. 15 of the Tully Presbyterian Church, and it was once part of Troop No. 1 and was chartered in 1924. Pictured here are the Scouts from Sharon Hill who participated in an outing at Camp Delmont on May 30, 1924.

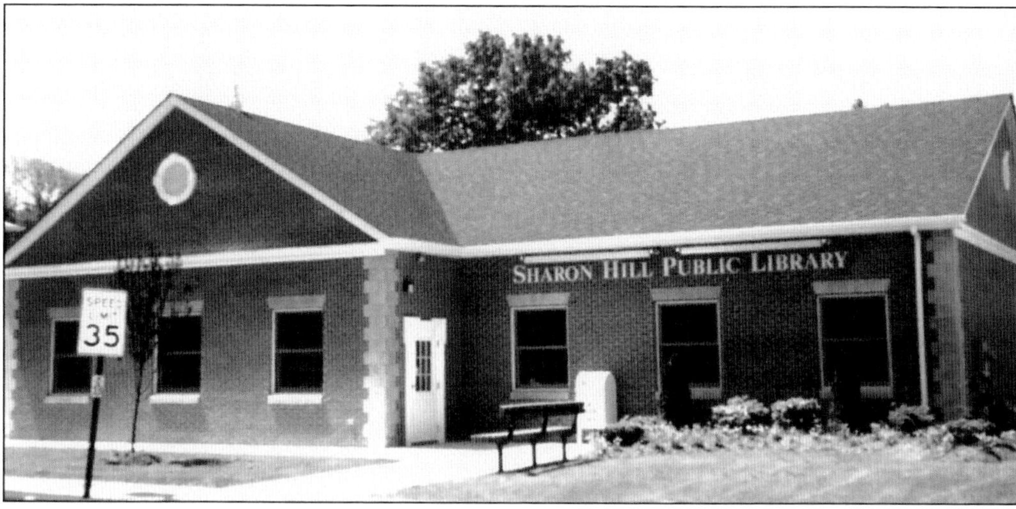

SHARON HILL PUBLIC LIBRARY, 1997. The first library was formed in 1936. Members of the library group first met in the building behind Beckett's drugstore. Volunteer members of the group staffed the library until the first paid librarian was hired in 1938. As the library grew, it was moved to the building beside the borough hall until the new building was built and dedicated in 1997.

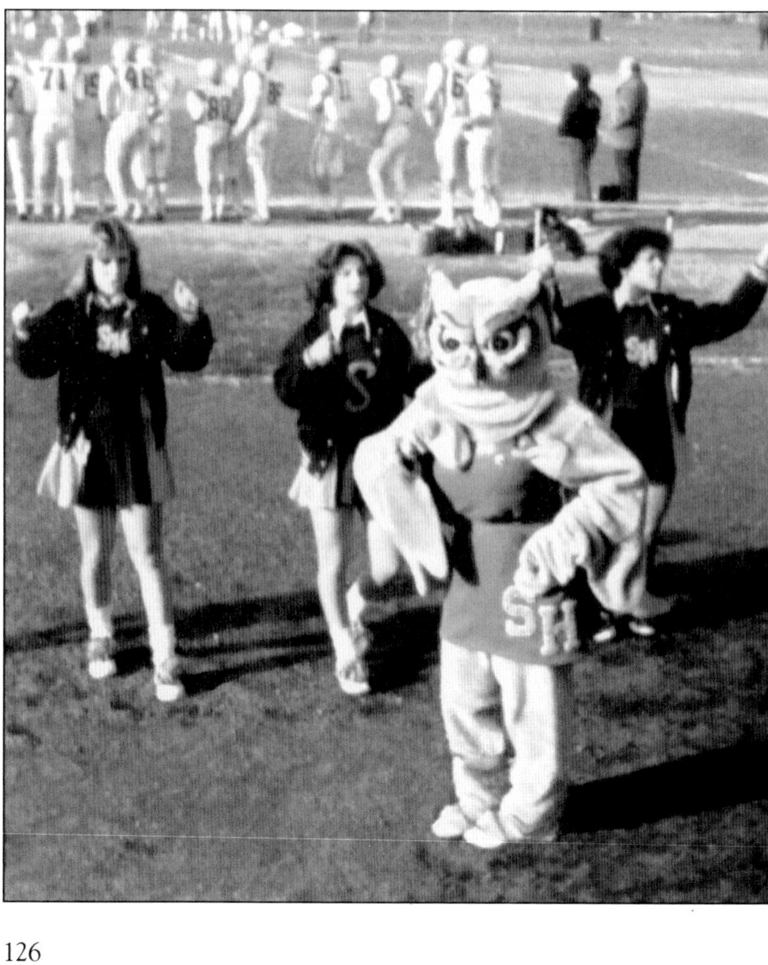

SHARON HILL HIGH SCHOOL MASCOT, 1977. The owl portrayed by Lola Rossi dances along with cheerleaders (from left to right) Barbara Hays, Kathy Powers, and Linda McCarron at a football game in November. The owl loved to entertain the crowds in the stands while rooting for Sharon Hill teams. (Courtesy of Lola Rossi.)

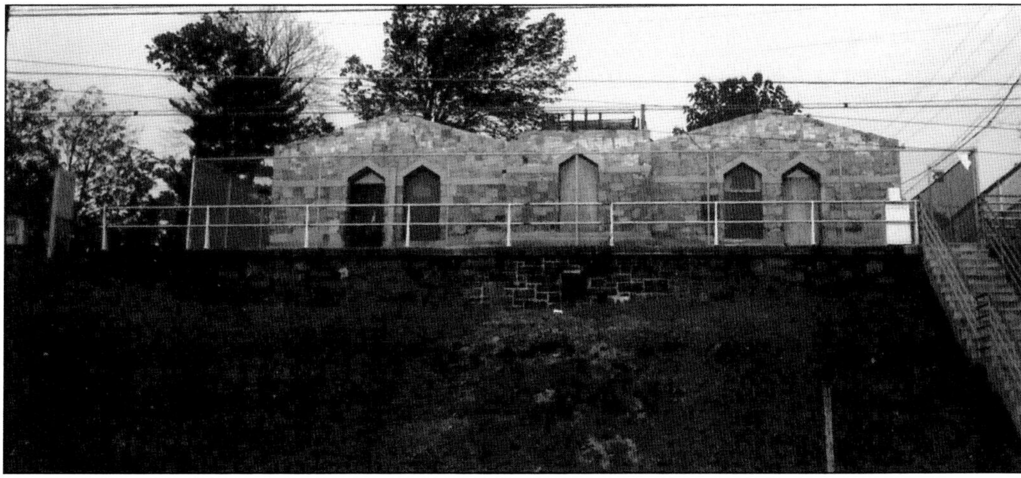

SHARON HILL TRAIN STATION RESTORATION, 1990S. During the repair of the roof of this 1872 train station on Sharon Avenue in 1991, the roof caved in, threatening the station with demolition. The Sharon Hill Historical Society was formed at this time to save the station and preserve the history of Sharon Hill. Research revealed that the station was eligible for the National Register of Historic Places. Its symmetrical design and use of locally acquired serpentine stone were recognized for their uniqueness. Of greater significance was the growth of Sharon Hill as a suburban area greatly influenced by transportation. The society has received funding and is in the process of restoring the site. Pictured below are charter members and members of the society. They are celebrating the placement of a new roof on the station. The historical society ended its parade march on the Fourth of July in 1997 at the station. Notice the red suspenders, neckerchiefs, and engineer hats.

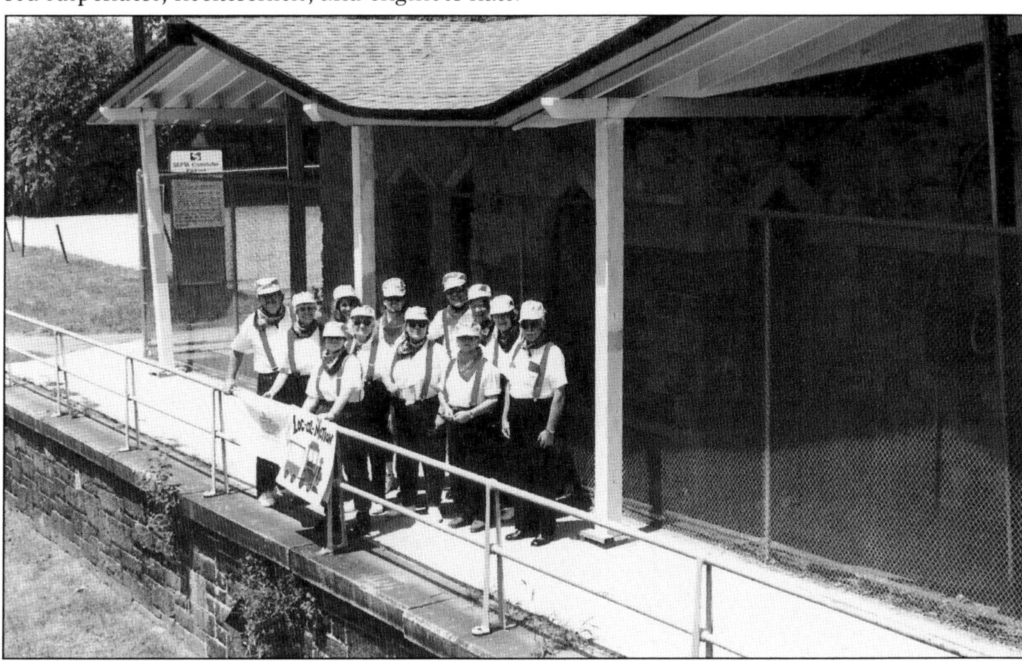